Handbook of Bankruptcy and Personal Insolvency

Sixth Edition

Steven A Frieze MA (Oxon)

Solicitor, Authorised Insolvency Practitioner and partner in the firm of Brooke North and Goodwin, Leeds and London — a QLG member firm

LAW & TAX

© Pearson Professional Limited 1996

ISBN 075200 2740

Published by
FT Law & Tax
21–27 Lamb's Conduit Street, London WCIN 3NJ

A Division of Pearson Professional Limited

Associated offices
Australia, Belgium, Canada, Hong Kong, India, Japan, Luxembourg, Singapore, Spain, USA

First published 1950
Sixth edition 1996

Steven A Frieze has asserted his right under the Copyright, Designs and Patents Act 1988 to be identified as the author of this work.

All rights reserved. No part of this publication may be reproduced, stored in a retrieval system, or transmitted, in any form or by any means, electronic, mechanical, photocopying, recording or otherwise, without the prior written permission of the publishers.

No responsibility for loss occasioned to any person acting or refraining from action as a result of the material in this publication can be accepted by the author or publishers.

The material herein which is Crown Copyright is reproduced with the permission of the Controller of Her Majesty's Stationery Office.

A CIP catalogue record for this book is available from the British Library.

Typeset by Kerrypress Ltd, Luton
Printed in Great Britain by Biddles Ltd, Guildford, Surrey

Contents

Preface xiii
Table of Cases xv
Table of Statutes xxi
Table of Statutory Instruments xxiv

1 Introduction 1

2 The Debtor and the Debt 4
   1 The debtor 4
   2 The debt 6

3 Grounds for Petitioning 8
   1 Introduction 8
   2 Form and contents of statutory demand 9
   3 Service of statutory demand 11
   4 Three weeks for compliance 13
   5 Defects 14
   6 Application to set aside a statutory demand 14
   7 Hearing of application to set aside 16
   8 The order 18

4 The Creditor's Petition 19
   1 The appropriate court 19
   2 Conditions for petitioning 20
   3 Form and contents 20
   4 The creditor 21
   5 Identification of the debtor 22
   6 Identification of the debt 23
   7 Verification of the petition 23
   8 Completion of the petition 24
   9 Procedure for presentation and filing 25
   10 Notice to chief land registrar 26
   11 Service of the petition 26
   12 Death of debtor 27

	13	Security for costs	28
	14	Consolidation of petitions	28
5	Hearing of the Petition	29
	1	Date of hearing	29
	2	Opposition by the debtor	29
	3	Amendment of petition	29
	4	Appearances at the hearing	29
	5	Extensions and adjournment	30
	6	Substitution of petitioner	31
	7	Change of carriage of petition	31
	8	Dismissal and withdrawal	32
	9	Certificate of debt	32
	10	Grounds for making a bankruptcy order	33
	11	The order	35
6	Debtor's Petition	37
	1	Grounds	37
	2	Court in which filed	37
	3	Form of petition	37
	4	Statement of affairs	38
	5	Procedure on issue	38
	6	Hearing of the petition	39
	7	Insolvency practitioner's report	39
	8	Making of the order	40
	9	Voluntary arrangements	41
	10	Action following the order	41
7	Dispositions, Proceedings and the Interim Receiver	42
	1	Restrictions on dispositions	42
	2	Restrictions on proceedings	43
	3	The interim receiver	44
	4	Receivership pending appointment of trustee	46
8	Investigations into the Bankrupt's Affairs	47
	1	Submission of statement of affairs	47
	2	Release and extension of time	47
	3	Assistance	48
	4	Failure to submit	48
	5	Limited disclosure	48
	6	Accounts	48
	7	Further disclosure	49
	8	Debtors' petitions	49
	9	Investigatory duties of the official receiver	49

CONTENTS   vii

9	Rescission and Annulment of Bankruptcy Order	50
	1 Rescission	50
	2 Annulment	51

10	Public Examination	54
	1 Application for examination	54
	2 Order for examination	54
	3 Bankrupt unfit for examination	55
	4 Procedure at hearing	55
	5 Adjournment	56
	6 Expenses of examination	57

11	Appointment and Removal of Trustee	58
	1 Power to make appointments	58
	2 Summoning of meeting to appoint first trustee	58
	3 Notice of the first meeting of creditors	59
	4 Rules governing meetings	60
	5 Proxies	61
	6 Business at first meetings	62
	7 Certifying the appointment of the trustee	63
	8 Resignation of trustee and vacancies	63
	9 Removal of trustee	64

12	The Creditors' Committee	66
	1 The right to establish a committee	66
	2 Membership and establishment of the committee	66
	3 Functions and rights of the committee	66
	4 Meetings of the committee	67
	5 Resolutions by post	68
	6 Termination of membership and vacancies	68
	7 Dealings with committee members	68
	8 Expenses of members	69
	9 No committee	69

13	Administration by the Trustee	70
	1 General functions of the trustee	70
	2 Vesting of bankrupt's estate	70
	3 After-acquired property	71
	4 Vesting of items of excess value	72
	5 Income payments order	72
	6 Acquisition of control	74
	7 Charge on bankrupt's home	74
	8 Powers of the trustee	75
	9 Priority of payment of expenses	76

CONTENTS

14 Disclaimer 77
   1 General power 77
   2 Exercise of power 77
   3 Time limits 78
   4 Communication of disclaimer 79
   5 Disclaimer of leaseholds 79
   6 Disclaimer of dwelling-house 79
   7 Disclaimer of land subject to rentcharge 80
   8 Vesting order 80
   9 Effect of disclaimer 81

15 Debts and Dividends 82
   1 Classes of debts 82
   2 Mode and form of proof 83
   3 Provable debts 83
   4 Contents of proof 84
   5 Debt payable at a future date and of a periodic nature 84
   6 Bills of exchange and promissory notes 85
   7 Time for proofs 85
   8 Admission and rejection of proofs 85
   9 Expunging proofs 86
   10 Interest 86
   11 VAT 86
   12 Secured creditors 87
   13 Dividends 87

16 Mutual Credit and Set-off 89
   1 The general law 89
   2 Application of bankruptcy law 89
   3 Definitions 90
   4 Where set-off allowed 90
   5 Where set-off not allowed 90
   6 Different classes of debt 91
   7 Contingent debts 91
   8 Crown set-off 92

17 Discharge 93
   1 Automatic discharge 93
   2 Suspension of discharge (rr 6.215 and 216) 93
   3 Application for discharge 94
   4 Certificate of discharge 95
   5 Effect of discharge 96

18 The Home 97
   1 Rights of occupation of the spouse 97
   2 Rights of the bankrupt 98

	3	Charge on the bankrupt's home (s 313)	99
	4	Determining the extent of the bankrupt's interest	99
19	Adjustment of Prior Transactions	101
	1	Transactions at an undervalue (ss 339 and 423)	101
	2	Voidable preference (s 340)	102
	3	The relevant time (s 341)	103
	4	Orders under ss 339 and 340	103
	5	Extortionate credit transactions (s 343)	104
	6	Avoidance of general assignment (s 344)	104
	7	Enforcement procedures (s 346)	105
	8	Distress (s 347)	105
	9	Liens on books and papers (s 349)	106
20	Bankruptcy Offences	107
	1	Liability to prosecution	107
	2	Defence of innocent intention	107
	3	Non-disclosure (s 353)	108
	4	Concealment of property (s 354)	108
	5	Explanations (s 354(3))	108
	6	Books and papers (s 355)	109
	7	False statements (s 356)	109
	8	Fraudulent disposal of property (s 357)	109
	9	Absconding (s 358)	110
	10	Fraudulent dealing with property obtained on credit (s 359)	110
	11	Obtaining credit or engaging in business (s 360)	110
	12	Failure to keep proper accounts (s 361)	111
	13	Gambling (s 362)	111
	14	Being a director of a limited company	112
	15	Contempt of court	112
	16	Evidence	112
	17	Criminal court action	112
21	Powers of the Court	114
	1	General powers of the court	114
	2	Power of arrest (s 364)	114
	3	Seizure of the bankrupt's property (s 365)	115
	4	Inquiry into the bankrupt's dealings and property	115
	5	Special manager (s 370)	116
	6	Redirection of mail (s 371)	117
22	Appeals	118
	1	General	118
	2	Who may appeal	119
	3	Rehearing	119

	4	Time limits	120
	5	Procedure	121
23		**Control of the Trustee**	124
	1	Control by the creditors	124
	2	Control by the court	125
	3	Control by the Department of Trade and Industry	125
	4	The rule in *ex p James*	126
	5	Maintenance and champerty	127
24		**General Procedure**	128
	1	Title of proceedings	128
	2	Applications	128
	3	Hearing of applications	128
	4	Transfer of proceedings	129
	5	Evidence	129
	6	Fee on issue	129
	7	Enforcement	129
	8	Computation of time	130
	9	Service by post	130
	10	Access to court file	130
	11	Paper, forms etc	130
	12	Costs rules	131
	13	Review	131
25		**Insolvent Partnerships**	132
	1	Introduction	132
	2	Winding up of an insolvent partnership	133
	3	Winding up the partnership and making the individual partners bankrupt	134
	4	Partner's own petition for bankruptcy order	135
	5	Petition against some of the partners	136
	6	Consolidation	137
	7	Loss of rights	138
26		**Deceaseds' Insolvent Estates**	139
	1	Introduction	139
	2	Where administration has begun	139
	3	Petition pending at time of death	140
	4	Where no administration is pending	141
	5	Modifications of the general law	141
27		**Individual Voluntary Arrangements**	143
	1	Introduction	143
	2	The proposal	144
	3	Application for an interim order	145

	4	Hearing of the application	146
	5	Action following the interim order	147
	6	The second hearing	148
	7	The creditors' meeting	148
	8	The third hearing	151
	9	Procedure in non-bankruptcy cases	151
	10	Challenge of meeting's decision	152
	11	Effect of approval	153
	12	Implementation of the arrangement	153
	13	Offence	154
	14	Default by the debtor	154
28	Deeds of Arrangement	155
	1	The nature of a deed	155
	2	Avoidance for non-compliance with the statutory conditions	156
	3	Registration of deeds of arrangement	156
	4	Effect of assent	157
	5	Trustees	157

Appendices

1	County Court Areas and Bankruptcy Courts	159
2	Alternative Courts for Debtors' Petitions in Bankruptcy	165
3	Forms	168

Index   251

Preface

This book was first published in 1950 as 'Handbook on Bankruptcy Law and Practice' under the authorship of Ivan Cruchley, who was also responsible for its second edition in 1964. The third edition was produced in 1977 by Michael Crystal and Brinsley Nicholson. Since 1977 there has been a fundamental change in bankruptcy law as a result of the passing of the Insolvency Act 1986, which came into effect on 29 December 1986. This had the effect of requiring a complete revision of this book for the fourth edition in 1988, although I followed the pattern and style of previous editions whilst at the same time trying to make reference to particular topics easier. The sixth edition incorporates the practical experience of the Act since it came into force.

It must be stressed that the law and procedure in this book relate only to bankruptcies commenced after 29 December 1986 and the old law continues to apply to those bankruptcies which commenced before that date. Since the new law has been in force for ten years, a number of cases have been decided giving helpful guidance and clarification to the Insolvency Act and the Insolvency Rules.

I have included in the forms section those forms which will more commonly be required, and two appendices, listing those county courts having bankruptcy jurisdiction together with those courts to which a debtor can present a bankruptcy petition if his 'home' court does not have a district judge available on a full-time basis.

The law is stated as at 1 March 1996.

Steven A Frieze
March 1996

Table of Cases

A & M, *Re* [1926] Ch 274; [1926] All ER Rep 350; (1926) 70 SJ 607 6
Abbey National v Moss (1993) 26 HLR 249; [1993] NPC 153; (1993) *The Times*,
   30 November 98
Abbott (A Bankrupt), *Re, ex p* The Trustee of the Property of the Bankrupt v
   Abbott (PM) [1983] Ch 45; [1982] 3 WLR 86; [1982] 3 All ER 181, DC 101, 102
Akeling Barford, *Re* [1988] 3 All ER 1019 106
AMC v Woodward (1994) BCC 688 102
Arbuthnot Leasing International v Havelet Leasing (No 2) (1990) BCC 636 102
Arden, *Re, ex p* Arden (1884) 14 QBD 121; [1884] 33 WR 460; (1884) 2 Morr 1 121
Atherton, *Re* [1912] 2 KB 251; [1912] 81 LJ KB 791; (1912) 106 LT 641 56
Aveling Barford, *Re* [1989] 1 WLR 360; [1988] 3 All ER 1019; (1988) 4 BCC 548 116
Bacon (MC), *Re* [1990] 3 WLR 646; (1990) BCC 78; [1980–90] IJ 292 102
Baker (A Bankrupt), *Re, ex p* Eastbourne Waterworks & Co v Official Receiver
   [1954] 1 WLR 1144; [1954] 2 All ER 790; (1954) 98 SJ 574 83
Barclays Bank v Eustice [1995] 1 WLR 1238 .... 102, 116
Barne, *Re, ex p* Barne (1886) 16 QBD 522; (1886) 54 LT 662; (1886) 3 Morr 33,
   CA 4
Beauchamp, *Re, ex p* Beauchamp [1904] 1 KB 572; [1904] 73 LJ KB 311; (1904)
   90 LT 594 9
Benson (A Debtor), *Re* (1971) unreported, 8 March 120
Betts, *Re, ex p* Official Receiver [1901] 2 KB 39; [1901] 70 LJ KB 511; (1901)
   84 LT 427, DC 40
Bird v IRC, *Re, ex p* The Debtor [1962] 1 WLR 686; [1962] 2 All ER 406; [1962]
   TR 173, CA 4, 5
Bishopsgate Investment Managers v Maxwell [1993] Ch 1; [1992] 2 WLR 991;
   [1992] 2 All ER 856; (1992) *The Times*, 29 January 56, 116
Bradley Hole, *Re* [1995] 4 All ER 865; [1995] BCC 418 .... 149, 154
Brauch (A Debtor), *Re, ex p* Brittanic Securities & Investments [1978] Ch 316;
   [1977] 3 WLR 354; [1978] 1 All ER 1004 5
Brickland v Newsome (1808) 1 Camp 474 22
British Anzani (Felixstowe) Ltd v International Marine Management (UK) Ltd
   [1980] QB 637; [1979] 3 WLR 451; [1979] 2 All ER 1063 89
British Eagle International Air Lines Ltd v Compagnie Nationale Air France [1975]
   1 WLR 758; [1975] 2 All ER 390; (1975) 119 SJ 368, HL 90
Brunner, *Re* (1887) 19 QBD 572; (1887) 56 LJ QB 606; (1887) 57 LT 418 56
Burford Midland Properties v Marley Extrusions [1994] BCC 604; [1994] EGCS
   108 149
Calor Gas v Piercy [1994] BCC 69; [1994] 2 BCLC 321 .... 44, 149
Campbell, *Re* [1984] BCLC 83 112
Cancol, *Re* [1996] 1 All ER 37 (1995) *The Independent*, 4 October 149
Carreras Rothman Ltd v Freeman Matthews Treasure Ltd [1985] Ch 207; [1984]
   3 WLR 1016; [1985] 1 All ER 155 91

xv

TABLE OF CASES

Charge Card Services Ltd, *Re* [1987] Ch 150; [1986] 3 WLR 697; [1986] 3 All ER 289 91
Chohan v Saggar (1992) BCC 306; [1991] NPC 111; (1991) *The Times*, 16 October 102
Citro (A Bankrupt), *Re* [1991] Ch 142; [1990] 3 WLR 880; [1990] 3 All ER 952 98
City Life Assurance Company Ltd, *Re* [1926] Ch 191; [1925] All ER Rep 453 90
Clark (A Bankrupt), *Re, ex p* The Trustee v Texaco; *sub nom* Clark (A Bankrupt), *Re, ex p* Trustee of the Property of the Bankrupt v Texaco [1975] 1 WLR 559; [1975] 1 All ER 453; (1975) 118 SJ 862 126
Cohen (A Bankrupt), *Re, ex p* The Bankrupt v IRC [1950] 2 All ER 36; [1950] WN 266; [1950] 66 TLR (Pt 1) 1207, CA 51, 120
Cole, *Re, ex p* Attenborough [1898] 1 QB 290; (1898) 67 LJ QB 302; (1898) 78 LT 23, DC 17
Combined Weighing & Advertising Machine Company, *Re* (1889) 43 ChD 99; [1886–90] All ER Rep 1044; (1886) 59 LJ Ch 26, CA 22
Condon, *Re, ex p* James (1874) 9 Ch App 609; [1874–80] All ER Rep 388; (1874) LJ Bcy 107 126
Cove (A Debtor), *Re* [1990] 1 WLR 708; [1990] 1 All ER 949 148
Credit Default Register Ltd, *Re* [1993] CCLR 59 12
Crispin, *Re, ex p* Crispin (1873) 8 Ch App 374; [1861–73] All ER Rep 190; (1861) 42 LJ Bcy 65 4
Curtis (DH) (Builders) Ltd, *Re* [1978] Ch 162; [1978] 2 WLR 28; [1978] 2 All ER 183 92
Curtis v Curtis [1969] 1 WLR 422; [1969] 2 All ER 207; (1969) 113 SJ 242, CA 84
Cushla Ltd, *Re* [1979] 3 All ER 415; [1979] STC 615 92
Daintrey, *Re, ex p* Mant [1900] 1 QB 546; [1895–9] All ER Rep 657; (1895) 69 LJ QB 207 90
Dalton (A Bankrupt), *Re, ex p* Herrington and Carmichael (A Firm) v The Trustee [1963] Ch 366; [1962] 3 WLR 140; [1962] 2 All ER 499, DC 42
Davenport, *Re, ex p* The Bankrupt v Eric Street Properties [1963] 1 WLR 817; [1963] 2 All ER 850; (1963) 100 SJ 457, CA 6
Debtor (32/SD/1991), A, *Re* [1993] 1 WLR 314; [1993] 2 All ER 991 51
Debtor (415 SD 1993), A, *Re* [1994] 1 WLR 917; (1993) *The Times*, 8 December 16
Debtor (51 SD 1991), A, *Re* [1992] 1 WLR 1294; [1993] 2 All ER 40 10
Debtor (No 1 of 1941), A, *Re* [1941] Ch 487; [1941] 3 All ER 11; (1941) 110 LJ Ch 220 6
Debtor (No 1 of 1987), A, *Re* [1989] 1 WLR 271; [1989] 2 All ER 46; [1988] 1 WLR 419; [1988] 1 All ER 959, CA 9, 14, 17
Debtor (No 2A of 1980, Colchester), A, *Re* [1981] Ch 148; [1981] 2 WLR 99; [1980] 3 All ER 641 50
Debtor (No 6 of 1941), A, *Re, ex p* Debtor v Petitioning Creditor and Official Receiver [1943] Ch 213; [1943] 1 All ER 553; (1943) 87 SJ 192, CA 21
Debtor (No 10 of 1992), A, *Re* [1995] BCC 529 149
Debtor (No 17 of 1966), A, *Re, ex p* The Debtor v Allen (An Infant by His Father and Next Friend NG Allen) [1967] Ch 590; [1967] 2 WLR 1528; (1967) 111 SJ 130 40
Debtor (No 20 of 1953), A, *Re, ex p* The Debtor v Scott and the Official Receiver [1954] 1 WLR 1190; [1954] 3 All ER 74; (1954) 98 SJ 589, CA 7
Debtor (No 26A of 1975), A, *Re* [1985] 1 WLR 6; [1984] 3 All ER 995; (1984) 128 SJ 685 20
Debtor (No 32 of 1993), A, *Re* [1994] 1 WLR 899; [1995] 1 All ER 628; (1994) BCC 438 33
Debtor (No 39 of 1974), A, *Re, ex p* Okill v Gething [1977] 1 WLR 1308; [1977] 3 All ER 489 21
Debtor (No 44 of 1978), A, *Re, ex p* The Debtor v Chantry Mont and Hawthorns [1980] 1 WLR 665; [1979] 3 All ER 265; (1979) 124 SJ 428, DC 23
Debtor (No 53 of 1991, Kingston upon Thames), A, *Re, ex p* FG Smith (Interiors) Ltd (1991) *The Independent*, 19 August 15, 25

TABLE OF CASES

Debtor (No 64 of 1992), A, *Re*, Bradford and Bingley Building Society v A Debtor [1994] 1 WLR 264; [1994] 2 All ER 177; [1994] BCC 55..................................148
Debtor (No 66 of 1995), A, *Re* [1956] 1 WLR 1226; [1956] 3 All ER 225; (1956) 100 SJ 649, CA..................................91
Debtor (No 68 of 1992), A, *Re* [1994] 1 WLR 264; (1993) *The Times*, 12 February 51
Debtor (No 82 of 1926), A, *Re* [1927] 1 Ch 410; (1927) 136 LT 349 91
Debtor (No 87 of 1993), A, *Re* (1995) *The Times*, 7 August..................................152
Debtor (No 162 of 1993), A, *Re* Doorbar v Alltime Securities No 1 [1994] BCC 994..................................149
Debtor (No 162 of 1993), A, *Re* Doorbar v Alltime Securities No 1 [1995] BCC 1149..................................149
Debtor (No 222 of 1990), A, *Re* [1992] BCLC 137; (1991) *The Times*, 27 June...............147, 152
Debtor (No 259 of 1990), A, *Re* [1992] 1 WLR 226; [1992] 1 All ER 641..................................1152
Debtor (No 310 of 1988), A, *Re* [1989] 1 WLR 452; [1989] 2 All ER 42; (1989) 133 SJ 848..................................17, 149
Debtor (No 340 of 1992), A, *Re* [1994] 3 All ER 269; [1994] 2 BCLC 171; (1995) *The Times*, 6 March..................................8
Debtor (No 400 of 1940), A, *Re*, *ex p* Debtor v Dodwell (Trustee) [1940] Ch 236; [1949] 1 All ER 510; (1949) 93 SJ 148..................................125
Debtor (No 490 of 1991), A, *Re* [1992] 1 WLR 507; [1992] 2 All ER 664; [1993] BCLC 164; (1992) *The Times*, 9 April..................................17
Debtor (No 564 of 1949), A, *Re*, *ex p* Customs and Excise Commissioners v The Debtor [1950] Ch 282; [1950] 1 All ER 308; (1950) 94 SJ 113, CA..................................6
Debtor (No 784 of 1991), A, *Re* [1992] Ch 554; [1992] 3 WLR 119; [1992] 3 All ER 376; [1992] STC 549..................................5
Debtor (No 799 of 1994), A, *Re* [1995] 3 All ER 723..................................35, 121
Debtor (No 991 of 1962), A, *Re*, *ex p* The Debtor v Tossun (H) [1963] 1 WLR 51; [1963] 1 All ER 85; (1963) 106 SJ 937, CA..................................17
Debtor (No 1036 of 1995), A, *Re* (1995) unreported, 28 July..................................150, 151
Debtor (No 2021 of 1995), A, *Re* (1995) unreported 62, 149
Debtor (No 2389 of 1989), A, *Re* [1991] Fam 326; [1991] 2 WLR 578; [1990] 3 All ER 984..................................34
Debtor, A v Focus Insurance, *Re* (1993) *The Times*, 12 July..................................14
Debtor, A v Sun Alliance, *Re* (1994) unreported, 12 January..................................44
Debtor, A, *Re*, *ex p* Official Receiver [1901] 2 KB 354; (1901) 17 TLR 536; *sub nom*, *Re*, WL (Debtor) (1901) 70 LJ KB 699; (1901) 8 Mans 247; *sub nom*, *Re*, Debtor, *ex p* Official Receiver (1901) 84 LT 666; (1901) 45 SJ 520, CA..................................36
Densham (A Bankrupt), *Re*, *ex p* Trustee of the Property of the Bankrupt v The Bankrupt [1975] 1 WLR 1519; [1975] 3 All ER 726; (1975) 119 SJ 774..................................100
Dent, *Re* [1994] 1 WLR 956; [1994] 2 All ER 904; (1993) EGCS 190, DC..................................104
Deveze, *Re* (1874) 9 Ch App 293; (1874) 43 LJ Bcy 87; (1874) 29 LT 858..................................91
Dunn, *Re*, *ex p* Official Receiver v Dunn [1949] Ch 640; [1949] 2 All ER 388; (1949) 93 SJ 576, CA..................................40
Easton, *Re*, *ex p* Dixon (1893) 9 TLR 408; (1893) 37 SJ 479; (1893) 10 Morr 111, DC..................................17
Eberhardt v Mair [1955] 1 WLR 1180..................................35
Eberle's Hotels & Restaurant Co v Jona s (1887) 18 QBD 459; (1887) 56 LJ QB 278; [1887] 35 WR 467, CA..................................90
Elgood v Harris [1896] 2 QB 419; (1896) 66 LJ QB 53; (1896) 75 LT 419..................................91
Erskine, *Re*, *ex p* Erskine (1893) 10 TLR 32; (1893) 38 SJ 144, CA..................................5
Everett v Robertson (1858) 28 LJ QB 23; (1858) 32 LT OS 74; [1858] 120 ER 813..................................47
Ezekiel v Orakpo [1977] QB 260, CA..................................43
Farnham, *Re* [1895] Ch 799; [1895–9] All ER Rep 897; (1895) 64 LJ Ch 717, CA..................................6
Field (A Debtor), *Re* [1978] Ch 371; [1977] 3 WLR 937; [1978] 2 All ER 981; (1977) *The Times*, 6 July, DC..................................34, 50
Fitch v Official Receiver [1966] 1 WLR 242; (1995) *The Times*, 21 November..................................50
Flint, *Re* [1993] Ch 319; [1993] 2 WLR 537; (1992) 136 SJ (LB) 221; (1992) *The Times*, 16 July..................................42

TABLE OF CASES

Forster v Wilson (1843) 12 M & W 191; (1843) 13 LJ Ex 209; [1843] 152 ER 1165 89
Gilmartin, *Re* (1988) *The Independent*, 21 November 118
Gissing v Gissing [1971] AC 886; [1970] 3 WLR 255; [1970] 2 All ER 780, HL..................100
Gorman (A Bankrupt), *Re* [1990] 1 WLR 616; [1990] 1 All ER 717; [1990] LS Gaz, 23 May, 41, DC...100
Government of India v Taylor [1955] AC 491; [1955] 2 WLR 303; [1955] 1 All ER 292, CA 7
Hanak v Green [1958] 2 QB 9; [1958] 2 WLR 755; [1958] 2 All ER 141, CA.....................89
Hans Place, *Re* (1992) BCC 737; [1992] 4 EG 143; [1993] BCLC 768 77
Hawkins, *Re*, *ex p* Hawkins [1894] 1 QB 25; (1894) 69 LT 769; [1894] 42 WR 202, DC 84
Heath v Tang [1993] 1 WLR 1421; [1993] 4 All ER 694; (1993) *The Times*, 11 August 51, 86
Helsby, *Re*, *ex p* Trustee [1894] 1 QB 742; [1891–4] All ER Rep Ext 1448; (1891) 63 LJ KB 265, CA...120
Heyworth, *ex p* (1888) 22 QBD 83...35
Hindcastle v Barbara Attenborough Associates [1996] 1 All ER 737.....................81
Holliday, *Re* [1981] Ch 405; [1981] 2 WLR 996; [1980] 3 All ER 385 98
Holmes v Official Receiver (1995) unreported, 7 July.....................................57, 94
Hough, *Re* (1990) *The Independent*, 26 April...134
Huddersfield Fine Worsteds Ltd v Todd (1925) 134 LT 82; (1925) 42 TLR 52.......157
Hussain, *Re* (1995) 8 *Insolvency Intelligence* 76..154
Jeavons, *Re*, *ex p* Brown (1874) 9 Ch App 304; (1874) 43 LJ Bcy 105; (1874) 30 LT 108 120
Jones (VA 289 of 1994), *Re* (1995) unreported, 24 March 147
Jones, *Re*, *ex p* Jones (1881) 18 ChD 109; [1881–5] All ER Rep 831; (1881) 50 LJ Ch 673 6
Judgment Debtor (No 1539 of 1936), A, *Re* [1937] Ch 137; (1937) 106 LJ Ch 183; (1937) 156 LT 16 ....13, 27
Keever (A Bankrupt), *Re*, *ex p* Trustee of the Property of the bankrupt v Midland Bank [1967] Ch 182; [1966] 3 WLR 779; [1966] 3 All ER 631..........................22
Kent, *Re*, *ex p* Official Receiver [1905] 2 KB 666...52
Kerr v Kerr [1897] 2 QB 439; [1895–9] All ER Rep 865; (1895) 66 LJ QB 838........84
Kouyoundjian (a Bankrupt), *Re*, *ex p* The Trustee v Lord [1956] 1 WLR 558; [1956] 2 All ER 286; (1956) 100 SJ 381...20
Kumar, *Re* [1993] 1 WLR 224; [1993] 2 All ER 700; [1993] BCLC 548 102
Leake (formerly Bruzzi) v Bruzzi [1974] 1 WLR 1528; [1974] 2 All ER 1196 ....99, 100
Leisure Study Group, *Re* [1994] 2 BCLC 65..154
Leonard, *Re*, *ex p* Leonard [1896] QB 473; (1896) 65 LJ QB 393; (1896) 74 LT 183 34
Levy, (AI) (Holdings), *Re* [1964] Ch 19; [1963] 2 WLR 1464; [1963] 2 All ER 556 42
Lewis, *Re*, *ex p* Harris (1876) 2 ChD 423; (1876) 45 LJ Bcy 71; (1876) 34 LT 261 22
Linton, *Re*, Linton v Linton (1885) 15 QBD 239; (1885) 54 LJ QB 529; (1885) 52 LT 782, CA..84
Lister v Hooson [1908] 1 KB 174; (1908) 77 LJ KB 161; (1908) 98 LT 75, CA.........91
Lloyd, *ex p* (1882) 47 LT 64, CA 125
Lowrie, *Re*, *ex p* The Trustee of the Bankrupt v The Bankrupt [1981] 3 All ER 353................98
McGreavey, *Re*, *ex p* McGreavey v Benfleet Urban District Council [1950] Ch 269; [1950] 1 All ER 442; (1950) 94 SJ 146, CA 7, 21
McKeen, *Re* [1995] BCC 412...154
McKinnon v Armstrong Brothers & Co (1887) 2 App Cas 531; (1887) 36 LT 482 91
McMullen v Cerrone (1994) BCC 25; (1993) 66 P&CR 351; [1994] 1 BCLC 152 145
Majory (A Debtor), *Re*, *ex p* The Debtor v Dumont (FA) [1955] Ch 600; [1955] 2 WLR 1035; (1955) 99 SJ 316...34
Maugham, *Re*, *ex p* Maugham (1888) 21 QBD 21; (1888) 57 LJ QB 487, DC 118
Midland Bank v Pike [1988] 2 All ER 434; (1986) *Financial Times*, 18 April 99

TABLE OF CASES

Mordant Mordant and Hallis, *Re* [1995] BCC 209 71
Myrtle v Reynolds (1995) unreported, 20 October 148
Naeem, *Re* [1990] 1 WLR 48; [1989] LS Gaz, 20 December 152, 153
National Westminster Bank v Halesowen Presswork and Assemblies Ltd [1972] AC 785; [1972] 2 WLR 455; [1972] 1 All ER 641, HL 90, 91
Noble (A Bankrupt), *Re*, *ex p* The Bankrupt v Official Receiver [1965] Ch 129; [1964] 3 WLR 206; [1964] 2 All ER 522 .... 35, 121
Norris, *Re*, *ex p* Norris (1890) 7 Morr 8, CA 50
Norris, *Re*, *ex p* Reymolds (1888) 4 TLR 452; (1888) 5 Morr 111, CA 5
Onslow, *Re*, *ex p* Kibble (1875) 10 Ch App 373; (1875) 44 LJ Bcy 63; (1875) 32 LT 138 35
Otway, *Re*, *ex p* Otway [1895] 1 QB 812; (1895) 64 LJ QB 521; (1895) 72 LT 452 35
Owen, *Re*, *ex p* Owen (1884) 12 QBD 113; (1884) 58 LJ Ch 863; (1884) 50 LT 514, CA 21
Paget, *Re*, *ex p* Official Receiver [1927] 2 Ch 85; [1927] All ER Rep 465; (1927) 96 LJ Ch 377, CA 56
Painter, *Re*, *ex p* Painter [1895] 1 QB 85; (1895) 64 LJ QB 22; (1895) LT 581, DC 40
Palmer, *Re* [1944] Ch 316 141
Penned v Rhodes (1846) 9 QB 114 34
Philippson, *Re*, 1993 Harrogate County Court, 7 *Insolvency Intelligence* 57 149
Porter v Freudenberg [1915] 1 KB 857; [1914–15] All ER Rep 918; (1914) 84 LJ KB 1001; (1914) 112 LT 313, CA 27
Practice Direction (Bankruptcy 4/86) *see* Practice Note (Bankruptcy: Substituted Service) (No 4 of 1986) 24
Practice Direction (Bankruptcy No 1 of 1991) [1992] 1 All ER 678 .... 146, 151
Practice Direction (Bankruptcy: Distribution of Business) [1987] 1 WLR 1202 32
Practice Direction (Bankruptcy: Petition) [1987] 1 All ER 602 24
Practice Direction (No 1 of 1995) (Insolvency Appeals: Individuals) [1995] BCC 1129; (1995) *The Times*, 14 August 118
Practice Direction [1988] 3 All ER 984 15
Practice Note (Bankruptcy: Certificate of Debt) [1987] 1 WLR 120; [1986] 2 All ER 864 33
Practice Note (Bankruptcy: Consent Orders) No 2 of 1992 [1992] 1 WLR 379; [1992] 2 All ER 300 128
Practice Note (Bankruptcy: Petition) [1987] 1 WLR 81; [1987] 1 All ER 602 23
Practice Note (Bankruptcy: Petition (No 2)) [1987] 1 WLR 1424; [1987] 1 All ER 602 23
Practice Note (Bankruptcy: Service Abroad) [1988] 1 WLR 461 12
Practice Note (Bankruptcy: Statutory Demand: Setting Aside) [1987] 1 WLR 119; [1987] 1 All ER 607 .... 13, 15, 16, 17
Practice Note (Bankruptcy: Substituted Service) (No 4 of 1986) [1987] 1 WLR 82; [1987] 1 All ER 604; (1987) 1331 SJ 1024 .... 11, 12, 26
R v Hayat (1976) 63 Cr App R 181; [1976] Crim LR 508; (1976) 120 SJ 434, CA 111
R v Leinster (Duke of) [1924] 1 KB 311; [1923] All ER Rep 187; (1923) 93 LJ KB 144 111
R v Maywhort [1955] 1 WLR 848; [1955] 2 All ER 752; (1955) 99 SJ 510 112
R v Salter [1968] 2 QB 793; [1968] 3 WLR 39; [1968] 2 All ER 951 112
R v Smith (1915) 11 Cr App Rep 81, CCA 111
R v Tuttle [1929] All ER Rep 107; (1929) 140 LT 701; (1929) 45 TLR 357, CA 112
Rainbow v Mortgage Properties Ltd [1995] 1 WLR 789 44
Ramsey v Hartley [1977] 1 WLR 686; [1977] 2 All ER 673; (1977) 121 SJ 319 127
Roberts Petroleum Ltd v Bernard Kenny Ltd [1983] 2 AC 192; [1983] 2 WLR 305; [1983] 1 All ER 564 44
Rogers v James (1816) 7 Taunt 147; (1816) 2 Marsh 425; (1816) 129 ER 59 22
Rolls Razor v Cox [1967] 1 QB 552; [1967] 2 WLR 241; [1967] 1 All ER 397 90
Rose, *Re* [1995] BCC 102 71
Sacker, *Re*, *ex p* Sacker (1888) 22 QBD 179; (1882) 58 LJ QB 4; (1882) 60 LT 344, CA 21

Saigol v Goldstein [1994] 1 WLR 1610; (1994) BCC 576; [1994] EGCS 95 149
Salaman (A Bankrupt), *Re* (1983) 127 SJ 763; (1983) 80 LS Gaz 2997, DC 32
Seagull Manufacturing Co Ltd (in liquidation), *Re* [1991] 3 WLR 307; [1991] 4
   All ER 257; [1993] BCC 41; (1991) 135 SJ (LB) 18..55, 116
Sheehan, *Re,* 1994 Swansea County Court, 7 *Insolvency Intelligence* 57....................................149
Smith v Braintree DC [1989] 3 WLR 1317; [1989] 3 All ER 897...43
Stacey v Hill [1901] 1 KB 660; (1901) 70 LJ KB 435; (1901) 84 LT 410, CA...........................81
Stein v Blake [1994] Ch 16; [1993] 3 WLR 718; [1993] 4 All ER 225; (1995)
   BCC 543, CA...89
Suttill v Graham [1977] 1 WLR 819; [1977] 3 All ER 1117; (1977) 121 SJ 408.....................100
T H Knitwear (Wholesale) Ltd, *Re* [1988] 1 All ER 860; (1988) 4 BCC 102 ....87, 126
Taylor, *Re*, *ex p* Taylor [1901] 1 KB 744; (1901) 70 LJ KB 531; (1901) 84 LT 426 52
Theophile v Solicitor-General [1950] AC 186; [1950] 1 All ER 405; (1950) 94 SJ
   208...5
Thomas, *ex p* (1747) 1 Atk 73; [1747] 26 ER 82..7
Tucker, *Re* [1990] 1 All ER 603 116
Tynte, *Re*, *ex p* Tynte (1880) 15 ChD 125; (1880) 42 LT 598; [1880] 28 WR 767....................7
Unit 2 Windows Ltd (in liquidation), *Re* [1985] 1 WLR 1383; [1985] 3 All ER
   647; (1986) PCC 194..91
Victor v Victor [1912] 1 KB 247; [1911–13] ER Rep 959; (1911) 81 LJ KB 354.....................84
Von Engel, *Re* (1988) *The Independent*, 21 August...51
Warnford Investments Ltd v Duckworth [1979] 1 Ch 127; [1978] 2 WLR 741;
   [1978] 2 All ER 517..81
Webber, *Re*, *ex p* Webber (1889) 24 QBD 313; (1889) 59 LJ QB 581; (1889) 62
   LT 485, CA..121
Wells, *Re* [1892] Ch 116...106
Wells v Girting (1819) 1 Brod & Bing 447; (1819) 4 Moore CP 78; [1819] 129
   ER 795..7
Wike, *Re*, *ex p* Keighley (1874) 9 Ch App 667; (1874) 44 LJ Bcy 13, LJJ 123
Winterbottom, *Re*, *ex p* Winterbottom (1886) 18 QBD 446; (1886) 56 LJ QB 238;
   (1886) 56 LT 168, DC 21
Wisepark, *Re* (1994) BCC 221...149
Woodstead Finance v Petrou (1985) 136 New LJ 188, CA...104
Wright, (SA & D), *Re* (1992) BCC 503...42

Table of Statutes

Administration of Justice Act 1988—
    ss 71, 77, 80 113
    s 84(1), (6) 113
    s 87 113
Bankruptcy Act 1869 .... 4, 143
Bankruptcy Act 1883 .... 1, 2, 143
Bankruptcy Act 1890 .... 2, 143
Bankruptcy Act 1914 .... 2, 5, 143
Bankruptcy (Amendment) Act 1926 2
Bills of Sale Act 1878 104
Changing Orders Act 1979—
    s 1 105
    s 3 75
    (5) 75
Companies Act 1985—
    s 375 61
Company Directors Disqualification Act
1986 .... 132, 136
    s 11 112
Consumer Credit Act 1974 104
Deeds of Arrangement Act 1913 2
Deeds of Arrangement Act 1914 .... 143, 155
    s 1 155
    (2) 156
    s 2 156
    s 3(1), (5) 156
    ss 11, 13, 14, 15 157
    ss 16, 17, 19 158
Finance Act 1983 86
    s 22(5) 87
Insolvency Act 1976 2
Insolvency Act 1985—
    sched 10 97
Insolvency Act 1986 .... 2, 11, 14, 16, 75, 78,
                              95, 101, 119, 120,
                                     135, 138
    Part I 132
    Part II 132
    s 31 112
    s 125A(6) 135
    s 175 137

Insolvency Act 1986 (contd)—
    s 175A 137
    (5)(b) 132
    s 221A 133
    Pt VIII 34
    ss 252–263 41
    s 252 39
    s 253 145
    (2) 144
    s 254(1), (2) 145
    s 255(1)(c) 145
    (5) 146
    s 258 150
    s 259 151
    s 260(2) 153
    (4), (5) 151
    s 261 151
    s 262 152
    (4) 152
    s 263(3) 153
    (5) 154
    s 264(1)(b) 37
    (c) 154
    s 265 (1) 4
    (2) 5
    s 266(3) 24
    s 267 7
    (2)(b) 6, 7
    (c) 6, 8
    (d) 8
    (4) 6
    s 268 .... 8, 20
    (1)(a) 8, 11, 13
    (b) 8
    (2) 9
    s 269 .... 21, 135
    (1)(a) 6, 22
    (b) 6
    s 270 .... 14, 15, 135
    s 271 141
    (1) 33
    (2) 14, 33

Insolvency Act 1986 (contd)—
- s 271(3), (c) 33
- (5) 29
- s 272(1), (2) 37
- s 273 .... 38, 39, 44, 46, 141
- s 274 39
- s 275 39
- (3) 40
- s 276 154
- s 279(1), (2) 93
- (3) 57, 93
- s 280 94
- (2), (3) 95
- s 281 96
- (5) 40
- s 282 52
- (1), (a) 51
- (b) 52
- (3) 51
- s 283 141
- (1) 70
- (2) 70–2
- s 284 42
- (1)–(3) 42
- (4) 141
- (a), (b) 42
- (5) 43
- s 285 .... 44, 74, 141
- (1), (2) 43
- (3) 43, 105
- (5) 44
- s 286 116
- (1) 44
- (2) 44, 45
- (3) 44
- (5) 45
- (7) 46
- s 287(1)–(4) 46
- s 288(1)–(3) 47
- (4) 48
- s 289(1) 49
- s 290(1), (2) 54
- (3) 55
- (4) 56
- (5) 55
- s 292(1) 58
- (2) 58, 139
- (3), (4) 58
- s 293(1), (2) 59
- s 294 59
- s 295(2) 58
- (3) 119
- s 296 63
- (2) 58, 119
- s 297 .... 46, 58
- (2) 40
- s 298(1) 64
- (5) 119

Insolvency Act 1986 (contd)—
- s 298(7) 63
- s 299 119
- s 300(2) 66
- (3) 64
- (6) 58, 119
- s 301(1) 66
- s 302(1) 21
- (2) 69, 124
- s 303 53
- (1), (2) 125
- (2A)–(C) 137
- s 304 53
- s 305(2), (3) 70
- s 306(2) 70
- s 307 .... 71, 78
- (4) 71
- s 308 .... 71, 72, 78
- (1)–(4) 72
- s 309 72
- s 310 .... 71, 73
- (1)–(4), (6), (7) 73
- s 311 .... 74, 116
- (3)–(5) 74
- s 312 .... 74, 116
- s 313 99
- (1) 74
- (3), (4) 75
- s 314 75
- (2) 75
- (4) 76, 124
- (6), (7) 76
- ss 315–319 79
- s 315 77
- (2) 77
- (3), (5) 81
- (6) 124
- s 316 78
- s 317 79
- (2) 79
- ss 318, 319 80
- s 320 79
- (2)–(4) 80
- s 321(1), (3) 80
- s 323 89
- s 324(3) 88
- s 325(2) 88
- s 328(4) 86
- s 329 83
- (6) 80
- s 330 88
- s 332 99
- s 333 71
- s 336 .... 75, 80
- (1), (2) 97
- (5) 97, 98
- s 337 .... 75, 80
- (2), (5) 98

TABLE OF STATUTES

Insolvency Act 1986 (contd)—
  s 338 99
  s 339 ....100–4, 113, 144
    (1) 101
    (2) 103
    (3) 101
  s 340 ....101–3, 144
    (2) 103
    (3), (4) 102
    (5), (6) 103
  s 341 103
    (2) 103
    (3) 103, 104
  s 342 103
    (1), (2A) 104
  s 343 ....104, 144
    (3) 104
  s 344 104
    (2), (3)(b) 104
  s 346 ....43, 105
    (1)–(6) 105
  s 347 ....43, 105
    (1) 105
    (2) 106
    (3) 43, 106
    (4), (5), (8) 106
  s 349 106
  s 350 107
  s 352 107–110
  s 353 108
  s 354 108
    (1)–(3) 108
  s 355 ....108, 109, 111
  s 356 109
    (1) 108
  s 357 ....108, 109
  s 358 ....108, 110
  s 359 110
    (1) 108
  s 360 110
  ss 361, 362 111
  s 363(1), (2), (3), (4) 114
  s 364 114
    (1) 129
  s 365 115
    (4) 115
  s 366 ....73, 115, 116, 129
    (1) 106
  s 367 116
    (3) 115
  s 369 116
  s 370 ....45, 46, 116

Insolvency Act 1986 (contd)—
  s 370(3), (4) 117
  s 371 117
  s 374 20
  s 375 ....119, 120, 131
    (1) 50, 118
    (2) 118
  s 376 ....15, 50, 78, 80, 85, 120, 128–130
  s 383 21
    (3), (4) 22
  s 386 ....82, 84, 86
  s 423 ....100–102, 113, 116
  s 435 103
  s 436 5
  Sched 4 137
  Sched 5 124
    Parts 1, II 75
  Sched 6 ....82, 84, 86, 142
  Sched 10 107
  Sched 11 2
    para 13(1), (2) 93
Land Charges Act 1972 75
Land Registration Act 1925 75
Law of Property Act 1925—
  s 30 97
  s 172 102
Law Reform (Married Women and Tort
  feasors) Act 1935 6
  s 1 22
Limitation Act 1939 47
Local Government Finance Act 1988 7
Magistrates' Courts Act 1980—
  s 32 107
Married Woman's Property Act 1882—
  s 17 100
Matrimonial Causes Act 1973—
  s 24 42
  s 39 101
Matrimonial Homes Act 1983 ....97, 98
  s 1 ....97, 98
    (1) 97
    (3) 98
Mental Health Act 1983 ....6, 55
Partnership Act 1890 137
Powers of Criminal Courts Act 1973 .....2, 113
Social Security Pensions Act 1975—
  Sched 3 82
Supreme Court Act 1981—
  s 16 118
Theft Act 1968 ....2, 112
Trustee Act 1925—
  s 41 157

Table of Statutory Instruments

Administration of Insolvent Estates of Deceased Persons Order 1986 (SI No 1999) 27, 139
   art 2 141
   art 4 139
      (2), (3) 139
   art 5 ....27, 140, 141
      (2) 140, 141
      (3), (4) 140
      (5) 141
   art 12 ....141, 142
   art 24 142
   Sched 1, Part II 140, 141
   Sched 2 28
      art 1 140
      Part II 141
   Sched 3 ....140, 141
Bankruptcy Rules 1952 (SI No 2113) 2
Conditional Fee Agreements Order 1995 (SI No 1674) 127
County Court Fees Order 1982 (SI No 1706) 3
County Court Rules 1981 (SI No 1687) 2
   Ord 38 131
Deeds of Arrangement Rules 1925 (SI No 795) 155
Insolvency Fees Order 1986 (SI No 2030)–
   arts 8, 9 ....3, 38
Insolvency Practitioners Regulations 1986 (SI No 1995) 45
Insolvency Proceedings (Monetary Limits) Order 1986 (SI No 1996) ....
                          3, 72, 105, 108
Insolvency Rules 1986 (SI No 1925) 2, 14, 16, 78, 119, 120, 125
   rr 5.3, 5.4 145
   r 5.5(1), (2), (4) 146
   r 5.5A 146
   r 5.6(4) 147
   r 5.7 147
   r 5.8 147

Insolvency Rules 1986 (SI No 1925) (contd)—
   r 5.8(4) 147
   r 5.9 147
   r 5.10 ....147, 148
      (4) 148
   r 5.13 148
   r 5.14 149
   r 5.17 ....149, 152
      (9) 152
   r 5.18(1), (2) 150
      (3)(*b*) 149
      (4), (5) 150
   r 5.19(1), (3) 150
   r 5.21 153
   r 5.22 151
      (2) 152
   r 5.29 153
   r 5.30 154
   r 6.1(1), (3), (4) 10, 17
      (5) 10
   r 6.2 23
      (2) 11
      (4) 10
   r 6.3 24
      (1) 12
      (2) 11
      (3) 12, 25
   r 6.4(1) 14
      (2) 15
      (3) 14, 16
   r 6.5(1)–(4) 16
      (6) 18
   r 6.7(1) 22
      (3) 23
   r 6.8(1) 23
      (*a*) 24
   r 6.8(3) 23
   r 6.9 37
      (1)–(5) 19
   r 6.10 26
      (6) 58

Insolvency Rules 1986 (SI No 1925)
(*contd*)—
r 6.11(1) 12, 13
    (3), (4) 12
    (5) 12, 13
    (6), (7) 13
    (8) 13, 25
r 6.12(1), (3)–(7) 24
r 6.13 26
r 6.14(1), (2), (4) 26
r 6.15 27
    (2) 27
r 6.16 27
r 6.17(2)–(4) 28
r 6.18(1), (2) 29
rr 6.21, 6.22 29
r 6.23 ....30, 31
r 6.24 30
    (3) 30
r 6.25(1) 34
    (2), (3) 35
r 6.26 30
r 6.28 30
    (4) 30
r 6.29 31
r 6.30 32
    (1), (2) 31
r 6.31 ....31, 32
    (1), (2) 31
r 6.32(1), (2) 32
    (3) 31, 32
r 6.33 35
    (4) 35
r 6.34 50
    (2) 35, 36
    (3), (4) 36
r 6.38 37
    (3) 38
r 6.39 38
    (2) 38
r 6.40 ....10, 37
    (3) 37
r 6.42 38
    (6) 38
    (7) 40
r 6.43 38
r 6.44 39
r 6.45 40
r 6.46 40
    (2) 40
    (3) 41
r 6.50 40
r 6.51(2), (3) 45
r 6.52(1) 45
r 6.53(2) 45
    (3) 45
rr 6.55, 6.56 45
r 6.57(1), (3) 46

Insolvency Rules 1986 (SI No 1925)
(*contd*)—
r 6.59 47
r 6.60(1)–(3) 47
r 6.61 ....48, 77
r 6.62(4), (5) 47
    (7) 48
r 6.63(1)–(3) 48
r 6.64(1), (2) 48
rr 6.65, 6.66, 6.71 49
r 6.79(1)–(3) 59
    (4) 59, 60, 62
    (5) 59
r 6.80 62
    (2) 63
r 6.81 59
r 6.84 ....60, 63
r 6.86 59
r 6.88 60
    (2) 63
r 6.89 60
r 6.92(1)–(3) 60
r 6.93 61
    (1), (3), (4) 60
r 6.94 60
    (3), (4) 60
r 6.96 83
    (2), (3) 83
r 6.97 83
    (2) 83
r 6.98(1), (3) 84
r 6.104 85
r 6.105 ....85, 125
r 6.107 86
r 6.108 85
r 6.111 84
r 6.112(1), (2) 84
r 6.113 86
    (3), (4) 86
r 6.114 84
rr 6.115, 6.116 87
r 6.117(4) 87
rr 6.118, 6.119 87
r 6.120(2)–(5) 63
r 6.122 119
r 6.126 63
    (3), (4) 64
r 6.127(3), (7) 64
r 6.128 64
r 6.129(3) 64
r 6.130 64
r 6.132 64
    (2) 65
r 6.133 ....65, 119
r 6.135(4) 119
r 6.138 125
    (3) 66
rr 6.140–142 125

Insolvency Rules 1986 (SI No 1925)
(*contd*)—
r 6.148(1) 62
    (2) 62, 67
r 6.150(2), (3) 66
r 6.151 66
    (3), (3A) 66
r 6.152(1) 67
r 6.153(1), (2) 67
    (3) 68
r 6.154 67
r 6.155 67
    (2) 68
r 6.156 ....66, 67
    (2) 66
rr 6.157, 6.158, 6.160 68
r 6.162(1), (3), (4) 68
r 6.163 67
r 6.164 69
r 6.165(4) 69
r 6.166(2) 119
r 6.172(3), (4) 55
r 6.173(1) 54
    (2) 57
    (4), (5) 54
r 6.174(1)–(3) 55
r 6.175(1)–(6) 56
r 6.176(1)–(3) 56
    (4) 57, 94
r 6.177 57
r 6.178 77
r 6.179 79
    (6) 79
r 6.180 79
rr 6.182, 6.184 78
r 6.185 79
r 6.186 80
    (3) 81
r 6.187(2) 72
r 6.188 72
r 6.189(2) 73
rr 6.190, 6.191 73
rr 6.192, 6.193 74
rr 6.194–196 116
r 6.200(1), (2) 71
    (4), (5) 72
r 6.201 71
r 6.206 51
    (4) 51
r 6.207(2)–(5) 52
rr 6.208–6.210 52
r 6.211(3), (4) 52
r 6.212 53
r 6.213 53
    (1) 53
r 6.215 ....93, 94
r 6.216 93
rr 6.217, 6.218 95

Insolvency Rules 1986 (SI No 1925)
(*contd*)—
r 6.219 85
rr 6.220, 6.221 95
r 6.224 ....38, 69, 76
    (1)(*e*) 45
r 6.236 28
r 6.237 99
rr 7.2–7.4 128
r 7.4(4) 51
    (6) 128
r 7.5 128
r 7.6 129
    (1), (2) 128
    (3), (4) 129
rr 7.7–7.9 129
r 7.11 ....20, 129
    (5) 20
r 7.12 ....20, 129
rr 7.19, 7.20 129
r 7.21 ....115, 129
r 7.22 115
r 7.23 129
r 7.26(2) 128
r 7.28(2) 130
r 7.31 130
r 7.33 131
r 7.34 131
    (2) 125
    (4), (5) 131
rr 7.35, 7.36 131
r 7.43 6
r 7.44 ....6, 21
r 7.48(1) 119
r 7.50 118
r 7.51 3
r 7.55 ....14, 17
r 7.56 43
r 7.57 83
r 8.1(3) 61
r 8.2 62
    (1), (2) 61
r 8.6(1), (1A) 62
r 8.7 61
    (3) 61
r 9.6(4) 115
r 11.2(1), (1A), (2), (3) 85
r 11.3(1), (2) 85
r 11.5(2) 88
r 11.6(2) 87
    (4) 88
rr 11.7, 11.11 88
r 11.13 84
r 12.3 83
    (7) 83
r 12.4A(2), (4) 60
r 12.7 130
r 12.8 67

Insolvency Rules 1986 (SI No 1925) (*contd*)—
  r 12.9..13, 130
  r 12.10...130
  r 12.11...14
  r 12.12...55
  r 13.7..14
  Sched 2 ....10, 37
  Sched 4 ....9, 12, 16–18, 20, 24, 26, 27,
            29–32, 37, 38, 45, 47, 55, 60, 61,
            67, 77, 83, 99, 128, 130, 145,
            148, 149, 151
  Sched 5 16
    para 2 21
Insolvent Partnerships Order 1994 (SI No 2421)................5, 6, 132, 137
  art 10...132
  art 11...135
  Sched 3 134

Insolvent Partnerships Order 1994 (SI No 2421) (*contd*)—
  Sched 4 137
  Sched 9 ....133, 134, 135
Rules of the Supreme Court 1965 (SI No 1776)..2
  Ord 3...130
    r 2..13
    rr 3, 6 130
  Ord 23...122
  Ord 59..120, 121
    r 10(5)..122
  Ord 62...131
  Ord 65, r 7 ....14, 24, 26, 29
  Ord 66, r 1 130
  Ord 81, r 5 ....5, 134, 136
    r 6..5
Supreme Court Fees Order 1980 (SI No 821)..3

Chapter 1

Introduction

Bankruptcy is the status of a debtor who has been declared by judicial process to be insolvent or unable to pay his debts as they fall due out of his assets. This sets in motion a statutory system which has two primary objects. The first is to vest all the property which the debtor has at the commencement of the bankruptcy or acquires before his discharge in a trustee for distribution amongst his creditors equitably according to their rights. The second is to release the debtor from his liability to those creditors at the end of a specified period subject to his conduct during the bankruptcy.

Bankruptcy legislation has a long history, commencing with a statute of Henry VIII which dealt with fraudulent debtors. Until 1861 the bankruptcy laws applied only to traders; non-traders who were unable to pay their debts came under another set of statutes relating to insolvent debtors. In 1869 an Act to amend and consolidate the existing law was passed, which contained many of the substantive bankruptcy law principles now in operation. It also provided for the administration of bankruptcy law and matters in the London bankruptcy district by judges of the High Court specially appointed by the Lord Chancellor, and by bankruptcy registrars, and in the country by the county court judges. There was no separation between the judicial and administrative functions, both of which were exercised by the court.

The administration of bankruptcy matters under the 1869 Act did not work efficiently owing to the lack of official control over the trustees in bankruptcy, a new office created by the Act in place of the former system of official assignees, and in 1883 the Bankruptcy Act of that year repealed the 1869 Act and amended and consolidated the law. This Act laid the basis of modern bankruptcy administration. It separated the judicial and administrative functions. The former remained vested in the High Court and the county courts, but the administrative functions were transferred to the Board of Trade. A new department was set up, entitled the Bankruptcy Department of the Board of Trade, under the Inspector-General in Bankruptcy. Its functions were to exercise a general supervision, under the direction of the Board of Trade and the ultimate control of Parliament, over all the administrative side of bankruptcy work, including control over the appointment and the work of trustees in bankruptcy. A necessary corollary was the provision in the Act for the appointment by the Board of Trade, now the Department of Trade and Industry, of officers to carry out these supervisory functions of the Department. These officers were, and are, entitled official receivers. They are officers of the Department who act in their respective districts under the general direction and authority of the Department, but they are also invested with the status of officers of the courts to which they are attached. There are proposals being considered to privatise the work of the Insolvency Service (as the official receivers' service is now called). From the 1883 Act also come the features in our present-day law of an investigation by the court into the debtor's conduct, punishment for bankruptcy offences, strict investigation of proof of debts and general supervision of proceedings, including the control of funds and independent audit of the trustee's accounts.

The Bankruptcy Act of 1890 and the Bankruptcy and Deeds of Arrangement Act of 1913 (the latter enacted to give effect to the recommendations of a committee of inquiry appointed some years before) introduced no sweeping reforms. The principal reform made by the earlier Act was in respect of the conditions relating to the discharge of a bankrupt. The 1913 Act made offences by bankrupts punishable summarily and in general tightened up the law as to criminal liability of bankrupts, as well as amending the law as to married women and the avoidance of settlements.

The Insolvency Act 1976 introduced, amongst other things, the concept of the automatic review of all bankruptcies after five years with the object of granting the bankrupt a discharge unless he had failed to comply with any of his obligations under the Act.

The Bankruptcy Act 1914, the Bankruptcy (Amendment) Act 1926, the Theft Act 1968, the Powers of Criminal Courts Act 1973 and the Insolvency Act 1976, together with the Bankruptcy Rules 1952 (SI No 2113) as amended from time to time, govern all bankruptcies commenced before 29 December 1986 when the Insolvency Act 1986 came into force. The Insolvency Act 1986 and the rules made under it are referred to in this book as 'the Act'; the Insolvency Rules 1986 (as amended) are referred to as 'the Rules'. Where section numbers or rule numbers are quoted without a reference to any act or rules, then they are sections or rules of the Act or the Rules as the case may be.

The Act only applies to those cases where the proceedings were begun on or after 29 December 1986, that is, where a petition was presented on or after that date. The old law continues to apply to those bankruptcies which commenced, that is, where a petition was presented or a receiving order was made, before that date subject to some transitional provisions set out in Sched 11 of the Act.

This book only deals with the bankruptcy law set out in the Act and the Rules, though previous case law where still applicable is referred to as appropriate. For the old law, which continues to apply as stated, reference should still be made to the Bankruptcy Act 1914 and the Bankruptcy Rules 1952, as amended, and to the third edition of this book.

Except so far as is inconsistent with the Insolvency Rules 1986, the Rules of the Supreme Court and the practice of the High Court apply to bankruptcy proceedings in the High Court and the County Court Rules and the practice of the county court apply to bankruptcy proceedings in the county court with the necessary modifications (r 7.51).

Court fees are prescribed by the Supreme Court Fees Order and the County Court Fees Order except for the requirements relating to deposits payable on the presentation of bankruptcy petitions which are to be found in the Insolvency Fees Order 1986 (SI No 2030), arts 8 and 9 as amended.

Monetary limits applicable to small bankruptcies, and references to an insolvency practitioner for a report on a possible voluntary arrangement etc are set out in the Insolvency Proceedings (Monetary Limits) Order 1986 (SI No 1996).

Chapter 2

The Debtor and the Debt

1 The debtor

A person can be made bankrupt subject to English bankruptcy law if a bankruptcy petition can be presented to the court against him. This applies whether the petition is presented by the debtor himself or by a creditor.

By s 265(1) of the Act, a petition may not be presented to the court unless the debtor:
(1) is domiciled in England and Wales; or
(2) is personally present in England and Wales on the day on which the petition is presented; or
(3) at any time in the period of three years ending with the day the petition was presented, has been ordinarily resident or has a place of residence in England and Wales or has carried on business in England and Wales.

The onus is on the petitioning creditor to establish the jurisdiction of the English bankruptcy court when an issue is raised by the debtor as to jurisdiction (*Re Barne* (1886) 16 QBD 522). Decisions on the interpretation of the jurisdictional sections have usually arisen from attempts to make a foreigner bankrupt.

Foreigners

At one time the English bankruptcy court would only exercise jurisdiction over a foreigner if the foreigner (a) came to England, (b) contracted debts in England and (c) committed an act of bankruptcy in England (*Re Crispin, ex p Crispin* (1873) LR 8 Ch 374, decided under the provisions of the Bankruptcy Act 1869). Now, although the foreigner must still owe a debt or debts which are enforceable in this country, the bankruptcy court will exercise jurisdiction over him even if he has never been personally in England provided that he has at any time in the three years before the presentation of the petition carried on business there by a manager or been a partner in a firm carrying on business in England.

Domicile

It is for the debtor to prove that he has changed his domicile if his domicile was in England and Wales and he says that he is no longer domiciled there. In *Re*

Bird [1962] 1 WLR 686, the debtor successfully proved that he had changed his domicile and so was outside the provisions of an alternative method of conferring jurisdiction on the English courts in the 1914 Act.

Ordinarily resident

For a debtor to fall within the term 'ordinarily resident', there must be some regularity in his stay within the jurisdiction during the relevant period; it must not be occasional although there is no requirement that it be for any great length of time (*Re Brauch (a Debtor)* [1977] 3 WLR 354). There are a number of reported decisions on the meaning of 'ordinarily resident' (see, for example, *Re Norris, ex p Reynolds* (1888) 5 Morr 111; *Re Erskine, ex p Erskine* (1893) 10 TLR 32) but in each case it is a question of fact and degree for the court on the basis of the evidence submitted to it (*Re Brauch*, above).

Carried on business in England

The debtor must have carried on his own business and not, for example, that of a limited company even if he is the majority shareholder or controlling director (*Re Brauch*, above). Once it is established that the debtor has carried on his own business, he is deemed to continue to carry on such business until he has satisfied all the obligations which the fact of carrying on that business has imposed on him (*Theophile v Solicitor-General* [1950] AC 186 and *Re a Debtor (No 784 of 1991)* [1992] Ch 554). Thus, in *Re Bird* [1962] 1 WLR 686, the debtor was held to continue to carry on his business because he had failed to pay income tax assessed on that business. Because of the extension of the period, at some time during which the debtor must have carried on business in England and Wales, to three years, the importance of the deemed continuance of carrying on business may have diminished.

Business is defined in s 436 of the Act as including a trade or profession.

Partnership

Although s 265(2) of the Act provides that 'carrying on business' includes the carrying on of business by a firm or partnership, a bankruptcy petition cannot be presented against an individual member of an insolvent partnership until after a winding up petition has been presented against the partnership as an unregistered company under the Insolvent Partnerships Order 1994 (SI No 2421). However, if the requirements of RSC Ord 81, rr 5 and 6 have been satisfied, proceedings in respect of a partnership debt can be taken against one or more of the partners and these would include bankruptcy proceedings. For proceedings against insolvent partnerships generally, see Chapter 26.

Minors

In the absence of a debt actually enforceable against a minor, he cannot be made bankrupt, whether the petition is presented by a person claiming to be a creditor

(*Re Jones, ex p Jones* (1881) 18 Ch D 109) or by the minor himself (*Re A and M* [1926] Ch 274; *Re Davenport* [1963] 1 WLR 817).

Where the debt incurred by the minor is in respect of necessaries, the minor can be made bankrupt (*Re a Debtor (No 564 of 1949)* [1950] Ch 282).

In the case of a partnership, where one of the partners is a minor, if there is no enforceable debt against him, a winding up order can be made against the partnership as an unregistered company under the Insolvent Partnerships Order 1994 but leave to enforce the partnership debts against the minor personally would be refused and so bankruptcy proceedings against him could not be taken.

Married women

The Law Reform (Married Women and Tortfeasors) Act 1935 provides that a married woman shall be subject to the law relating to bankruptcy and to the enforcement of judgments and orders in all respects as if she were a single woman.

Mentally disordered persons

Mentally disordered persons within the meaning of the Mental Health Act 1983 are liable to be made bankrupt (*Re Farnham* [1895] Ch 799; *Re a Debtor (No 1 of 1941)* [1941] Ch 487). The concurrence of the Court of Protection will be required (see *Re a Debtor (No 1 of 1941)*, above).

Where bankruptcy proceedings are taken against such a person and it appears to the court that the person is incapable of managing and administering his property and affairs, the court may appoint such person as it thinks fit to appear for, represent or act for that person (rr 7.43 and 7.44).

2 The debt

The debt on which a creditor petitions must satisfy the following conditions:
 (a) it must equal or exceed the 'bankruptcy level'—currently £750 (s 267(4)) (or, if two or more creditors join in the petition, the aggregate amount of the debts owing to the several petitioning creditors must equal or exceed this minimum);
 (b) it must be a liquidated sum, payable either immediately or at some certain future time and be unsecured (s 267(2)(*b*)); and
 (c) it must be a debt which the debtor appears either unable to pay or to have no reasonable prospect of being able to pay (s 267(2)(*c*)).

If the creditor holds security but it is insufficient in value to cover the debt due to him, he can petition for the shortfall provided that this is above the minimum level (£750) and provided that the petition is expressed not to be made in respect of the secured part of the debt and the creditor states the estimated value of his security (s 269(1)(*b*)). If the creditor is willing to give up his security he can petition for the entire debt due to him (s 269(1)(*a*)).

Where the petition is based on a judgment debt for damages and costs, the costs must have been taxed at the date of the presentation of the petition to be included as part of the minimum debt (*Re a Debtor (No 20 of 1953)* [1954] 1 WLR 1190). The debt, however, need not have been due to the petitioning creditor when it was incurred provided that it is vested in him at the time of the presentation of the petition (*Ex p Thomas* (1747) 1 Atk 73).

If a bill of exchange has not matured, a petition can still be presented based upon the debt, as it is due at some certain time in the future, under s 267(2)(*b*).

Neither a statute-barred debt (*Ex p Tynte* (1880) 15 Ch D 125) nor a debt founded on an illegal consideration (*Wells v Girling* (1819) 1 Brod & Bing 447) will support a petition. Likewise a foreign revenue debt which is not enforceable in this country (*Government of India v Taylor* [1955] AC 491) cannot support a petition.

In *Re McGreavey* [1950] Ch 269 it was held that an unpaid demand for rates, though enforceable only by distress or committal, and not by action at law, is a 'debt' and would support a bankruptcy petition. A liability order obtained from a magistrates' court for non-payment of the community charge or poll tax under the Local Government Finance Act 1988 is to be treated as a debt for the purposes of s 267 of the Act. Arrears of maintenance under the matrimonial legislation cannot support a bankruptcy petition but a lump sum order which remains unsatisfied can.

It follows that a good petitioning creditor's debt is a liquidated sum of the required amount which is provable in bankruptcy proceedings and which could have been enforced by legal process.

Chapter 3

Grounds for Petitioning

1 Introduction

Under the old law a bankruptcy petition could only be presented to the court when the debtor had committed an act of bankruptcy, the most common one of which was failure to comply with the requirements of a bankruptcy notice based upon an unsatisfied judgment debt. Now a creditor's petition can be presented if it is in respect of a liquidated debt above the minimum level and two other conditions are satisfied:
  (1) The debt upon which it is based is a debt which the debtor appears to be unable to pay or to have no reasonable prospect of being able to pay (s 267(2)(c)).
  (2) There is no outstanding application to set aside a statutory demand served (under s 268) in respect of the debt (s 267(2)(d)).

If the debt is payable immediately, the debtor appears to be unable to pay a debt if:
  (a) the petitioning creditor has served on the debtor a demand (known as 'the statutory demand') in the prescribed form requiring him to pay the debt or to secure or compound for it to the satisfaction of the creditor, at least three weeks have elapsed since the demand was served and the demand has neither been complied with nor set aside in accordance with the rules; or
  (b) execution or other process issued in respect of the debt on a judgment or order of any court in favour of the petitioning creditor has been returned unsatisfied in whole or in part (s 268(1)(a) and (b)).

For this latter requirement to be satisfied, it is necessary for the sheriff or bailiff to have obtained access to the debtor's premises and satisfied himself that there were goods of insufficient value to meet the judgment debt. If access to the debtor's premises is not obtained, this requirement will not have been satisfied (*Re a Debtor* (*No 340 of 1992*) (1995) *The Times*, 6 March).

If the debt is not immediately payable, the debtor appears to have no reasonable prospect of being able to pay a debt if:
  (a) the petitioning creditor has served on the debtor a statutory demand in the prescribed form requiring him to establish to the satisfaction of the

creditor that there is a reasonable prospect that the debtor will be able to pay the debt when it falls due;
(b) at least three weeks have elapsed since the demand was served; and
(c) the demand has neither been complied with nor set aside in accordance with the Rules (s 268(2)).

2 Form and contents of statutory demand

Which form

Schedule 4 to the Rules contains three forms of statutory demand:
>   Form 6.1   Statutory demand for a debt presently due but not based on a judgment or order.
>   Form 6.2   Statutory demand for a debt presently due based on a judgment or order.
>   Form 6.3   Statutory demand for a debt due at a future time. For all these forms, see Appendix 3, forms 1 to 3.

If the debtor is a partnership and it is desired to wind up the partnership and make the partners bankrupt as well, a different form of statutory demand is required (see Chapter 25, section 3). If the debt is partly the subject of a judgment and partly not, Form 6.1 should be used though the use of the incorrect form will not lead to the demand being set aside if the debtor was not misled by the error (*Re a Debtor (No 1 of 1987)* [1989] 2 All ER 46).

Debtor

The full name and address of the debtor must be given where known but it is sufficient to say 'A B JONES (MALE)' or even 'SMITH (MALE)' where no other details are known.

Creditor

The full name and address of the creditor making the demand should be given. If the address is one at which the debtor can find the creditor, the demand will not be invalidated because it was a temporary home of the creditor who had no permanent home, or by the fact of the occasional absence of the creditor from the place even for the whole day, unless the absence is such as to deprive the debtor of a reasonable opportunity of complying with the demand (*Re Beauchamp, ex p Beauchamp* [1904] 1 KB 572).

The debt

Only one debt can be included in the demand and the amount of the debt must be stated and the consideration for it (or, if there is no consideration, the way in which it arises), details of the judgment or order on which the demand is founded (if any), the grounds upon which it is alleged that the debtor appears to have no reasonable prospects of paying and, if the amount claimed included interest or other charges accruing from time to time, the amount or rate of such charge separately identified and the grounds on which payment of it is claimed (r 6.1(3) and (4)). The amount of such charge is limited to that which has accrued due at the date of the demand (r 6.2(4)). A statutory demand can claim a sum in foreign currency provided that the sterling equivalent as at a stated date is given (*Re a Debtor (51 SD 91)* [1992] 1 WLR 1294).

If the debt is overstated in the demand, the demand will not be set aside as to the undisputed amount (see 7 below).

The Crown

The Crown have a right to petition in the High Court if their petition is based upon an unsatisfied execution, or if based on a statutory demand, that an intention to do so is expressed in the demand, and there is a part of the form for completion to this effect.

Security

If the creditor holds any security in respect of the debt, the full amount of the debt must be specified but the nature of the security and the value which the creditor puts upon it as at the date of the demand must also be stated and the amount for which payment is claimed by the demand must be the full amount of the debt less the amount specified as the value of the security (r 6.1(5)).

Signature and date

The demand must be dated and signed either by the creditor himself or by a person stating himself to be authorised to make the demand on the creditor's behalf (r 6.1(1)). If the creditor has solicitors acting for him, the individual solicitor or legal executive of that firm should sign the demand adding details of his firm together with a reference and telephone number.

Appropriate court

On page two of the demand, there must be completed details of the appropriate court to which the debtor can apply, if he so wishes, for the statutory demand to be set aside. The appropriate court is the court to which the debtor could present his own bankruptcy petition. The appropriate court is the High Court if the debtor has resided or carried on business in the London insolvency district for the greater part of the six months immediately preceding the presentation of the petition or if the debtor is not resident in England and Wales, or the county court for the insolvency district in which the debtor has resided or carried on business (r 6.40). Not all county courts have bankruptcy jurisdiction and for a list of the county courts exercising bankruptcy jurisdiction and over which areas, see Appendix 1. The alternate court in Sched 2 to the Rules which can be used by a debtor in presenting his own petition cannot be utilised.

Assignment

If the creditor is entitled to the debt by way of assignment from the original creditor, the section of the demand must be completed with details of the original creditor and date of assignment.

Compliance

The prescribed form states that the debtor has 21 days after service upon him to comply. Only the creditor who served the demand (and not any other creditor (s 268(1)(*a*)) can rely upon non-compliance to found a petition. The period for applying to set aside the demand is 18 days after service. If the demand is served abroad, these time limits will need to be altered (see **3** below).

Future debt

If the demand is based upon a debt payable at a future time, Form 6.3 must be used and the creditor must set out why he believes the debtor has no reasonable prospects of paying the debt when it falls due. There is no guidance in the Act as to what constitutes reasonable prospects or what are the criteria for the creditor to be reasonably satisfied.

Information

The demand must include an explanation of the purpose of the demand and the fact that, if the debtor does not comply with it, bankruptcy proceedings may be commenced against him, the time within which the demand must be complied with if that consequence is to be avoided, the methods of compliance which are open to the debtor and his right to apply to the court for the demand to be set aside. The demand must also specify with whom the debtor may enter into communication with a view to securing or compounding for the debt to the satisfaction of the creditor or, as the case may be, establishing to the creditor's satisfaction that there is a reasonable prospect that the debt will be paid when it falls due. Any person so named in the demand must also state his address and telephone number (if any) (r 6.2(2)). See also p 9 above.

3 Service of statutory demand

The creditor is under an obligation to do all that is reasonable for the purpose of bringing the demand to the debtor's attention *and*, if practicable in the circumstances, to cause personal service of the demand to be effected (r 6.3(2)). Where it is not possible to effect personal service promptly, service may be effected by other means such as first class post or insertion through a letter box (*Practice Note* (*Bankruptcy: Substituted Service*) [1987] 1 WLR 82). In all cases where substituted service is effected, the creditor must have taken all those steps which would suffice to justify the court making an order for substituted service of a bankruptcy petition (above). If the creditor fails to discharge this obligation, the court may decline to allow a bankruptcy petition to be filed (r 6.11(1)). It is an abuse of the process of the court and harassment of debtors to send out statutory demands by post with no intention of relying on them for the purposes of bankruptcy proceedings and such practice has cost a collection agency its Consumer Credit Act licence (*Re Credit Default Register Ltd* (1993) unreported, 31 March).

Generally, the rules as to service of a statutory demand are the same as for bankruptcy petitions (r 6.3(1)). If substituted service of a petition by first class post is used, service is deemed to have been effected on the seventh day after posting. It is suggested that the same method of calculating the date of service of a demand be used (*Practice Note (Bankruptcy: Substituted Service)*, above).

Where a statutory demand is for payment of a sum due under a judgment or order of the court and the creditor knows or believes with reasonable cause that the debtor has absconded or is keeping out of the way with a view to avoiding service and there is no real prospect of the sum due being recovered by any other execution or process, then the demand may be advertised in one or more newspapers and the time for compliance runs from the date of the advertisement's first or only appearance (r 6.3(3)). A form of advertisement is set out in the *Practice Note (Bankruptcy: Substituted Service)* (above) and can be found in Appendix 3, form 4.

A statutory demand, not being a court document, can be served out of the jurisdiction without leave. However, where it is to be served out of the jurisdiction, the time for compliance must be altered to give the debtor more time to comply in accordance with the Extra Jurisdiction Tables in the *Supreme Court Practice* (see *Practice Note (Bankruptcy: Service Abroad)* [1988] 1 WLR 461).

Proof of service

If the statutory demand has been served personally on the debtor, the affidavit of service must be made by the person who effected service (r 6.11(3)). If service of the demand (however effected) has been acknowledged in writing, the affidavit of service must be made by the creditor or by a person acting on his behalf (r 6.11(4)). Otherwise the affidavit of service must be made by the person having direct knowledge of the means adopted for serving the demand (r 6.11(5)).

There are two forms of affidavit of service in Sched 4 to the Rules. Form 6.11 (Appendix 3, form 5) should only be used unamended where the demand has been served personally and acknowledged in writing and should be made by the creditor or the person acting for him. If service has not been acknowledged, the affidavit should be made by the person who effected service and paras 2 and 3 (part) should be omitted. There is no particular form that an acknowledgment must take except that it must be in writing. It can be given by the debtor himself or by someone stating himself to be authorised to accept service on the debtor's behalf (r 6.11(4)).

Form 6.12 (Appendix 3, form 6) should be used where substituted service of the demand was effected and can be used whether or not service has been acknowledged in writing. Paragraphs 4 and 5 (part) provide for the alternatives. The appropriate person to make the affidavit may, however, not be the same in both cases. If the demand has been acknowledged in writing, it is the creditor or the person acting on his behalf; if the demand has not been acknowledged in writing, the person making the affidavit must be someone having direct knowledge of the means adopted for serving the demand. The affidavit should give particulars of the steps which have been taken with a view to serving the demand, the means whereby (those steps having been ineffective) it was sought to bring the demand to the debtor's attention and a date by which, to the best of the knowledge of the person making the affidavit, the demand will have come to the debtor's attention (r 6.11(5)). The steps referred to above must be such as would have sufficed to justify an order for substituted service of a bankruptcy petition (r 6.11(6)). Substituted service of a bankruptcy petition would not be ordered unless there is a probability that it will come to the notice of the debtor; see, eg, *Re a Judgment Debtor (No 1539 of 1936)* [1937] Ch 137.

The date by which it is believed the demand would have come to the attention of the debtor is the date deemed to have been the date of service (r 6.11(7)).

If an enquiry agent is merely used to carry out investigations as to the whereabouts of the debtor, para 1 of the affidavit Form 6.12 should be deleted and the following substituted: '1 Attempts have been made to serve the demand, full details of which are set out in the accompanying affidavit of.... '

The above notes on completion of the prescribed forms of affidavit of service are set out in the *Practice Note (Bankruptcy: Statutory Demand: Setting Aside)* [1987] 1 WLR 119.

The affidavit of service must exhibit the demand itself and any acknowledgment in writing. If the demand has been served by advertisement, a copy of the advertisement must be exhibited to the affidavit of service (r 6.11(8)).

If a bankruptcy petition is based upon the failure to comply with a statutory demand, the affidavit of service of the demand must be filed at court at the time the petition is filed (r 6.11(1)).

4 Three weeks for compliance

A debtor appears unable to pay his debts if a statutory demand has been served on him and 'at least three weeks' have elapsed since the demand was served (s 268(1)(*a*)). By analogy with the old bankruptcy rules and under the provisions of RSC Ord 3, r 2 incorporated into bankruptcy law by r 12.9 of the Rules, the day the demand was served and the day the bankruptcy petition is presented to the court should be excluded so that there are 21 clear days between service and presentation of the petition based on failure to comply with the demand. Similar rules apply to the calculation of the 18-day period after service of the demand within which the debtor must apply to the court if he wishes to have the demand set aside.

Under RSC Ord 65, r 7 (which applies to bankruptcy proceedings by virtue of r 12.11 of the Rules), any document served after 4 pm or on a Saturday or Sunday is deemed to have been served on the next business day. This rule would appear to apply to the service of a statutory demand and care must be taken in the calculation of the period for compliance.

If the creditor can show that there is a serious possibility that the debtor's property or value of any of his property will be significantly diminished during the three-week period after service of the demand, he may present a petition before the expiration of the three-week period (s 270) but a bankruptcy order cannot be made until after the three-week period has elapsed (s 271(2)). A petition based upon a statutory demand can be presented in these circumstances even if there is an application pending to set aside the demand (*Re a Debtor v Focus Insurance* (1993) *The Times*, 12 July).

5 Defects

Under r 7.55 no insolvency proceedings are to be invalidated by reason of any formal defect or by any irregularity, unless the court considers that substantial injustice has been caused by the defect or irregularity and the injustice cannot be remedied by any other order of the court. Insolvency proceedings are defined by r 13.7 as meaning any proceedings under the Act or the Rules. Statutory demands are not therefore covered by r 7.55. Bankruptcy notices under the old law were dealt with strictly and all a debtor had to prove was that the defect in question could mislead or was capable of misleading him and not that it actually did mislead or embarrass him. Any mistake in the statutory demand will not invalidate it unless the error actually misled the debtor (*Re a Debtor (No I of 1987)* [1989] 2 All ER 46) (the date of the guarantee given by the debtor had been misstated in the demand but the court had a degree of flexibility when confronted with an application to set aside the defective demand though this was not to be taken by creditors as a charter for slipshod work).

6 Application to set aside a statutory demand

If the debtor wishes to apply for the statutory demand to be set aside, he must do so within the period of 18 days from the date of service of the demand upon him or the date of first advertisement of the demand (r 6.4(1)). Care must be taken in calculating the date by which the application need be made if the demand was not personally served (see **4** above).

The application must be supported by an affidavit specifying the date on which the demand came into the debtor's hands, stating the grounds on which he claims that it should be set aside, and must exhibit a copy of the demand (r 6.4(3)). The application is made to a bankruptcy registrar or district judge, and no fee is payable. Four copies of the application and affidavit should be lodged so that the court can serve all those entitled to be notified.

If the debtor wishes to apply to set aside the demand after the period of so doing (18 days) has elapsed, he may do so under s 376 which gives the court power to extend the time, either before or after it has expired, for doing any act. The application to extend time is made *ex p* to a registrar or district judge supported by an affidavit giving, in addition to the reasons for applying to set aside the demand, the reasons why the application was not made in time (see *Practice Direction* [1988] 3 All ER 984). It would seem that reasons like 'I forgot to apply in time' or 'I was too busy to apply on time' will be sufficient. The affidavit should have a paragraph added to it stating whether to the debtor's knowledge or belief the creditor has either presented or not presented a petition, and asserting, if it be true, that unless restrained by injunction, the creditor may present a petition. The application for an extension of time is made to the registrar or district judge but if an injunction is also required, then the application is made to a judge. There is a fee payable on this application of £20. For the procedure on applying to set aside a demand and for an extension of time to apply to set aside, see the *Practice Note (Bankruptcy: Statutory Demand: Setting Aside)* [1987] 1 WLR 119.

The court to which these applications are to be made is the bankruptcy court to which the debtor could present his own bankruptcy petition (see Chapter 6) except that if the demand was served by a government department, is based on a judgment or order, and an intention to petition in the High Court is stated in the demand itself, then the appropriate court to which application to set aside must be made is the High Court (r 6.4(2)).

An application for leave to apply to set aside a statutory demand is considered an application to set aside the demand so that any petition based upon that demand is liable to be dismissed (*Re a Debtor (No 53 of 1991)* (1991), *The Independent*, 19 August), but a petition may still be presented under s 270 (see **4** above).

The prescribed form of affidavit in support of the application to set aside the demand gives eight possible reasons for applying to have the demand set aside but these reasons are not meant to constitute an exhaustive list. They are:

(*a*) the debtor does not admit the debt because...;
(*b*) the debtor admits the debt but it is not payable now;
(*c*) part of the debt is admitted and the debtor will pay it now but denies the balance of the debt;
(*d*) part of the debt is admitted but is less than the minimum sum (currently £750) and the balance is disputed;
(*e*) the debtor admits the debt and is prepared to secure or compound for it to the creditor's satisfaction by [stating nature of satisfaction];
(*f*) the debt is fully secured or the unsecured element is below the minimum sum (currently £750);
(*g*) the debtor has a counterclaim or set-off equal to or exceeding the claim;
(*h*) execution of the judgment has been stayed;
(*i*) the demand does not comply with the Rules in that....

All the above reasons are self-explanatory except for (f). It is clear that if a creditor offers security of sufficient value for a debt then the demand should be set aside. However, where a creditor offers a charge over assets which cannot be realised immediately, the creditor is not under an obligation even to consider the offer (*Re A Debtor (415 SD 1993*) (1993) *The Times*, 8 December). A debtor does not have a right to a satisfactory written reply from the creditor in response to any offer. If the court was required to decide whether a creditor's refusal to consider an offer was unreasonable, it would turn the statutory demand procedure into an elaborate affair (above). But it is not clear what to compound for a debt involves. If the debtor offers his creditors 50p in the £ he is proposing a composition with his creditors and that would not be a ground for setting aside a demand. If the debtor offers to pay the creditor who served the demand by instalments that might constitute compounding for the debt and the court has to decide whether the offer was reasonable or not.

The application to set aside automatically causes the time for compliance with the demand to cease to run until after the hearing of the application (r 6.4(3)). For the form of application (Form 6.4 in Sched 4 to the Rules), the affidavit in support (Form 6.5 in Sched 5 to the Rules) and the additional paragraphs to add to the affidavit if application to extend time is also sought (in the *Practice Note* (*Bankruptcy: Statutory Demand: Setting Aside*)), see Appendix 3, forms 7, 8 and 9.

On receipt of an application to set aside, the court may, if satisfied that no sufficient cause is shown for it, dismiss it without giving notice to the creditor. As from the date of dismissal, the time limited for compliance with the demand runs again (r 6.5(1)). It is therefore very important that an application to set aside a demand is supported by an affidavit setting out fully the grounds of the application and those grounds are within the scope of the Act and the Rules for setting aside a demand.

7 Hearing of application to set aside

If an application to set aside a demand is not dismissed under r 6.5(1) (see above), the court will fix a venue for it to be heard and the court must give at least seven days' notice to the debtor (or his solicitor), the creditor and whoever is named in the demand with whom the debtor can enter into communications with reference to it (r 6.5(2)).

On the hearing of the application, the court may determine the matter summarily or adjourn it, giving such directions as it thinks fit (r 6.5(3)).

Rule 6.5(4) sets out four grounds upon which the court may grant the application to set aside:

(1) If the debtor appears to have a counterclaim, set-off or cross demand which equals or exceeds the amount of the debt or debts specified in the demand, the debtor does not have to show that the counterclaim, set-off or cross demand could not be set up in the action in which the judgment or order (if any) giving rise to the demand was made (*Practice Note* (*Bankruptcy: Statutory Demand: Setting Aside*), above).

If the creditor disputes the debtor's counterclaim, set-off or cross demand, the court may allow the debtor to adduce further evidence in chief in support of his application before reaching a decision on the genuineness of his allegation (*Re a Debtor (No 991 of 1962)* [1963] 1 WLR 51).

(2) If the debt (not being the subject of a judgment or order) is disputed on grounds which appear to the court to be substantial, the court will normally set aside a demand if, in its opinion, on the evidence there is a genuine triable issue (*Practice Note (Bankruptcy: Statutory Demand: Setting Aside)*, above). If only part of the debt is disputed or the debt is overstated, the demand should not be set aside provided that there is a sum equivalent to the minimum debt (currently £750) which is admitted (*Re a Debtor (No 1 of 1987)* above and *Re a Debtor (No 490 of 1991)* (1992) *The Times*, 9 April. If the demand is founded on a judgment or order, the court will not at this stage go behind the judgment or order and enquire into the validity of the debt, nor, as a general rule, will it adjourn the application to await the result of an application to set aside judgment or order (*Practice Note* as above). The debtor still has the opportunity to attack the validity of the debt and/or the judgment at the hearing of the petition (*Re Easton, ex p Dixon* (1893)10 Morr 111). However, if an application to set aside the judgment on which the demand is based has already been made, the court is likely to adjourn the hearing of the application to set aside until after the application to set aside the judgment has been heard.

(3) If it appears that the creditor holds some security in respect of the debt claimed in the demand and either the creditor has not complied with r 6. 1(5) by disclosing and valuing his security and claiming the shortfall or unsecured part of his debt only, or the court is satisfied that the value of the security equals or exceeds the full amount of the debt—if the failure to reveal the security held is by inadvertence, the court may waive irregularity under r 7.55 and give the creditor leave to amend the demand to the unsecured part of the debt, dismiss the debtor's application but order that the debtor have a further three weeks to comply with the demand as amended. The court is now allowed to evaluate the correctness of the creditor's estimate of the value of his security, which under the old law was not the case. The court can now require the creditor to amend his demand but without prejudice to his right to petition based upon the original demand. A debt is secured to the extent that security is held over any property *of the debtor* whether by mortgage, charge or lien but the assignment to the creditor of a claim which the debtor has against a third party is not security as against the debtor (*Re a Debtor (No 310 of 1988)* [1989] 2 All ER 42).

(4) If the court is satisfied, on other grounds, that the demand ought to be set aside, guidance as to what might constitute other grounds is to be found in the marginal notes to the form of affidavit set out in Sched 4 to the Rules (Form 6.5; see Appendix 3, form 8). These marginal notes are referred to in **5** above.

An application to set aside a demand should not be adjourned merely on the ground that if further time is given to the debtor, he or someone on his behalf will be able to pay the debt (*Re Cole, ex p Attenborough* [1898] 1 QB 290).

It is no longer considered good law for the court to set aside a statutory demand conditionally, the condition being the payment into the joint names of the parties' solicitors of the sum in question to await the outcome of proceedings over the debt.

If the court dismisses the application, it must also make an order authorising the creditor to present a bankruptcy petition either forthwith or on or after a date specified in the order (r 6.5(6)). A copy of the order must be sent forthwith by the court to the debtor (r 6.5(6)). It would appear that the court should only postpone the right of the creditor to present a petition if there is likely to be an appeal against the order dismissing the application or perhaps because there are real prospects of the debtor complying with the demand if a little extra time is given to him.

8 The order

If a statutory demand is set aside, the order should be in Form 6.6 in Sched 4 to the Rules (see Appendix 3, form 10).

Chapter 4

The Creditor's Petition

1 The appropriate court

By r 6.9(1), the petition must be presented in the High Court in the following cases:
  (1) If the debtor has resided or carried on business within the London insolvency district for the greater part of the six months immediately preceding the presentation of the petition, or for a longer period during those six months than in any other insolvency district.
  (2) If he is not resident in England and Wales.
  (3) If the petitioning creditor is unable to ascertain the debtor's residence or place of business.
  (4) If the petition is presented by a government department and either follows an unsatisfied execution or intention to petition in the High Court was indicated in the statutory demand.

Otherwise, the petition must be presented in the county court for the insolvency district in which the debtor has resided or carried on business for the longest period during the six months preceding the presentation of the petition (r 6.9(2)). If the debtor has carried on business in one insolvency district and resided in another, the petition must be presented to the court for the insolvency district in which he has carried on business (r 6.9(3)) but if the debtor has carried on business in the six-month period in more than one insolvency district, the petition should be presented to the court for the insolvency district in which he has his principal place of business or has had his principal place of business for the longest period (r 6.9(4)). But if there is a voluntary arrangement in force (see Chapter 27), the petition must be presented to the court dealing with that voluntary arrangement irrespective of where the debtor now lives or carries on business.

The petition must contain sufficient information to establish the correctness of the choice of court (r 6.9(5)).

The London insolvency district comprises all places within the City of London and the districts of the following county courts:

Barnet	Brentford
Bow	Central London

Clerkenwell
Edmonton
Ilford
Lambeth
Mayor and City of London
Marylebone
Shoreditch
Southwark
Wandsworth
West London
Whitechapel
Willesden

Not all county courts have bankruptcy jurisdiction. For a list of all county courts and those courts exercising bankruptcy jurisdiction for them, see Appendix 1.

A petition is not necessarily invalidated by reason of it having been presented to the wrong court. The court may (under r 7.12):

(1) transfer the proceedings to the correct court;
(2) order the proceedings to continue in the court where they were begun provided that that court has been designated a court for bankruptcy proceedings by the Lord Chancellor under s 374;
(3) order the proceedings to be struck out.

The petition and any proceedings in bankruptcy may at any stage be transferred from one court to another provided the transferee court has bankruptcy jurisdiction (r 7.11). Transfer of 'any proceedings' in r 7.11 refers to the transfer of the whole of the bankruptcy proceedings and does not confer jurisdiction to transfer to the High Court a motion pending in bankruptcy proceedings that have been initiated and are continuing in a county court (*Re Kouyoundjian (a Bankrupt)* [1956] 1 WLR 558 and *Re a Debtor (No 26A of 1975)* [1985] 1 WLR 6). The transfer may be ordered by the court of its own motion, on the application of the official receiver or on the application of a person having an interest, eg, the debtor or a creditor (r 7.11(5)).

2 Conditions for petitioning

By s 268 a creditor is not entitled to present a bankruptcy petition against a debtor unless:

(a) the debt owed to him by the debtor, or if there are joint petitioners the aggregate of the debts owed to them, equals or exceeds the bankruptcy level, currently £750;
(b) the debt is a liquidated sum payable immediately or at some certain future time; and
(c) the debtor is unable to pay the debt or has no reasonable prospect of being able to pay.

These requirements have been discussed in Chapter 2.

3 Form and contents

There are four forms of bankruptcy petition set out in Sched 4 to the Rules:

Form 6.7 Creditor's petition on failure to comply with a statutory demand for a liquidated sum payable immediately

Form 6.8   Creditor's petition on failure to comply with a statutory demand for a liquidated sum payable at a future date
Form 6.9   Creditor's petition where execution or other process on a judgment has been returned unsatisfied in whole or in part
Form 6.10   Petition for default in connection with voluntary arrangement.
These forms are to be found in Appendix 3 as forms 11 to 14.

4 The creditor

For the purpose of a bankruptcy petition the expression 'creditor' clearly includes a person to whom a debt is due from the debtor and who can sue the debtor immediately for that debt in an action at law or in equity (*Re Sacker, ex p Sacker* (1888) 22 QBD 179). Since *Re McGreavey* [1950] Ch 269 (p 7) it also includes a local authority to whom a sum is due in respect of unpaid rates or community charge (see Chapter 2, **2**) and any person to whom a sum is due from the debtor which is provable in bankruptcy proceedings and which could have been enforced by legal process.

The right of the following classes of persons to present a creditor's petition should be noted:

A trustee in bankruptcy—he may petition in respect of a debt due to the bankrupt or the estate but he must first obtain permission of the creditors' committee (Sched 5, para 2) or the Department of Trade (acting via the official receiver) if there is no committee (s 302(1)).

Partners—a petition may be presented in the name of the firm. Where one of the partners becomes bankrupt before the petition is heard, his trustee should be joined as a co-petitioner (*Re Owen, ex p Owen* (1884) 13 QBD 113).

Companies—the petition must be in the name of the company whether it is a going concern or in liquidation; a petition in the name of the liquidator cannot be sustained (*Re Winterbottom, ex p Winterbottom* (1886) 18 QBD 446).

Mentally disordered persons—such a person may petition by a person appointed by the court to act either generally or for the particular purpose of presenting a petition (r 7.44).

Secured creditors—under s 269, a secured creditor may present a petition but he must state in his petition that he is willing to give up his security for the benefit of the creditors in the event that a bankruptcy order is made or give an estimate of the value of his security. In the latter case, he may be admitted as a petitioning creditor to the extent of the balance of the debt due to him, after deducting the value so estimated, in the same manner as if he were an unsecured creditor. The creditor does not forfeit his security on non-compliance with this provision, but on the facts coming to light, the petition is likely to be dismissed unless the court exercises its discretion and permits an amendment of the petition.

Amendment may be allowed where the petitioner's omission was due to inadvertence or some reasonable excuse (see *Re a Debtor* (*No 39 of 1974*) [1977] 3 All ER 489 but compare *Re a Debtor* (*No 6 of 1941*) [1943] Ch 213). A secured creditor is defined in s 383 as a person holding a mortgage, charge, lien or other security over the property of the debtor. A bank holding a cheque for collection on behalf of a debtor has been held to be a secured creditor (*Re Keever* [1967] Ch 182). But security does not include a lien on books, papers, or other records unless they are documents of title (s 383(4)). If a secured creditor petitions and states, under s 269(1)(*a*), that he is willing to give up his security and a bankruptcy order is subsequently made, he is deemed to have given up his security (s 383(3)). See also Chapter 3.

Trustees—a bare trustee of a debt, without any beneficial interest, must join the beneficial owner since the latter is the person capable of dealing with the debt.

Executors—an executor may present a petition in respect of a debt due to the estate and even before taking out probate (*Rogers v James* (1816) 7 Taunt 147).

Receivers—a receiver can be a petitioner where he has an independent cause of action, eg, as holder of a bill of exchange (*Re Lewis, ex p Harris* (1876) 2 Ch D 423), but he cannot petition on a sum due to him as a receiver. The same applies to administrative receivers who act as agent of the company of which they have been appointed even where the company has gone into liquidation and their agency has, therefore, ended.

Assignee—a legal or equitable assignee of a debt may petition without joining his assignor. But a garnishee order does not create, as between the garnishor and garnishee, any debt and a judgment creditor who has obtained such an order against a person indebted to the judgment debtor cannot present a bankruptcy petition against that person (*Re Combined Weighing & Advertising Machine Company* (1889) 43 Ch D 99).

Joint creditors—they should all join in the petition (*Brickland v Newsome* (1808) 1 Camp 474).

Married women—a married woman can present a petition in respect of any debt which is her property (Law Reform (Married Women and Tortfeasors) Act 1935, s 1).

Minors—a minor should petition through his next friend.

5 Identification of the debtor

The petition must contain the following information with respect to the debtor, so far as it is within the knowledge of the petitioner:

(a) the debtor's name, place of residence and occupation (if any);
(b) the name or names in which he carries on business, if other than his true name, and whether alone or jointly with others;
(c) the nature of his business and the address or addresses at which he carried it on;
(d) any name or names, other than his true name, in which he has carried on business at or after the time when the debt was incurred and whether alone or jointly with others;
(e) any address or addresses at which he has resided or carried on business at or after that time and the nature of that business (r 6.7(1)).

If to the petitioner's *personal* knowledge the debtor has used any other name, this fact must also be stated (r 6.7(3)).

In the title, it is not necessary to recite the debtor's name. Any alias or trading name will appear in the body of the petition.

6 Identification of the debt

For what constitutes a debt upon which a petition can be based, see p 6. In the petition, there must be stated:
 (a) the amount of the debt, the consideration for it and the fact that it is owed to the petitioner;
 (b) when the debt was incurred or became due;
 (c) if the debt includes any charge by way of interest not previously notified to the debtor as a liability of his or any other charge accruing from time to time, the amount or rate of the charge (separately identified) and the grounds on which it is claimed to form part of the debt provided that the amount or rate must in the case of a petition based upon a statutory demand be limited to that claimed in the demand;
 (d) either:
  (i) that the debt is for a liquidated sum payable immediately and the debtor appears unable to pay it, or
  (ii) that the debt is for a liquidated sum payable at some certain future time and the debtor appears to have no reasonable prospect of being able to pay;
  and in either case, that the debt is unsecured (r 6.8(1)).

If the petition is based on a debt in respect of which a statutory demand has been served, the date and manner of service of the demand and the fact that, to the best of the creditor's knowledge and belief, the demand has neither been complied with nor is there any application to have the demand set aside outstanding, must also be stated (r 6.2). By analogy with the old law, an application to set aside a demand is not outstanding when it has been dismissed by the registrar or district judge even though an appeal may be pending (*Re a Debtor* (*No 44 of 1978*) [1980] 1 WLR 665).

If the petition is based on a statutory demand, only the debt claimed in the demand may be included in the petition and not any interest or other charges accrued since the demand was served (*Practice Note* (*Bankruptcy: Petition*) [1987] 1 WLR 81 as amended by *Practice Note* (*Bankruptcy: Petition* (*No 2*)) [1987] 1 WLR 1424).

If the petition is based upon an unsatisfied execution, the court from which the execution was issued and the particulars relating to the return must be stated (r 6.8(3)). See also Chapter 3.

7 Verification of the petition

A bankruptcy petition must be verified by an affidavit that the statements in the petition are true, or are true to the best of the deponent's knowledge, information and belief (r 6.12(1)). The affidavit verifying the petition must be sworn before the presentation of the petition and lodged with it. Indeed, the proposed petition must be exhibited to the affidavit (r 6.12(3)).

The affidavit must be sworn by the petitioner or by some person such as a director, company secretary or similar officer, or a solicitor (who has been concerned in the matters giving rise to the presentation of the petition) or by some responsible person who is duly authorised to make the affidavit and has the requisite knowledge of those matters (r 6.12(4)). It is doubted whether a clerk or trainee solicitor in the employment of the petitioning creditor's solicitors is the right person to swear such an affidavit. If the affidavit is not sworn by the petitioner himself, the person making the affidavit must state his capacity, his authority and means of knowledge of the matters sworn to (r 6.12(5)).

The affidavit is *prima facie* evidence of the truth of the statements in the petition to which it relates (r 6.12(6)).

If the petition is based on failure to comply with a statutory demand and more than four months have elapsed since the demand was served, the reasons for the delay must also be given in the affidavit (r 6.12(7)). If an adequate explanation for the delay is not given, the court may dismiss the petition under s 266(3) where there has been a breach of the Rules 'or for any other reason' and the staleness of the grounds for petitioning may be a sufficient other reason for the petition to be dismissed. The court has no power to refuse to seal a petition on this ground but the petition may be dismissed at the hearing.

Schedule 4 to the Rules contains an affidavit verifying the petition, Form 6.3 (see Appendix 3, form 15).

8 Completion of the petition

A *Practice Direction (Bankruptcy: Petition)* [1987] 1 All ER 602 has set out very useful guidelines for completing the petition and is set out below in its entirety (except for the parts which are no longer applicable):

1. The petition does not require dating, signing or witnessing.
2. In the title it is only necessary to recite the debtor's name, eg Re John William Smith or Re J W Smith (male). Any alias or trading name will appear in the body of the petition. This also applies to all other statutory forms other than those which require the 'full title'.
3. Where the petition is based on a statutory demand, only the debt claimed in the demand may be included in the petition.
4. When completing para 2 of the petition, attention is drawn to r 6.8(1)(*a*) to (*c*), particularly where the 'aggregate sum' is made up of a number of debts.
5. Date of service of the statutory demand (para 4 of the petition): (a) In the case of personal service, the day of service as set out in the affidavit of service should be recited and whether service is effected *before/after* 1600 hrs on Monday to Friday or *before/after* 1200 hrs on Saturdays: see RSC Ord 65, r 7. (b) In the case of substituted service (otherwise than by advertisements), the date alleged in the affidavit of service should be recited. (As to the date alleged, see *Practice Direction (Bankruptcy 4/86)* [1987] 1 All ER 604) (c). In the strictly limited case of substituted service by advertisement under r 6.3

of the 1986 rules, the date to be alleged is the date of the advertisement's appearance or, as the case may be, its first appearance: see rr 6.3(3) and 6.11(8).
6. There is no need to include in the preamble to or at the end of the petition details of the person authorised to present the petition.
7. Certificates at the end of the petition: (a) the period of search for prior petitions has been reduced to *three* years.
8. Deposit on petition. The deposit will now be taken by the court and forwarded to the Official Receiver. The petition fee and deposit should be handed to the Supreme Court Accounts Office, Fee Stamping Rooms, who will record the receipt and will impress two entries on the original petition, one in respect of the court fee and the other in respect of the deposit [*applies to High Court only*]. Cheque(s) for the whole amount should be made payable to 'HM Paymaster General'.

There is no provision in the Rules as there was in the 1952 Rules for searches for prior petitions at the county court to see if the debt was paid but the *Practice Direction* refers to carrying out these searches and the certificates to be endorsed on the petition of their result. Before a court issues a petition, it searches its own records to see if a prior petition exists but enquiries are not made of any other courts which also properly could have jurisdiction. If a petition is based upon failure to comply with a statutory demand and if there is pending an application for an extension of time in which to apply to have the demand set aside, such an application will be treated as an application to set aside the demand and the petition will be dismissed. The petitioning creditor's solicitors should therefore search for applications to set aside statutory demands and for applications for leave to apply out of time before petitioning (*Re a Debtor (No 53 of 1991)* (1991) *The Independent*, 19 August). See also Chapters 3 and 4.

9 Procedure for presentation and filing

As to which court a petition should be presented to, see p 19. Requirements:
(1) The petition together with two copies (one for service on the debtor and the other for exhibiting to the affidavit of service of the petition) and a further copy for the supervisor of any voluntary arrangement entered into by the debtor.
(2) If the petition is based upon the failure to comply with a statutory demand, the affidavit of service of the demand—if the court staff are in any doubt as to whether a statutory demand has been properly served, they will ask the registrar or district judge if the petition can be issued (and see also Chapter 3 Section 4 for the provisions relating to expedited petitions).
(3) A receipt for the deposit payable on presentation. The deposit is payable to the official receiver but the court will accept this on behalf of the official receiver and pass it on to the appropriate person; the amount is currently £300;
(4) The court fee, currently £55.

A petition does not need to be signed by or on behalf of the petitioning creditors.

Each copy of the petition lodged at court is sealed and all but one copy are handed back to the petitioner. The date and time of filing is endorsed by the court on every copy together with the venue (time, date and place) for the hearing as fixed by the court (r 6.10).

10 Notice to chief land registrar

When a petition is filed, the court must immediately send notice of the petition to the chief land registrar in Form 6.14 in Sched 4 to the Rules together with a request that the notice may be registered in the register of pending actions (r 6.13). A search against a person against whom a bankruptcy petition has been presented will reveal an entry 'PA(B)' together with details of the court to which the petition has been presented etc.

11 Service of the petition

The petition must be served personally on the debtor by an officer of the court, the petitioning creditor or his solicitor, or by a person instructed by the creditor or his solicitor for that purpose and service must be effected by delivering a sealed copy of the petition to him (r 6.14(1)).

If service is effected after 4 pm on a business day or after 12 noon on a Saturday, it is deemed to have been effected on the next business day (RSC Ord 65, r 7). If, to the petitioner's knowledge, a voluntary arrangement is in force (see Chapter 27), a copy of the petition must be served on the supervisor as well (unless it is the supervisor who is the petitioner) (r 6.14(4)).

If the court is satisfied by affidavit *or other evidence on oath* that prompt personal service cannot be effected because the debtor is keeping out of the way to avoid service of the petition, *or for any other cause*, it may order substituted service to be effected in such manner as it thinks fit (r 6.14(2)). *Practice Note* (*Bankruptcy: Substituted Service*) [1987] 1 WLR 82 sets out guidelines as to the evidence sufficient to justify an order for substituted service:

(1) One personal call at the residence and place of business of the debtor where both are known or at either of such places as is known. Where it is known that the debtor has more than one residential or business address, personal calls should be made at all addresses.

(2) Should service by this means fail, a first class prepaid letter should be written to the debtor referring to the calls made, the purpose of them, the failure to meet the debtor and adding that a further call will be made at a time and at a place specified of which at least two business days' notice should be given. The letter should also state that if the time and place are not convenient, the debtor should name some other time and place reasonably convenient for the purpose and if the debtor fails to keep the appointment, application will be made to the court for an order

for substituted service either by advertisement or in such other manner as the court may think fit.
(3) In attending any appointment made by letter, inquiry should be made as to whether the debtor has received all letters left for him and if the debtor is away, inquiry should be made as to whether or not letters are being forwarded to an address within England and Wales or elsewhere.
(4) If the debtor is represented by a solicitor, an attempt should be made to arrange an appointment for personal service through that solicitor—it should be noted that service of a petition (as opposed to a statutory demand) cannot be accepted by a solicitor.
(5) The affidavit in support of the application for an order for substituted service should deal with all the above matters including all relevant facts as to the debtor's whereabouts and whether the appointment letters have been returned.

Substituted service should not be ordered unless there is good reason to believe that the petition will come to the notice of the debtor.

The principles governing the use of substituted service generally were stated in *Porter v Freudenberg* [1915]1 KB 857 (at pp 889 *et seq*) and were adopted and applied in bankruptcy law in *Re a Judgment Debtor* (*No 1539 of 1936*) [1937] Ch 137 and later cases.

Where the court makes an order for substituted service by first class ordinary post, the order will normally provide that service is deemed to be effected on the seventh day after posting.

A form of order for substituted service is contained in Sched 4 to the Rules as Form 6.15 (see Appendix 3, form 16). If substituted service includes a notice in the *London Gazette*, Form 6.16 (see Appendix 3, form 17) sets out the form of advertisement.

Whatever form of service is adopted, service must be proved by affidavit. The affidavit of service must exhibit a sealed copy of the petition and if substituted service has been ordered, a sealed copy of the order for substituted service must also be exhibited (r 6.15). The affidavit of service must be filed in court immediately after service (r 6.15(2)). If personal service has been effected, the affidavit must be in Form 6.17 in Sched 4 to the Rules and if substituted service has been utilised, Form 6.18 in Sched 4 to the Rules. For both these forms of affidavit, see Appendix 3, forms 18 and 19.

12 Death of debtor

If the debtor dies before service of the petition, the court may order service to be effected on his personal representatives, or on such other person as it thinks fit (r 6.16).

This rule does not affect the general jurisdiction over the estates of deceased debtors. Where a debtor has died before a petition had been presented against him the Administration of Insolvent Estates of Deceased Persons Order 1986 (SI No 1999) applies. Under art 5 of that Order, unless the court orders otherwise, where a petition has been presented against a debtor who subsequently died, the proceedings are to be continued against him as if he were alive subject to the modifications set out in Sched 2 to that order (see Chapter 26).

13 Security for costs

Only in the case of a petition based upon a debt payable at some future time and the debtor having no reasonable prospect of being able to pay it can security for costs be ordered. The petitioning creditor can, on the debtor's application, be ordered to give security for costs, the nature and amount of which is at the court's discretion (r 6.17(2) and (3)). If an order for security is made, no hearing of the petition can take place until the whole amount of the security ordered has been given (r 6.17(4)).

14 Consolidation of petitions

Where two or more petitions are presented against the same debtor, the court can order the consolidation of the different sets of proceedings on such terms as it thinks fit (r 6.236).

Chapter 5

Hearing of the Petition

1 Date of hearing

A petition must not be heard until at least 14 days have elapsed since it was served on the debtor unless the court is satisfied that it is a proper case for an expedited hearing, or it appears that the debtor has absconded or the debtor consents to a hearing within the 14 days (r 6.18(1) and (2)).

It must be remembered that service of the petition after 4 pm on a business day or 12 noon on Saturday is deemed to have been effected on the next business day (RSC Ord 65, r 7). Care must therefore be taken to ensure that the petition is served in plenty of time before the hearing.

2 Opposition by the debtor

If the debtor wishes to oppose the petition, he must not later than seven days before the hearing file at court a notice specifying the grounds on which he proposes to object to the making of a bankruptcy order against him and send a copy of that notice to the petitioning creditor or his solicitor (r 6.21). The notice is Form 6.19 in Sched 4 to the Rules (see Appendix 3, form 20).

3 Amendment of petition

A petition may be amended at any time after presentation by the omission of any creditor or any debt with leave of the court (s 271(5) and r 6.22). This provision will be of assistance where a petition has been presented on behalf of two or more creditors, one or more of whom have subsequently been paid or had their debts compounded to their satisfaction. However, if the remaining debts are below the bankruptcy level (currently £750), then it would appear that the petition must fail.

4 Appearances at the hearing

Every creditor who intends to appear on the hearing must give notice of his intention to the petitioning creditor and the notice must specify his name and address, and the telephone number and reference for communication with him or anyone authorised to speak on his behalf. The notice must also state the amount and nature of his debt and whether he intends to support or oppose the petition. The notice must be sent so as to reach the addressee not later than 4 pm on the business day before the hearing and anyone failing to comply with these rules may only appear on the hearing with leave of the court (r 6.23). Schedule 4 to the Rules prescribes the form of notice, Form 6.20 (see Appendix 3, form 21).

The petitioning creditor must prepare for the court a list of the creditors (if any) who have given notice of their intention to appear under r 6.23. The list must contain their names, addresses, the amount of their debts and whether they support or oppose the petition (r 6.24). If no creditors have contacted the petitioning creditor, the list should still be prepared stating 'None' on its face. Schedule 4 to the Rules prescribes the form of list, Form 6.21 (see Appendix 3, form 22). The list is handed to the court before the commencement of the hearing (r 6.24(3)).

It does not follow that if there are more creditors either in number or value opposing the petition than supporting it that a bankruptcy order will be refused and accordingly the purpose behind the preparation of the list, other than to inform the court of the identity and debts of those who appear, is uncertain.

If the petitioning creditor fails to appear on the hearing, the petition will be dismissed and no subsequent petition against the same debtor, either alone or jointly with any other creditor, may be presented by the same creditor in respect of the same debt, without the leave of the court to which the first petition was presented (r 6.26). This rule follows a similar rule in the old bankruptcy law but there is no provision in the Rules for the attendance of the petitioning creditor to be excused on application as there was in the old law. There is also no provision for the petitioning creditor's solicitor to appear instead of the petitioning creditor even if the petition was presented by that solicitor on behalf of his client. However, it is the practice that attendance of the petitioning creditor's solicitor will suffice.

5 Extensions and adjournment

If the petition has not been served or not served more than 14 days before the hearing, the petitioning creditor may apply to the court to appoint another hearing date. The application must state the reasons why service has not been effected. No costs occasioned by the application will be allowed in the proceedings except with leave of the court (r 6.28).

The courts are unwilling to adjourn a petition more than once since it must not be allowed to hang over the debtor's head indefinitely. If the debtor is proposing to pay the debt by instalments, the petition should not be adjourned indefinitely to see if the proposal is implemented. The petition should be dismissed in these circumstances.

If the court appoints another hearing date (ie, the originally fixed hearing never takes place), the petitioning creditor must inform any creditor who has given him notice of intention to appear on the hearing (r 6.28(4)).

If the court adjourns the hearing of the petition, the petitioning creditor must send notice of the making of an order adjourning the petition (containing details of the new hearing date) to the debtor and any creditor who has given him notice of intention to appear on the hearing (r 6.29). Schedule 4 to the Rules contains an order adjourning the petition (Form 6.23) and the notice of the adjournment (Form 6.24) (see Appendix 3, forms 23 and 24). The court prepares Form 6.23 and the petitioning creditor sends out the notice in Form 6.24.

6 Substitution of petitioner

The court may order, on such terms as it thinks fit, that another creditor be substituted for the petitioning creditor. Only a creditor who has given notice of his intention to appear on the hearing under r 6.23, wishes to prosecute the petition and at the date the petition was presented would have been in a position to have petitioned himself, is entitled to ask to be substituted (r 6.30(2)). This means that for a creditor to be substituted as petitioner, he must not only have been owed a debt equal to bankruptcy level (currently £750), but must also either have had an execution returned unsatisfied before the date on which the petition was presented or have served his own statutory demand at least three weeks, and not more than four months before that date. He cannot rely on the statutory demand served by another creditor.

The court can only order substitution where a creditor petitions and is subsequently found not to be entitled to do so or where the petitioner consents to withdraw his petition or allows it to be dismissed, consents to an adjournment, fails to appear on the hearing or appears on the hearing but does not ask for a bankruptcy order (r 6.30(1)).

If the court does order substitution of a petitioning creditor, the petition will need amendment and it will have to be re-served and the hearing adjourned to a future date. This contrasts with the effect of a change of carriage of the petition under r 6.31 (see below).

The order for substitution of a petitioner on a creditor's petition is Form 6.24A in Sched 4 to the Rules.

7 Change of carriage of petition

On the hearing of a petition, any person who claims to be a creditor and who has given notice of his intention to appear on the hearing under r 6.23 may apply to the court for an order giving him carriage of the petition in place of the petitioning creditor but without requiring any amendment of the petition (r 6.31(1)). The court may make such an order if it is satisfied that the applicant is an unpaid and unsecured creditor and the petitioning creditor intends to seek the adjournment or withdrawal of his petition or does not intend to prosecute the petition either diligently or at all (r 6.31(2)). The court must not make such an order if satisfied that the petitioning creditor's debt has been paid, secured or compounded for by a third party or by the disposition of the debtor's own property made with the approval of the court (r 6.32(3)).

For the debt to have been paid, secured or compounded for by a third party, there must in effect have been a gift to the debtor from the third party since if there had been some arrangement for the debtor to repay the third party, the effect would be the same as if the debtor's own assets had been utilised (*Re Salaman (a Bankrupt)* (1983) 127 SJ 763).

For there to be a change in carriage of the petition, the 'new' creditor need not have been able to present a petition himself at the date the petition was presented nor need be be owed a sum equal to the bankruptcy level (currently £750).

The change of carriage order is Form 6.24B in Sched 4 to the Rules.

8 Dismissal and withdrawal

No order giving leave to withdraw a petition will be made before the petition is heard (r 6.32(3)).

If the petitioner applies to the court for his petition to be dismissed or for leave to withdraw, he must, unless the court orders otherwise, file in court an affidavit setting out why he wants the petition dismissed or withdrawn and the circumstances in which the application to dismiss or withdraw are made (r 6.32(1)). The affidavit must also include details of any payments made by the debtor to the petitioner or any arrangements entered into for securing or compounding the debt together with details of what dispositions of property of the debtor have been made for the purpose of the settlement or arrangement with the petitioner and whether the petitioner was paid by a third party or the debtor himself and that if any property of the debtor was used to make the payment or secure the settlement or arrangement, the court's approval had been obtained to it (r 6.32(2)).

Where application for dismissal or withdrawal is made, it seems that the practice of the High Court is to adjourn the petition to a new hearing and for the petition to be relisted under the debtor's name, marked 'For dismissal' so as to enable any other creditor to make application to be substituted as petitioning creditor or to have the carriage of the petition changed to him under rr 6.30 and 6.31 (*Practice Direction (Bankruptcy: Distribution of Business)* [1987] 1 WLR 1202).

9 Certificate of debt

On the hearing of a petition, to satisfy the court that the debt on which the petition is founded has not been paid or secured or compounded for, the court will normally accept as sufficient a certificate signed by the person representing the petitioning creditor (this could be the local solicitor agent for the petitioning creditor's solicitor) in the following form:

> I certify that I have/my firm has made inquiries of the petitioning creditor(s) within the last business day prior to the hearing/adjourned hearing and to the best of my knowledge and belief the debt on which the petition is founded is

still due and owing and has not been paid or secured or compounded for (save as to ....).

Signed_____ Dated_____

This certificate will be printed on the attendance slips used in the High Court but should, perhaps, be prepared by petitioning creditors' representatives in connection with proceedings pending in the county courts. A fresh certificate is required on each adjourned hearing (Practice Note (Bankruptcy: Certificate of Debt) [1987] 1 WLR 120).

10 Grounds for making a bankruptcy order

The court must not make a bankruptcy order unless it is satisfied that the debt, or one of the debts, in respect of which the petition was presented is either:
    (a) a debt which has been neither paid nor secured nor compounded for; or
    (b) a debt due at a future time which the debtor has no reasonable prospect of being able to pay when it falls due (s 271(1)).

The court must not make a bankruptcy order if the petition is based on a statutory demand and three weeks have not elapsed since it was served (s 271(2)). See Chapter 3 Section 4 as to when permission to petition before the expiry of three weeks after service of a statutory demand will be allowed.

The court will not make a bankruptcy order and will dismiss the petition if it is satisfied that the debtor is able to pay all his debts or is satisfied:
    (a) that the debtor has made an offer to secure or compound for a debt in respect of which the petition is presented;
    (b) that the acceptance of that offer would have required the dismissal of the petition; and
    (c) that the offer has been unreasonably refused;
and in determining whether the debtor is able to pay all his debts, his contingent and prospective liabilities must also be taken into account (s 271(3)).

There is no guidance in the Act or the Rules as to how the courts are to apply s 271(3). It is relatively straightforward for the court to be satisfied that the debtor can pay all his debts (subject to being able to raise the necessary cash to meet the debts).The debtor would presumably detail all his assets and liabilities and if there was a positive balance, then he must be able to pay his debts, the petition must be dismissed and the creditor would have sufficient information to enable him to take suitable enforcement action which would ensure payment for him.

If the debtor has made an offer to secure the debt, this too should present a straightforward picture to the court. If the offer to secure is good in that it offers full security to the creditor, any refusal of security would be unreasonable and the petition should be dismissed, or if the offer of security is not sufficient the petitioning creditor is entitled to the order he is seeking. In *Re A Debtor (No 32 of 1993)* [1995} 1 All ER 628 it was held that in order to determine whether the creditor's refusal of a lesser sum in settlement was unreasonable within s 271(3)(*c*) the court had to be satisfied that no reasonable hypothetical creditor in the position of the petitioning creditor and in the light of the actual history of the matter as disclosed to the court, would have refused the offer.

A problem is caused by the third reason for not making a bankruptcy order, namely, the offer to compound for the debt. In *Penned v Rhodes* (1846) 9 QB 114, compounding was described as 'such a bargain with the creditors that they were satisfied then with what they hoped to obtain afterwards'. This expression suggests that if the debtor makes an offer to the petitioning creditor of less than the total amount of his debt but the offer is one which, in all the circumstances, is better than the petitioning creditor could expect to achieve as a result of the bankruptcy of the debtor, the petitioning creditor's refusal of the offer would be considered unreasonable by the court and his petition would be dismissed. To make a decision of this nature, the court would need a great deal of information about the debtor's affairs, including whether there were any matters affecting the debtor which, if a bankruptcy order were made, might result in assets being clawed back for the benefit of the debtor's estate and divided amongst his creditors. The court would have to approach the matter in much the same way as a trustee in bankruptcy would do after the trustee had carried out his investigation into the debtor's affairs and collected in all his assets. This, it is submitted, is something which the court is unable to do in the context of the hearing of the bankruptcy petition. It has been held that the fact that the debtor had no assets available for distribution amongst his creditors was not sufficient cause to obtain the dismissal of the petition as, *inter alia*, his public examination might lead to the discovery of assets (*Re Leonard* [1896] QB 473; *Re Field (a Debtor)* (1977) *The Times*, 6 July). See also Chapter 6 on the interpretation of the offer to secure in the context of applications to set aside statutory demands.

A proposal for a voluntary arrangement under Part VIII of the Act (see Chapter 27) which is not acceptable to the petitioning creditor (holding the effective right of veto because of the amount of the debt owed to him) is not an offer to secure and compound which has been unreasonably refused such that the court should dismiss the petition (*Re a Debtor (No 2389 of 1989)* [1990] 3 All ER 984).

If the court is satisfied that the statements in the petition are true and that the debt on which it is founded has not been paid, or secured or compounded for, then it *may* make a bankruptcy order (r 6.25(1)). Note that the rule gives the court a discretion whether or not to make the order.

Where the petition is presented for the purpose of extorting money or to put pressure on the debtor for some collateral or inequitable purpose the court may dismiss the petition for other sufficient cause (*Re Majory, a Debtor* [1955] Ch 600). It is a question of fact in every case whether in all the circumstances there has been conduct of the creditor of a nature which established that the creditor has used or threatened bankruptcy proceedings oppressively, eg, to obtain some payment or promise from the debtor or some collateral advantage properly attributable to the use of the threat of bankruptcy proceedings (*Re Majory*, above).

There may be other sufficient causes where the effect of the bankruptcy order will be to destroy the debtor's only asset (*Re Otway, ex p Otway* [1895] 1 QB 812).

If the petition is brought in respect of a judgment debt and there is an appeal pending against that judgment or execution on that judgment has been stayed, the court *may* stay or dismiss the petition (r 6.25(2)). The court should adjourn the hearing of the petition pending the hearing of an appeal against the judgment debt if satisfied that the appeal was serious or *bona fide* and was being prosecuted with due diligence (*Re a Debtor (No 799 of 1994)* [1995] 3 All ER 723). If the court considers an appeal against the judgment to be frivolous, then it may make a bankruptcy order as in *Ex p Heyworth* (1888) 22 QBD 83 and *Re Noble* [1965] Ch 129. Where the court is satisfied that an appeal is *bona fide*, it should order the petition to be stayed generally with liberty to apply. The court has power to go behind a judgment debt on which a petition is founded and to inquire into the consideration for such a debt. The object of this power is to procure the distribution of the debtor's estate among his just creditors, for if a judgment were conclusive a person might allow judgments to be obtained against him in collusion with friends or relations without any debt being due to them at all (*Re Onslow, ex p Kibble* (1875) 10 Ch App 373).

A petition preceded by a statutory demand will not be dismissed on the ground only that the amount of the debt was overstated in the demand unless the debtor, within the time allowed for complying with the demand, gave notice to the creditor disputing the validity of the demand on that ground. In the absence of such notice, the debtor is deemed to have complied with the demand if he has within the time allowed paid the correct amount (r 6.25(3)). Although in the course of bankruptcy proceedings, an issue estoppel was created by the dismissal of the debtor's application to set aside a statutory demand (where the judge found no substantial ground on which the debt could be disputed) a bankruptcy court could on the full hearing of the petition go behind that issue estoppel and in effect decide again whether or not there were grounds to dispute the debt (*Eberhardt v Mair* [1995] 1 WLR 1180).

11 The order

The bankruptcy order is prepared by the court and must include the date and time of the making of it and the date of the presentation of the petition and must contain a notice requiring the debtor forthwith after service of it on him to attend the specified office of the official receiver (r 6.33). The name, address, telephone number and reference of the petitioning creditor's solicitor if he has one must be endorsed on the order (r 6.33(4)).

At least two sealed copies of the order must be sent by the court to the official receiver whose obligation it is to send one to the debtor and advertise the making of the order in such local newspaper as he thinks fit and in the *London Gazette*. The official receiver must also inform the Chief Land Registrar so that an entry is made in the register of writs and orders affecting land (r 6.34(2)).

On the application of the debtor or a creditor, the court may order the official receiver to suspend action under r 6.34(2) pending a further order of the court (r 6.34(3)) but the application for such an order must be supported by an affidavit stating the grounds on which it is made and if an order is made, a copy of it must be delivered to the official receiver (r 6.34(4)). The usual ground for such an application and order being made is that the debtor intends applying for the bankruptcy order to be rescinded because it was made in error, the debt having been paid, or the debtor was unable to attend the hearing of the petition and would have explained to the court that he was able to pay his debts in full etc.

But the court should not, in the exercise of its discretion, grant the debtor's application simply because the petitioning creditor and the other creditors assent thereto. It should take into consideration all the circumstances of the case and have regard to the interests of the public of which the Department of Trade is the guardian (*Re a Debtor, ex p Official Receiver* [1901] 2 KB 354).

Chapter 6

Debtor's Petition

1 Grounds

A debtor may present his own bankruptcy petition (s 264(1)(b)) but only on the grounds that he is unable to pay his debts (s 272(1)) and the petition must be accompanied by a statement of his affairs in the prescribed form (Form 6.28 in Sched 4 to the Rules; see Appendix 3, form 25). The statement of affairs must contain such particulars of the debtor's creditors and of his debts and other liabilities and of his assets together with such further information as may be prescribed (s 272(2)). Copies of this form can be obtained from court offices and the official receiver.

2 Court in which filed

The same rules as to jurisdiction in relation to creditors' petitions (r 6.9) apply to debtors' petitions (r 6.40); see Chapter 4. However, under 6.40(3) except in a case where the High Court is the appropriate court to which to present the petition, if it is more expedient for the debtor with a view to expediting his petition, it may be presented to whichever county court is specified in Sched 2 to the Rules as being in relation to the debtor's own county court the nearest full-time court. See Appendix 2 for the list of county courts specified in Sched 2. The petition must contain sufficient information to establish that it is brought in the appropriate court.

3 Form of petition

The petition must state:
    (1) The name, place of residence and occupation of the debtor.
    (2) The names in which business is carried on, if different and whether business is carried on alone or with others.
    (3) The nature of the business and business addresses.
    (4) The names in which business was carried on, if different, and whether business was carried on alone or with others.
    (5) Any former addresses during the period when the debts were incurred (r 6.38).

If the debtor has at any time used a name different from that specified in (1) above, that fact must be stated in the petition (r 6.38(3)).

Form 6.27 in Sched 4 to the Rules is a debtor's petition. Copies can be obtained from the court and the official receiver's office.

The petition must contain a statement that the petitioner, that is, the debtor, is unable to pay his debts and requests that a bankruptcy order be made against him and if there is in force a voluntary arrangement (see Chapter 27), this fact must also be stated, including the name and address of the supervisor (r 6.39). If the debtor has within the last five years been bankrupt, made a composition with his creditors, been subject to a county court administration order or entered into a voluntary arrangement, particulars must be given (r 6.39(2)).

4 Statement of affairs

The debtor's petition must be accompanied by a statement of affairs in the prescribed form (Form 6.28) verified by affidavit (which can be sworn before an officer of the court). Although this document is not a simple one to complete, and may therefore be outside the capability of the debtor to complete himself, the cost of obtaining professional assistance to complete the statement of affairs may not be allowed out of the debtor's estate (r 6.224) although if the debtor obtains legal aid to cover the cost of legal advice in connection with his bankruptcy proceedings, his solicitor may be able to include the cost of accountancy help with the statement of affairs as a disbursement for which the legal aid fund will be responsible.

5 Procedure on issue

When issuing a debtor's petition, the following are required:
  (a) the petition and statement of affairs with three copies of the petition and two copies of the statement of affairs (r 6.42);
  (b) receipt for the deposit of £250 (Insolvency Fees Order 1986 (SI No 2030), arts 8 and 9);
  (c) fee—£25.

One copy of the petition is returned to the debtor endorsed with the hearing date (if the court does not hear the petition forthwith). Copies of the petition and the statement of affairs are forwarded to the official receiver or insolvency practitioner if one is appointed under s 273 (see 7 below). The court retains one copy of the petition.

If there is a voluntary arrangement in force (see Chapter 27) at least 14 days' notice of the hearing must be given to the supervisor.

In cases of urgency the court can direct the debtor to deliver documents to the official receiver (r 6.42(6)).

The court notifies the chief land registrar for registration in the register of pending actions (r 6.43).

6 Hearing of the petition

On the hearing of the petition, the court may:
  (a) make a bankruptcy order; or
  (b) make a bankruptcy order and issue a certificate for the summary administration of the bankrupt's estate (where the total debts do not exceed the 'small bankruptcies level', currently £20,000, and the bankrupt has not been adjudicated bankrupt before in the last five years nor has he entered into any composition with his creditors or scheme of arrangement) (s 275); or
  (c) appoint an insolvency practitioner to prepare a report under s 273.

The registrar or district judge will go through the petition and statement of affairs with the debtor to ensure that he understands what he is doing and that a bankruptcy order will achieve what the debtor understands it to achieve. For example, if a debtor believes that bankruptcy will rid him of liability under a judgment for damages for personal injuries caused by him, a maintenance order in family proceedings or liability for fines, none of which is correct, then the debtor may think again. Also if a voluntary arrangement with creditors seems a sensible alternative, this will be suggested to the debtor instead of making a bankruptcy order (even in those cases when the court is not required under s 273 to appoint an insolvency practitioner to investigate the possibility of a voluntary arrangement).

7 Insolvency practitioner's report

On the hearing of a debtor's petition, the court must not make a bankruptcy order where the total of the debtor's debts would be less than the 'small bankruptcies level', currently £20,000, the minimum value of the debtor's assets would be equal to or more than the 'minimum amount', currently £2,000, the debtor has not been adjudicated bankrupt nor entered into any composition with his creditors or scheme of arrangement within the last five years and it would be appropriate to appoint an insolvency practitioner to prepare a report (s 273).

If the court appoints an insolvency practitioner to prepare a report, a copy of the order, the petition and the statement of affairs must be sent to him and the court must also fix a venue for the report to be considered with notice of this being given to the practitioner and the debtor (r 6.44). The debtor is entitled to attend when the report is being considered and make any representations he wishes.

The insolvency practitioner appointed to prepare a report must inquire into the debtor's affairs and submit a report to the court within the time limited by the court stating whether the debtor is willing to enter into a voluntary arrangement (see below) and whether a meeting of the debtor's creditors should be convened and if so, where and when. Upon receiving the report, the court can make an interim order under s 252 so as to facilitate the implementation of the proposed voluntary arrangement or make a bankruptcy order (s 274).

8 Making of the order

The bankruptcy order is settled by the court and once sealed is sent to the official receiver who must send a copy to the bankrupt (rr 6.45 and 6.46). The official receiver notifies the chief land registrar, gazettes the order and causes it to be advertised in such local newspaper as he thinks fit (r 6.46(2)).

On the making of a bankruptcy order the court can, if it appears appropriate to do so, issue a certificate for the summary administration of the debtor's estate (see above).

The certificate of summary administration can be revoked on the court's own motion or on the application of the official receiver (r 6.50) if it appears that the certificate should not have been issued (s 275(3)).

The effect of a certificate of summary administration is on the procedure for the administration of the debtor's estate by the official receiver (no outside trustee is appointed unless the court directs under s 297(2)). There is no obligation on the official receiver to investigate the debtor's conduct and affairs, and the period of time before the debtor can expect an automatic discharge from bankruptcy is reduced from three to two years.

If the petition contains a request for the supervisor of a voluntary arrangement (see Chapter 27) to be appointed trustee, a report must be filed by the supervisor at least two days before the hearing stating that he has notified creditors at least ten days before filing his report of his intention to seek the appointment as trustee and detailing the response of creditors including any objections received (r 6.42(7)).

In *Re a Debtor (No 17 of 1966)* [1967] Ch 590 a debtor filed his own petition on the basis of a judgment for £2,400 obtained against him for personal injury damages in respect of which a consent order had been made for payment by weekly instalments of £1.25 which the debtor could satisfy. The Divisional Court upheld the registrar's decision to grant an annulment on the ground that the debtor had no reasonable grounds for alleging that he was unable to pay his debts presently payable (see also *Re Betts, ex p Official Receiver* [1901] 2 KB 39). Under s 281(5) discharge from bankruptcy does not release the former bankrupt from liability to pay damages for personal injuries ordered against him and in respect of which the bankrupt might have been seeking to avoid payment by his bankruptcy, unless the court otherwise orders, and so bankruptcy may no longer be an attractive alternative. On the other hand, it has been held not to be an abuse of the process of the ocurt for a debtor to present a petition with the object of evading pressure of a judgment payable by instalments which the debtor could not meet (*Re Painter, ex p Painter* [1895] 1 QB 85). In considering whether the presentation of a petition by a debtor is an abuse of the process of the court, the test to be applied is whether the debtor honestly believed on reasonable grounds 'that he was unable to pay his debts' (*Re Dunn, ex p Official Receiver* [1949] Ch 640; *Re a Debtor (No 17 of 1966)*, above).

9 Voluntary arrangements

Under ss 252–263, a debtor can obtain what is, in effect, a moratorium from the court pending the preparation of proposals to be put to his creditors via an insolvency practitioner for the payment of their debts or part of them as an alternative to the debtor's bankruptcy. If a 75 per cent majority of creditors, present in person or by proxy at a meeting of creditors, agree to the proposals, then they become binding on all creditors and the insolvency practitioner who assisted the debtor or another such practitioner nominated by the creditors supervises the implementation of the proposals. See also Chapter 27.

10 Action following the order

At least two copies of the sealed order must be sent by the court to the official receiver who must send one of them to the debtor.

The court may, on the application of either the debtor or a creditor, order the official receiver to suspend his action in advertising the making of the order in the *London Gazette* and a local newspaper pending a further order of the court (r 6.46(3)) but such an application must be supported by an affidavit stating the grounds on which it is made. If the court makes an order requiring the official receiver to suspend his actions, he must be sent a copy of the court order.

Chapter 7

Dispositions, Proceedings and the Interim Receiver

1 Restrictions on dispositions

If a person is adjudged bankrupt, any disposition of his property or payment made by him after the date of the presentation of the petition for the bankruptcy order is void (except to the extent that it was made with the consent of the court or ratified subsequently by the court) (s 284(1) and (3)) unless the recipient acted in good faith, for value, without notice of the petition and before the bankruptcy order was made (s 284(4)(*a*)). In company winding up, where similar provisions to this exist, the payment of wages, rent, and the purchases of goods have all been authorised by the court or ratified subsequently; see, eg, *Re A I Levy (Holdings) Ltd* [1964] Ch 19 and *Re SA and D Wright* [1992] BCC 503. Even a court order (whether or not by consent) under s 24 Matrimonial Causes Act 1973 ordering the transfer of property by a person against whom a petition had been presented amounts to a disposition and is void under s 284 (*Re Flint* (1992) *The Times*, 16 July).

If a payment to a third party is void, that party holds the money received for the bankrupt as part of his estate (s 284(2)).

It would seem that even payment of the petitioning creditor's debt by the debtor would require consent of the court if it is to be safe from the action of any other creditor who might take over the bankruptcy petition and obtain a bankruptcy order on it.

Notice of a statutory demand is not the same as notice of the petition for the purpose of s 284(4), though perhaps notice of a statutory demand that the debtor has not complied with might constitute lack of good faith as suggested in *Re Dalton* [1963] Ch 366.

If A acquired property from B who in turn had acquired it from the debtor in circumstances where the exception in s 284(4) applies, then even though A may have acquired the property after he received notice of the petition against the debtor, A can retain the property provided that B acquired the property in good faith etc (s 284(4)(*b*)).

If a banker has allowed the debtor's debt to him to be increased by virtue of a payment to a third party notwithstanding the making of a bankruptcy order against the debtor, in so far as the payment to that third party is void, the banker can still prove in the bankruptcy for the debt provided that he had no notice of the bankruptcy order or it is not reasonably practicable for the payment to be recovered (s 284(5)).

It will be remembered that bankruptcy petitions are not advertised (unless substituted service is ordered) and even though a bankruptcy order has been made, it may be some time before notice to the world by insertion of the appropriate notice in the *London Gazette* is given. In the meantime, the debtor may have continued to deal with his estate and protection for those who have dealt with the debtor in good faith during this period in ignorance of his status needs to be given.

2 Restrictions on proceedings

After a bankruptcy petition has been presented, any court *may* stay any action, execution or other legal process against the debtor or his property (s 285(1)). This includes action against the person of the debtor, eg, committal for non-payment of rates (*Smith v Braintree District Council* [1989] 3 All ER 897). On proof that a bankruptcy petition has been issued, the court in which any proceedings are pending *may* stay the proceedings or allow them to continue on such terms as it thinks fit (s 285(2)). It will be seen that the granting of a stay is not automatic and is at the discretion of the court having regard to all the circumstances.

If the court dealing with the bankruptcy proceedings makes an order staying any action, execution or other legal process against the debtor, service of the order can be effected by sending a sealed copy to the address of the plaintiff (or whoever) in the proceedings stayed (r 7.56).

After a bankruptcy order has been made, no person who is a creditor of the bankrupt has any remedy against the person or property of the debtor or may commence any action against the bankrupt except with leave of the court (s 285(3)). This rule is subject to two exceptions. First, under s 347, if rent is owing by the bankrupt, his landlord can levy distress for a maximum of six months rent accrued due before the bankruptcy order was made whether the distress was completed before or after the making of the bankruptcy order. However, if the distress was levied less than three months before the bankruptcy order was made, the goods distrained or their proceeds stand charged for the benefit of the bankrupt's estate with the preferential debts of the bankrupt to the extent that the other assets of the estate are insufficient to meet them (s 347(3)). An action by a lessor claiming possession of a property from a lessee against whom a bankruptcy order has been made does not require the leave of the court (*Ezekiel v Orakpo* [1977] QB 260).

Secondly, under s 346, the benefit of executions cannot be retained by the execution creditor unless the execution was completed (by seizure and sale of goods or the making of a charging order *nisi* in the case of property or the payment of a debt under a garnishee order) before the making of the bankruptcy order (not the date of presentation of the petition). But at the hearing of the application to make the charging order *nisi* absolute, the court has a discretion to refuse to make the order absolute if doing so will give one creditor priority where the debtor is insolvent (see *Roberts Petroleum v Bernard Kenny* [1983] 1 All ER 564) and *Rainbow v Moorgate Properties Ltd* [1995] 1 WLR 789). In *Calor Gas v Piercy* ([1994] BCC 69) a creditor obtained a charging order *nisi* prior to the debtor obtaining an interim order in connection with his proposal for a voluntary arrangement. The order *nisi* was made asbolute whilst the interim order was still in effect even though the debtor's proposal for a voluntary arrangement was rejected. The court nonetheless held that the creditor should not be allowed to retain the benefit of the charging order and discharged the same. In *Re a Debtor v Sun Alliance* (1994), unreported, 12 January the court decided that it was wrong to give one creditor priority over the others where the debtor was clearly insolvent even when those creditors did not attend court, the matter being left to the debtor to argue.

If execution was completed between the date of the presentation of the petition and the making of the bankruptcy order, the creditor would be able to retain the benefit subject to the rule requiring the sheriff to hold the proceeds of seizure and sale for 14 days (except in regard to sums under the prescribed sum, currently £500) by which time a bankruptcy order may have been made. See also Chapter 19.

A secured creditor can enforce his security after the presentation of a petition or the making of a bankruptcy order and is not affected by s 285 except as regards any unsecured shortfall. However, where goods of a bankrupt are held by a creditor by way of pledge, pawn or other security, the official receiver may give notice in writing of his intention to inspect the goods. In this event, the secured creditor cannot realise his security without leave of the court unless the official receiver or trustee in bankruptcy has been given a reasonable opportunity of inspecting the goods and of exercising the bankrupt's right of redemption (s 285(5)).

3 The interim receiver

If it is shown to be necessary for the protection of the debtor's property, the court may at any time after the presentation of a petition (and before the making of a bankruptcy order) on the application of either the debtor himself or a creditor appoint the official receiver as interim receiver (s 286(1)). If an insolvency practitioner has been appointed by the court at the hearing of a debtor's petition to prepare a report and act in relation to a voluntary arrangement (under s 273), the court may appoint that insolvency practitioner (and not the official receiver) as the interim receiver if the debtor's property is in need of protection pending the insolvency practitioner's report and the convening of a creditors' meeting (s 286(2)).

On making an order appointing an interim receiver, the court may direct that the interim receiver's powers be limited or restricted in any respect but otherwise the interim receiver has all the same powers as a receiver and manager of the bankrupt's estate (see below) (s 286(3)). The debtor is under an obligation to give the interim receiver an inventory of his property and generally to assist the interim receiver as he may reasonably require (s 286(5)).

To obtain an order for the appointment of an interim receiver, an application must be made supported by an affidavit setting out the grounds on which the appointment is sought, whether or not the official receiver has been informed of the application and given a copy of it, whether or not there is in force a voluntary arrangement, and the applicant's estimate of the value of the property in respect of which the interim receiver is to be appointed (r 6.51(2)). If it is proposed that an insolvency practitioner be appointed interim receiver because the case falls within s 286(2), the consent of that insolvency practitioner to being appointed must also be stated in the affidavit (r 6.51(3)). The petitioning creditor or the debtor himself are parties who can make such an application.

The order appointing an interim receiver is Form 6.32 in Sched 4 to the Rules. It must state the nature and short description of the property covered by the appointment and the duties to be performed by the interim receiver (r 6.52(1)). The court on making the order sends two sealed copies to the interim receiver who must send one of them to the debtor.

Before appointing the official receiver as interim receiver, the court may direct that the applicant for the order deposit with the official receiver, or otherwise secure to his satisfaction, a sum of money to cover his remuneration and expenses and if the sum directed proves to be insufficient and further monies are ordered by the court to be paid and are not paid, the court may discharge the order appointing an interim receiver (r 6.53(2)). The monies deposited, in the event of a bankruptcy order being made, if not required to meet the remuneration and expenses of the interim receiver because there are other assets in the estate, will be repaid to the applicant in the prescribed order of priority as set out in r 6.224(1)(*e*) (r 6.53(3)).

If an insolvency practitioner is appointed interim receiver, he is required to give security for the proper performance of his functions. The security to be provided must meet the prescribed requirements as set out in the Insolvency Practitioners Regulations 1986 (SI No 1995). If the interim receiver fails to give or keep up security, the order appointing him may be revoked and another person may be appointed interim receiver or the order appointing an interim receiver may be discharged (r 6.55).

Where the official receiver has been appointed interim receiver, he can apply to the court for some person to be appointed special manager to undertake such duties and providing such security as the court directs (s 370). A special manager can be an authorised insolvency practitioner or some other suitable person.

The interim receiver's remuneration is payable out of the debtor's property or estate and from the deposit lodged and is fixed by the court from time to time on the interim receiver's application (r 6.56).

The appointment of an interim receiver is terminated if and when:
(a) the bankruptcy petition is dismissed;
(b) a bankruptcy order is made on the petition; or

(c) the court, on application by the interim receiver, the official receiver, a creditor or the debtor, directs (s 286(7) and r 6.57(1)).

If the interim receiver's appointment terminates because the petition has been dismissed, the court may give directions relating to the interim receiver's accounts of his administration and authorise him to retain such of the property of the debtor as is necessary to meet his remuneration and expenses (r 6.57(3)).

4 Receivership pending appointment of trustee

Between the making of a bankruptcy order and the time when the bankrupt's estate vests in a trustee (be it the official receiver or an insolvency practitioner), the official receiver is the receiver and manager of the estate (unless a special manager has been appointed under s 370) (s 287(1)). As receiver and manager, the official receiver is under a duty to protect the estate in the same way as if he were a receiver appointed by the High Court and he is only entitled to sell perishable goods and any other goods whose value is likely to diminish if not disposed of (s 287(2)). He is not obliged to do anything which might involve his incurring expenditure unless directed to by the Secretary of State and may, if he thinks fit, summon a general meeting of the bankrupt's creditors (s 287(3)).

The official receiver as receiver and manager is immune from action whilst so acting (s 287(4)).

The official receiver does not become receiver and manager in those cases where there is an immediate vesting order under s 297 on the making of a bankruptcy order. This happens where the court decides to make a bankruptcy order as a result of the insolvency practitioner's report under s 273 and to appoint that insolvency practitioner as trustee, or where the supervisor of a failed voluntary arrangement is appointed trustee.

Chapter 8

Investigations into the Bankrupt's Affairs

1 Submission of statement of affairs

Except in the case of a bankruptcy order made on a debtor's petition (where the statement of affairs has to be lodged at court with the petition itself), a bankrupt must submit a statement of affairs to the official receiver within 21 days of the making of a bankruptcy order (s 288(1)).

The statement of affairs must contain particulars of the bankrupt's creditors, debts and other liabilities and of his assets together with such other information as may be prescribed (s 288(2)). There is a prescribed form (Form 6.33 in Sched 4 to the Rules) and by r 6.59 the statement of affairs must be in this form and must contain all the particulars required by that form.

The official receiver must give the bankrupt the forms for preparation of his statement of affairs together with instructions on how to complete them (r 6.60(1)). The statement of affairs must be verified by an affidavit and delivered to the official receiver together with a copy (r 6.60(2) and (3)).

The inclusion in the statement of affairs of a statute-barred debt appears not to constitute an acknowledgment under the Limitation Act 1939 (*Everett v Robertson* (1858) 28 LJQB 23).

2 Release and extension of time

The official receiver may release the bankrupt from his duty to submit a statement of affairs or extend the period for him to do so and if the official receiver refuses to do either, the court may, on the application of the bankrupt, do so (s 288(3)). If the court considers the bankrupt's application has no merit, it may dismiss it, but only after the bankrupt has been given the opportunity to attend court on an *ex p* hearing of which he has been given at least seven days' notice. If the court considers that the application has some merit, then the application can proceed to a hearing and the bankrupt must give at least 14 days' notice of that hearing to the official receiver and the official receiver must be served with any evidence that the bankrupt intends to adduce in support. The official receiver may file a report in answer and must serve it on the bankrupt at least five days before the hearing (r 6.62(4) and (5)).

Perhaps the only grounds on which the official receiver or the court would be prepared to dispense with the requirement to submit a statement of affairs would be if the bankrupt was physically or mentally incapable of doing it.

Whatever the outcome of the application, the bankrupt must pay his own costs unless the court orders otherwise (r 6.62(7)).

Bearing in mind that the bankrupt will not, by this stage, have any assets of his own to discharge any costs he may incur, it would seem that unless he can get legal aid to make the application or some friend or relative of his is prepared to assist, he would not be able to obtain legal assistance in the making of this application.

3 Assistance

If the bankrupt himself cannot prepare a proper statement of affairs, the official receiver may employ someone at the expense of the estate to assist in its preparation (r 6.63(1)). Alternatively, the official receiver may authorise an allowance out of the estate toward the expenses incurred by the bankrupt in employing someone to assist in its preparation. Before doing so, the official receiver must receive from the bankrupt an estimate of the costs and only a named person, approved of by the official receiver, can be authorised to do the work (r 6.63(2) and (3)).

These provisions do not relieve the bankrupt of the obligation to submit a statement of affairs; he remains the person primarily responsible for the preparation and submission on time of the statement of affairs.

4 Failure to submit

If the bankrupt, without reasonable excuse, fails to lodge a statement of affairs either within the time limited or at all, he is guilty of contempt of court and is liable to be punished accordingly (s 288(4)).

5 Limited disclosure

If the official receiver thinks it would prejudice the conduct of the bankruptcy for the whole of the statement of affairs to be disclosed, he may apply to the court for an order for limited disclosure (r 6.61).

6 Accounts

If the official receiver requests the bankrupt to do so, he must furnish the official receiver with accounts relating to his affairs of such nature, as at such date and for such period as the official receiver may specify except that, unless the court orders otherwise, only accounts for periods less than three years before the date of the presentation of the petition need be supplied (r 6.64(1) and (2)).

If the bankrupt is unable to prepare such accounts, then the official receiver may employ someone or authorise an allowance out of the estate to enable the bankrupt to employ someone to do the work in the same way as regards statements of affairs referred to in **3** above.

Accounts must be verified by affidavit (if so required by the official receiver) and delivered within 21 days of the request (or such longer period as the official receiver may allow). Two copies of the accounts and the affidavit (if required) must be delivered to the official receiver (r 6.65).

7 Further disclosure

The official receiver may from time to time require the bankrupt to submit in writing further information explaining or amplifying anything contained in his statement of affairs or accounts and the bankrupt must, if requested, provide the further information within 21 days of the official receiver's request or such further time as the official receiver may allow (r 6.66).

8 Debtors' petitions

The obligations in relation to a statement of affairs in the case of a person made bankrupt as a result of his own petition are to complete it (in the prescribed form, Form 6.28) and lodge it at court with the petition at the time of its presentation. No allowance for the cost of assistance in the preparation of the statement of affairs is to come out of the estate but there is no reason why the bankrupt should not have used some of his assets, prior to the presentation of his petition and the making of a bankruptcy order on his petition, to pay for the costs of assistance in the preparation of his statement of affairs.

The obligation to prepare accounts, submit them and provide further information is the same for bankrupts made bankrupt on their own petition as on creditors' petitions and an allowance for the cost of preparing accounts can be made out of the estate as with bankrupts made bankrupt on creditors' petitions (r 6.71).

9 Investigatory duties of the official receiver

Except in the case of a bankruptcy where a certificate of summary administration is in force (in which the duties of the official receiver are not mandatory), the official receiver must investigate the pre-bankruptcy conduct and affairs of every bankrupt and make such report to the court as he thinks fit (s 289(1)).

Chapter 9

Rescission and Annulment of Bankruptcy Order

1 Rescission

Every court having jurisdiction in bankruptcy under the Act may review, rescind or vary any order made by it under its bankruptcy jurisdiction (s 375(1)). The court has the power to rescind a bankruptcy order under this section. The court to which proceedings have been transferred from another court after the making of the bankruptcy order also has this power (*Re a Debtor* (*No 2A of 1980*) [1981] Ch 148, reversing the previously held view of the law and practice).

The circumstances that justify a court in rescinding a bankruptcy order are closely analogous to the circumstances which enable the court to annul a bankruptcy order (see below) and include the fact that all the debts have been paid. The jurisdiction of a court to rescind its own orders is very wide but has been exercised subject to the same time limits which apply if the aggrieved party wishes to appeal against a bankruptcy order, namely, the application must be made within the time limited for appeals which is four weeks. But all the time limits can be extended by the court under s 376.

A bankruptcy order should not be rescinded merely because the debtor alleges that he has no assets nor any prospect of having any assets with which to discharge his liabilities (*Re Field* [1978] Ch 371).

If an application to rescind a bankruptcy order is to be made, an application should be considered also, as a preliminary measure, for an order requiring the official receiver to suspend the action which he is otherwise obliged to take immediately after a bankruptcy order has been made, namely, to send notice of the order to the chief land registrar, to advertise the order in a local newspaper and to gazette the order (r 6.34).

The power to rescind is discretionary. In exercising his discretion to rescind, the registrar or district judge is not bound to do so merely because the petitioning creditor (*Re Norris* (1890) 7 Morr 8) or the general body of creditors consent. However, in *Fitch v Official Receiver* [1996] 1 WLR 242 it was held that a change of attitude of the petitioning creditor to the making of a bankruptcy order was a sufficient change of circumstances such as to entitle the court to review the bankruptcy order and to consider whether the order ought to be rescinded.

For a precedent of an application to rescind the bankruptcy order or to require the official receiver to suspend action, see Appendix 3, form 26. Fresh evidence may be lodged (*Re Cohen* [1950] 2 All ER 36 and *Re a Debtor* (32 DS 1991).

2 Annulment

The court may annul a bankruptcy order if at any time it appears to the court that the order ought not to have been made (on any grounds existing at the time the order was made) or the debts and expenses of the bankruptcy have all been either paid or secured to the satisfaction of the court since the making of the order (s 282(1)).

The court may annul a bankruptcy order even after the bankrupt has obtained his discharge (s 282(3)).

The court is limited when dealing with an application to annul to a consideration of the facts extant at the time of the making of the bankruptcy order (*Re von Engel*, (1988) *The Independent*, 21 August).

The application to annul must be served on the official receiver or trustee (if one has been appointed) and, probably, under the general power in r 7.4(4), on the petitioning creditor.

The application must specify on which of the two alternative grounds in s 282(1) it is made and in either case must be supported by an affidavit (r 6.206). The applicant must give at least 28 days' notice (unless the application is based on s 282(1)(*a*), that the order ought not to have been made, in which case 'sufficient notice' must be given) to the official receiver and (if other) the trustee and the petitioning creditor and supply them with copies of the application and affidavit (r 6.206(4)).

For a bankruptcy order to be annulled on the grounds that at the time the order was made there existed some reason why the order ought not to be made, there must have been some irregularity or invalidity in the proceedings. Examples of these include the fact that there was no longer a sufficient petition debt, some defect in the status of the debtor (eg, that he was a minor) or some irregularity in the service of a statutory demand. All these grounds would also constitute grounds for an appeal against the making of the order. If the application for annulment is made on these grounds, no report from the official receiver or trustee need be prepared prior to the hearing of the application. There is no general discretion to annul a bankruptcy order only on the basis of facts existing at the date of the hearing (*Re a Debtor*) (*No 68 of 1992*) (1993) *The Times*, 12 February).

However, once a bankruptcy order has been made, the bankrupt has no *locus standi* to apply to the court for the judgment on which the bankruptcy order was based to be set aside with the object, if successful, of applying for an annulment of the bankruptcy order. Only the trustee can apply for the judgment to be set aside (*Heath v Tang* (1993) *The Times*, 11 August.

If the application for annulment is made because all the debts and expenses have been paid or secured, at least 21 days before the hearing fixed for the application to be heard, the trustee, or the official receiver if no trustee has been appointed, must file a report containing details of the assets and liabilities of the bankrupt, the circumstances leading to the bankruptcy and any other matters thought fit (r 6.207(2)). If the debts and expenses have not been paid but have been secured, the report must state whether it is considered that the security is satisfactory (r 6.207(3)). The report must be sent to the bankrupt at least 14 days before the hearing and if the trustee is other than the official receiver then the official receiver must also be sent a copy of the report. The official receiver may file an additional report which must be sent to the bankrupt at least seven days before the hearing (r 6.207(4) and (5)).

In advance of the hearing, the court may make an interim order staying any proceedings and this order can even be made *ex parte* (r 6.208).

If the application is made on the grounds that debts have been paid or secured and it is known that there are creditors who have not proved their debts, the court may direct that notice be given to them of the application and order the trustee to advertise the application and, in the meantime, adjourn the application for not less than 35 days (r 6.209).

Before annulling the bankruptcy order, the court must be satisfied that all bankruptcy debts and expenses of the bankruptcy have been paid in full or secured to the satisfaction of the court (s 282(1)(*b*)) but if there are disputed debts or untraced creditors, the court may require security, in the form of a bond or money in court, should the creditors prove their debts or be traced ultimately (r 6.211(3)). The court may direct that particulars of the alleged debt be advertised and if no claim on the security is made within 12 months, the court can, on application, order the release of the security (r 6.211(4)).

The trustee must attend the hearing but where the official receiver is the trustee or has filed a report, he need not attend but may do so (r 6.210).

It is a ground for annulment that the bankruptcy proceedings are an abuse of the process of the court, and this point has been taken where the debtor had presented his own petition.

Release under seal by creditors, without any consideration, of the bankrupt from the debts owing to them is not 'payment in full' within the meaning of s 282 (*Re Kent, ex p Official Receiver* [1905] 2 KB 666). Similarly, if creditors are persuaded to assign their debts to an associate of the debtor for a nominal consideration and the assignee then only seeks to prove for the nominal sum he paid, payment of such a sum will not be sufficient to enable the bankrupt to secure an annulment.

The jurisdiction conferred on the court to annul a bankruptcy order is discretionary and an order may be refused if, having regard to the conduct of the bankrupt, it seems right to do so. In *Re Taylor, ex p Taylor* [1901] 1 KB 744, the bankrupt did not disclose in his statement of affairs or on his public examination a sum of money which was part of his assets. Afterwards he handed to the official receiver a portion of it sufficient to pay his debts and the costs in full and subsequently applied for an order annulling the bankruptcy order. The order of the lower court refusing the annulment was upheld.

If the bankruptcy order is annulled, the official receiver must, if he has notified the creditors of the debtor's bankruptcy, notify them of the annulment (r 6.212). The court must inform the Secretary of State and the former bankrupt can require the Secretary of State, at the expense of the former bankrupt, to advertise and gazette the making of the annulment order (r 6.213).

The order must include provision permitting the vacation of the bankruptcy order at the Land Registry (r 6.213(1)).

When a bankruptcy order has been annulled, this does not release any trustee from his obligation to prepare an account of his dealings with the former bankrupt's property and to submit it to the Secretary of State. The former bankrupt is not, however, directly involved in this, though he may be very seriously affected by it, for instance, because of the costs and expenses incurred while he was bankrupt. If he is aggrieved, then he may apply to the court under ss 303 and 304 for the actions of the trustee to be reviewed.

Chapter 10

Public Examination

1 Application for examination

Unlike under the old law, there is now no automatic public examination of a bankrupt. After a bankruptcy order has been made and before the discharge of the bankrupt, the official receiver may make application to the court for the public examination of the bankrupt (s 290(1)).

If notice is received by the official receiver from a creditor requiring him to make application for an order that the bankrupt be examined publicly and the notice has been sent with the concurrence of not less than half in value of all the creditors of the bankrupt, then the official receiver must make application to the court for such an order unless the court otherwise orders (s 290(2)).

The notice must be in writing and must be accompanied by a list of the creditors concurring, the amount of their claims, written confirmation of their concurrence and a statement of the reasons why the examination is requested (r 6.173(1)). If the creditor making the request himself constitutes more than half in value of all the creditors, then these requirements are modified accordingly.

Before making application to the court pursuant to such a request, the creditor making the request must lodge security for the expenses of the public examination with the official receiver. The official receiver must make the application within 28 days of receiving the request unless he is of the opinion that the request is unreasonable, in which case he can apply to the court for an order relieving him from the obligation to make the application for a public examination (r 6.173(4)). If the court, on the official receiver's *ex parte* application, agrees with him, notice must be given by the official receiver to the creditor who made the request. If the court disagrees with the official receiver, then he is obliged to make application for the public examination forthwith (r 6.173(5)). It is implicit in this rule that the court may direct that the official receiver's request to be relieved from the obligation to apply for a public examination be heard *inter partes*.

2 Order for examination

If the court orders a public examination to be held, it must appoint a day on which it is to be held and the bankrupt must attend on that day and be publicly examined as to his affairs, dealings and property (s 290(3)). If the bankrupt fails at any time to attend his public examination, he is guilty of contempt of court and is liable to be punished accordingly (s 290(5)).

A copy of the court's order must be sent forthwith to the bankrupt by the official receiver. The order is in Form 6.55 in Sched 4 to the Rules. The official receiver must give the bankrupt at least 14 days' notice of the hearing and must also give the same notice to any trustee, nominated or appointed, any special manager if one has been appointed and, unless the court directs otherwise, to every creditor known to the official receiver or identified in the bankrupt's statement of affairs (r 6.172(3)). The official receiver may also, if he thinks fit, advertise the forthcoming public examination in one or more local newspapers but if he does so, it must be at least 14 days before the date fixed for the examination (r 6.172(4)).

Leave to serve the order on a bankrupt resident abroad will be granted under r 12.12 (*Re Seagull* [1993] BCC 41).

3 Bankrupt unfit for examination

If the bankrupt is suffering from any mental disorder or physical disability rendering him unfit to undergo or attend a public examination, the court may stay the order for his public examination or direct that the public examination be conducted in such manner and at such place as it thinks fit (r 6.174(1)).

For the court to act in this way, application must be made to it either by the official receiver or by a relative or friend of the bankrupt whom the court considers to be a proper person to make such an application or by a person appointed by a court in the UK to manage the affairs of, or to represent, the bankrupt. In these latter two cases, at least seven days' notice of the application must be given to the official receiver and the trustee and, unless the bankrupt is a patient within the meaning of the Mental Health Act 1983, the application must be supported by an affidavit by a doctor as to the bankrupt's mental and physical condition (r 6.174(2) and (3)) . If extra cost is likely to be occasioned by the manner in which it is sought to have the public examination conducted, before any order is made on the application, such sum as the official receiver thinks will be sufficient to cover the extra costs must be deposited with him. Where the official receiver himself makes the application, it may be made *ex parte* and supported by a report (not affidavit) from him.

4 Procedure at hearing

The following may take part in a public examination and may question the bankrupt concerning his affairs, dealings and property and the causes of his failure:
  (a) the official receiver (and, if the bankruptcy comes about as a result of a criminal bankruptcy order, the official petitioner);
  (b) the trustee of the bankrupt's estate if his appointment has taken effect;

(c) any person who has been appointed special manager of the bankrupt's estate or business; and
(d) any creditor of the bankrupt who has tendered a proof of debt in the bankruptcy (s 290(4)).

Any of these persons may with the approval of the court (given at the hearing itself or in advance) appear by solicitor or counsel, or may authorise in writing another person to question the bankrupt on his behalf (r 6 175(2)).

The bankrupt must take the oath and must answer all such questions as the court may put, or allow to be put, to him (r 6.175(1)). The bankrupt may at his own expense employ a solicitor with or without counsel who may put to him such questions as the court may allow for the purpose of enabling him to explain or qualify any answers given by him and may make any representations on his behalf (r 6.175(3)) . The bankrupt is not entitled to refuse to answer questions put to him at the examination (and allowed by the court) on the ground that by so doing he may incriminate himself (*Re Atherton* [1912] 2 KB 251 and *Bishopsgate Investment Managers v Maxwell* [1992] 2 All ER 856) but the court can adjourn the examination if criminal proceedings have been instituted against the bankrupt and the court is of the opinion that the continuance of the examination would be calculated to prejudice a fair trial of those proceedings (r 6.175(6)). Before a question put to the bankrupt can be disallowed, the court has to be satisfied by the bankrupt that the answer could not secure any further assets or rights to the creditors or any protection to the public (*Re Paget, ex p Official Receiver* [1927] 2 Ch 85).

A written record of the proceedings must be made but the form of this is a matter for the court. The record must be read over either to or by the bankrupt, signed by him and verified by affidavit at a later date as fixed by the court (r 6.175(4)). This written record may be used as evidence against the bankrupt in any proceedings of the statements made by the bankrupt in the course of his examination (r 6.175(5)). The statements made by the bankrupt are not admissible in proceedings as against third parties even in the bankruptcy (*Re Brunner* (1887) 19 QBD 572).

5 Adjournment

The public examination may be adjourned by the court from time to time, either to a fixed date or generally (r 6.176(1)).

Where the examination has been adjourned generally, the court may at any time fix an adjourned hearing and give directions as to the manner in which the adjourned hearing will take place (in terms as to notice to interested persons and when and where it is to take place) either on the application of the official receiver or the bankrupt. If it is the bankrupt who makes the application, the court can direct that the adjourned hearing only take place after the bankrupt has lodged with the official receiver such sum as the official receiver considers necessary to cover the expenses of the adjourned hearing (r 6.176(2) and (3)).

Where the public examination is adjourned generally, the official receiver may, there and then, and without prior notice to the bankrupt, make application under s 279(3) for the relevant period for the automatic discharge of the bankrupt to cease to run (r 6.176(4)). It would seem that the conclusion of the bankrupt's public examination, if one has been ordered to be held, is still a prerequisite for his obtaining a discharge whether under the provisions for automatic discharge or after application to the court. In *Holmes v Official Receiver* (1995) unreported, 7 July, the judge upheld a district judge's decision to adjourn a public examination on short notice and to suspend the bankrupt's automatic discharge pending the happening of the first of his public examinations being concluded or a period of nine months elapsing.

6 Expenses of examination

Where an examination has taken place as a result of a request from a creditor, the court may order that the whole or part of the expenses of the examination are to come out of the deposit lodged by the creditor under r 6.173(2) (see **1** above) instead of out of the estate (r 6.177).

Chapter 11

Appointment and Removal of Trustee

1 Power to make appointments

The power to appoint a trustee is exercisable (s 292(1)):
  (a) by a general meeting of the bankrupt's creditors, except at a time when there is in force a certificate of summary administration;
  (b) by the court (under s 297 when a bankruptcy order is made at a time when there is a supervisor of a voluntary arrangement in office and the court wishes to appoint the supervisor as trustee) but if the supervisor desires to be appointed trustee by the court, the petition must contain such a request; however, the former supervisor cannot be appointed trustee unless a report has been filed at court not less than two days before the hearing of the petition stating that creditors have been informed, at least ten days before the report was filed, of the intention to seek such an appointment as trustee of the supervisor and giving details of the response from creditors including any objections to the appointment (r 6.10(6)); and
  (c) by the Secretary of State (where the meeting of creditors has failed to appoint a trustee or where a vacancy occurs and the official receiver refers the need for the appointment of a new trustee to the Secretary of State) (ss 295(2), 296(2) and 300(6)).

No person may be appointed a trustee unless he is a qualified insolvency practitioner (s 292(2)).

Two or more trustees can be appointed to act jointly but if more than one person is appointed as trustee, whether or not each trustee can act for the others in defined circumstances must be provided for (s 292(3)).

The appointment of any person as trustee takes effect from the time when he accepts the appointment but otherwise is at the time specified in his certificate of appointment (s 292(4)).

2 Summoning of meeting to appoint first trustee

Except where a certificate for summary administration has been issued, as soon as practicable in the 12-week period after the making of a bankruptcy order, the official receiver must decide whether or not to summon a meeting of creditors for the purpose of choosing someone to be the trustee of the estate in his place (s 293(1)). If he decides to summon such a meeting, the meeting must be held not more than four months from the date of the bankruptcy order (r 6.79(1)), and the official receiver must inform the court and give at least 21 days' notice to all creditors (r 6.79(2)). Notice must also be given by public advertisement (r 6.79(5)). Where the official receiver receives a request for a meeting of creditors to be held in a case where he had decided not to summon such meetings, he must withdraw any notices given by him that he did not intend to summon such a meeting and fix a date and venue for the meeting not more than three months from the date of the request and proceed as if he had decided to summon a meeting. The form of request for such a meeting is to be found in Sched 4 to the Rules as Form 6.34.

If the official receiver decides not to summon a meeting, he must inform the court and creditors (s 293(2)). If a request is made for a meeting to be summoned and the request is supported by at least 25 per cent in value of the creditors, the official receiver must summon a meeting (s 294). The meeting must be held within three months (r 6.79(4)).

Until such time as a meeting is held to appoint a trustee, there is no trustee. During this period, the official receiver is receiver and manager of the estate.

None of the foregoing has any application to bankruptcies where a certificate of summary administration is in force. The official receiver does have power to summon meetings of creditors at any time even in relation to this type of bankruptcy for the purposes of ascertaining the wishes of creditors (r 6.81).

3 Notice of the first meeting of creditors

If the official receiver decides to summon a meeting of creditors under s 293(1), he must fix a date and venue for the meeting which must be held not more than four months from the date of the bankruptcy order (r 6.79(1)). The official receiver has 12 weeks in which to make up his mind whether or not to summon a meeting and so, if he utilises the whole of that 12-week period, the meeting must be held within four weeks.

Notice of the first meeting of creditors must be given to all creditors at least 21 days before the date fixed for the meeting (r 6.79(3)).

In fixing the venue of a meeting, the official receiver must have regard to the convenience of those who are to attend (r 6.86) and meetings must be held between 10 am and 4 pm on business days unless the court orders otherwise (r 6.86). With every notice summoning a meeting there must be included forms of proxy (Form 8.4 in Sched 4 to the Rules; see Appendix 3, form 27).

The notice to creditors must state a time and date not more than four days before the meeting by which the creditors must lodge their proofs of debt (Form 6.37 in Sched 4 to the Rules; see Appendix 3, form 28) and, if applicable, proxies in order to entitle them to vote at the first meeting (r 6.79(4)). The official receiver must give at least 21 days' notice of the meeting to the bankrupt and may require him to attend the meeting (r 6.84).

4 Rules governing meetings

(1) The official receiver (or someone nominated in writing by him) is the chairman of the first meeting. Once a trustee is appointed, he or an employee of his or another authorised insolvency practitioner chairs meetings.

(2) At a meeting of creditors, a resolution is deemed to be passed when a majority in value of the creditors present personally or by proxy have voted in favour of the resolution (r 6.88).

(3) The quorum is at least one creditor in person or by proxy (r 12.4A(2)). If there is no quorum, then the only business that can be transacted is the election of a chairman, the proving of debts and the adjournment of the meeting (r 6.92(1)). If there is no quorum present within half an hour of the time appointed for the meeting, it must be adjourned for not more than 21 days (r 6.91(3)) to such a date and place as the chairman thinks fit (r 6.91(2)). If the chairman by himself or with one creditor would constitute a quorum and the chairman is aware that other creditors intend to attend, then the meeting must not commence until at least 15 minutes after the appointed time (r 12.4A(4)).

(4) No creditor can vote at any meeting unless he has lodged with the official receiver not later than the time mentioned for this purpose in the notice convening the meeting a proof of debt, that is, a statement in the appropriate form (see Chapter 15) of the amount claimed by him as due to him and the claim has been admitted for the purpose of entitlement to vote (r 6.93(1)). Acceptance by the official receiver of a proof of debt for voting purposes is not the same as acceptance of a proof by the trustee to rank for dividend. Creditors are not allowed to vote if their debts are unliquidated (r 6.93(3)) nor if their debts are secured (r 6.93(4)). For the purposes of voting, a secured creditor must value his security and can vote for the excess of his debt over the security held. If the chairman agrees to put an estimated minimum value on an unascertained debt, the claimant of such a debt can vote for that value (r 6.93(3)).

(5) The official receiver as chairman of the meeting can decide to reject a proof for voting purposes but that decision is subject to appeal (r 6.94). If the official receiver is in doubt as to the validity of a claim, he should mark the proof and allow the creditor to vote subject to his vote being subsequently declared invalid if the objection is sustained (r 6.94(3)). If on appeal the official receiver's decision to reject a proof is reversed, the court may order a further meeting (r 6.94(4)).

(6) Where the chairman holds a proxy requiring him to vote for a particular resolution, if no one else proposes that resolution, he must do so unless he considers that there is good reason for not doing so (r 6.89).

5 Proxies

Need for a proxy

A creditor may vote either in person or by proxy. Only a sole trader or other individual creditor can appear in person. If such a creditor wishes to appoint another person to attend a meeting on his behalf, he too must give the person attending his proxy. All other entities, that is, partnerships, companies or corporations, can only vote via representatives authorised to vote on their behalf by a proxy form. The court may in exceptional circumstances allow otherwise (r 6.93).

Where a person is authorised by s 375 of the Companies Act 1985 to represent a corporation or company at any meeting of creditors, he must produce to the official receiver a copy of his authority. That copy must either be under the seal of the corporation or company or must be certified to be a true copy by the secretary or a director of that organisation (r 8.7) but the authority need not be in the form of a resolution of the company (r 8.7(3)). Utilisation of this procedure would seem to be an alternative to completing and lodging a proxy.

Though there is no appeal procedure laid down if the chairman of the meeting rejects a proxy duly lodged and therefore does not allow that creditor's vote, it is open to the creditor affected to apply to the court for the chairman's decision to be reversed and for a new meeting to be held.

Form of proxy

Proxy forms must be sent out to creditors with the notice summoning their meetings (r 8.2(1)) and no form of proxy can be used except the one sent out with the notice or a substantially similar one (r 8.2(2)). Schedule 4 to the Rules includes a form of proxy for use in connection with meetings following a bankruptcy order (Form 8.4; see Appendix 3, form 27).

Neither the name nor the description of the official receiver, trustee or any other person may be printed or inserted in the body of any proxy form before it is sent out (r 8.2(1)).

A creditor may give a proxy to any person of full age (who himself need not be a creditor or contributory) (r 8.1(3)), requiring the proxy holder to use his discretion on voting (*a general proxy*) or requiring him to vote for or against any specified resolution (*a special proxy*). A creditor may appoint the official receiver to be his general or special proxy. If the official receiver has a number of general proxies given to him, it is usual for him to vote with these proxies in accordance with the wishes of the majority as expressed at the meeting itself or by virtue of special proxies lodged.

Lodging proxies

A proxy which the holder intends to use at any meeting of creditors must be lodged with the official receiver not later than the time mentioned for that purpose in the notice convening the meeting or the adjourned meeting. That time must be not more than four business days before the date fixed for the meeting (r 6.79(4)). The official receivers have been directed not to accept faxed proxies as they have been advised that they do not comply with the Rules being, in effect, facsimilies of an original document and therefore not signed originals. However, in a number of cases (largely unreported), faxed proxies have been held to be valid for use in connection with voluntary arrangements and in *Re A Debtor (No 2021 of 1995)* [1996] BCC 189 unreported, it was held that a proxy form has been signed for the purposes of r 8.2 if it bears some distinctive or personal marking which has been placed on it by or with the authority of the creditor and when that creditor faxes that proxy, he both sends the contents of the form and the signature applied to it. Whilst the case relates to an IVA, the same rules apply as in bankruptcy.

Solicitation for proxies and voting by proxy holders

Where the court is satisfied that any improper solicitation has been used by or on behalf of a trustee in obtaining proxies or in procuring his appointment as trustee, it may order that no remuneration be allowed to the person by whom or on whose behalf the solicitation was exercised (r 6.148(1)). This is so notwithstanding any resolution of the creditors' committee or of the creditors to the contrary (r 6.148(2)). A distinction must be drawn between proper and improper solicitation since it is only the latter which disentitles the trustee from his remuneration.

No person acting under a proxy may vote in favour of any resolution which would directly or indirectly place him or any associate of his in a position to receive any remuneration out of the estate of the bankrupt (r 8.6(1)). However, where any person holds proxies requiring him to vote for the appointment of himself as trustee he may use those proxies and vote accordingly provided that if the proxy holder himself has signed the proxy in his own favour, he produces to the chairman of the meeting written authorisation from the principal sufficient to show that he was authorised to sign (r 8.6(1A)).

6 Business at first meetings

The primary purpose of such meetings is to appoint a trustee. In fact, pursuant to r 6. 80, no resolutions can be taken at the meeting of creditors other than:
(a) a resolution to appoint a named insolvency practitioner to be trustee or two or more insolvency practitioners as joint trustees;
(b) a resolution to establish a creditors' committee;
(c) (unless a creditors' committee has been established) a resolution specifying the terms of the trustee's remuneration or to defer consideration of that matter;
(d) if two or more trustees are appointed, a resolution specifying whether acts are to be done by both or all of them or by only one;
(e) a resolution adjourning the meeting for not more than three weeks; and

(f) any other resolutions which the chairman thinks it right to allow for special reasons.

At the meeting no resolution can be proposed which has as its object the appointment of the official receiver as trustee (r 6.80(2)). Thus, the official receiver will only become the trustee of the bankrupt if no nominations for the appointment of a trustee are put forward and the official receiver does not decide to ask the Secretary of State (under s 296) to appoint another person as trustee.

The official receiver as convener of the meeting can require the bankrupt to attend the meeting (r 6.84) and so it must be presumed that matters regarding the bankrupt's activities can be raised by either the official receiver or those present. Bankrupts rarely, however, are asked to attend such meetings.

If there are a number of nominations for the position of trustee, then a vote is taken in accordance with the rules as set out on p **60**, but if there are three or more nominees, the chairman must continue taking votes until one nominee has a clear majority with the nominee obtaining the least support dropping out each time (r 6.88(2)).

No person can be appointed as trustee unless he is a qualified insolvency practitioner. Qualified insolvency practitioners are those who hold licences from the various authorised professional bodies (such as those governing Chartered Accountants and Certified Accountants, the Law Society or the Insolvency Practitioners Association) or from the Department of Trade.

The creditors' committee is appointed (except where the official receiver is trustee) to assist the trustee generally and in particular to determine the trustee's remuneration, though this power is subject to the overriding jurisdiction of creditors generally and the court. See Chapter 12 for fuller details of the duties and functions of the creditors' committee.

7 Certifying the appointment of the trustee

The official receiver or whoever is the chairman of the meeting must certify the appointment of the trustee, but not until the person appointed has provided him with a written statement that he is a qualified insolvency practitioner and consents to act (r 6.120(2)). The official receiver must send a certificate of appointment to the trustee (and file it at court) (r 6.120(4) and (5)) and the trustee's appointment is effective from the date endorsed on the certificate (r 6.120(3)).

There is no longer any requirement for the trustee to provide a separate fidelity bond for each appointment as trustee that he holds.

8 Resignation of trustee and vacancies

In the prescribed circumstances a trustee may resign his office by giving notice to the court (s 298(7)). Before resigning, the trustee must call a meeting of creditors and the notice of the meeting must be accompanied by an account of his administration (r 6.126). A trustee may only resign because of ill-health, ceasing to be a qualified insolvency practitioner or because of some conflict of interest (r 6.126(3)). Where two or more trustees were originally appointed, any one can seek to resign if he and the others are of the opinion that it is no longer expedient to have that number of joint trustees (r 6.126(4)) . If there is no quorum at the meeting of the creditors, the trustee's resignation is deemed to have been accepted and his release given.

Notice of the meeting must also be given to the official receiver and the chairman of the meeting must inform the official receiver of the resolutions passed at the meeting, namely, to accept the resignation of the trustee, that a new trustee be appointed and that the resigning trustee be or be not given his release (r 6.127(3)). The trustee's resignation is effective from the date the notice of it is filed by the official receiver at court (r 6.127(7)). If the creditors refuse to accept the trustee's resignation, the court may, on the trustee's application, give him leave to resign (r 6.128).

During any vacancy in the post of trustee (such as that caused by the death of the trustee), the official receiver is the trustee by virtue of his office (s 300(2)). He must then decide whether to summon a meeting of creditors to replace the trustee having regard to the stage in the administration reached by the previous trustee (s 300(3)). If one-quarter in value of the creditors request him to convene a meeting to appoint a new liquidator, he must do so (s 300(3)).

9 Removal of trustee

A trustee (other than the official receiver) can be removed by resolution of the creditors at a meeting duly summoned of which proper notice specifying the purpose of the meeting has been given (s 298(1)). Someone other than the trustee or his nominee may be elected chairman but if the trustee is the chairman, he may not adjourn the meeting without the consent of at least half in value of those present (in person or by proxy) and entitled to vote (r 6.129(3)). If the trustee is removed, the creditors can also resolve not to give him his release.

If the trustee does not summon a meeting to consider the resolution to remove him, the court can order such a meeting to be held and give directions as to the way it is to be conducted (r 6.130). However, if an application is made to the court for an order requiring the trustee to summon a meeting to consider a resolution for his removal as trustee, the court may, if it thinks no 'sufficient cause' has been shown for the application, dismiss it but not until after an *ex parte* hearing of the application (r 6.132). If the court considers the application should proceed, a date will be fixed.

The court can remove a trustee on the application of an interested person and r 6.132(2) applies to such an application as well. Sufficient cause would have to be shown for such an application. In this context, 'sufficient cause' would appear to mean no more than in accordance with the Rules, ie, the applicant has the required minimum of support from creditors, 25 per cent of the total value of all creditor's claims. Thus a trustee is always at risk of being removed at a meeting of creditors if he is required to call such a meeting and more than 50 per cent of creditors want his removal. No reasons need be given nor is blameworthy conduct on the part of the trustee required.

The Secretary of State can remove a trustee but before doing so must notify the trustee and the official receiver of his decision and his reasons and specify a period within which the trustee can make representations against his removal (r 6.133).

In all the above cases, the trustee removed from office may or may not be given his release.

Chapter 12

The Creditors' Committee

1 The right to establish a committee

A general meeting of a bankrupt's creditors may establish a committee (known as 'the creditors' committee') to exercise the functions conferred on it by the Act (s 301(1)).

A creditors' committee cannot be established at any time when the official receiver is the trustee of the bankrupt's estate, except in connection with an appointment made by a general meeting of creditors of a person to be trustee instead of the official receiver (s 300(2)).

2 Membership and establishment of the committee

Any creditor (other than a secured creditor) is eligible to be a member of the committee provided that he has lodged a proof of debt and his proof has not been wholly disallowed for voting purposes nor for the purposes of distribution and dividend (r 6.150(2)).

A body corporate may be a member of the committee (r 6.150(3)) but it can only act through a representative duly authorised in accordance with r 6.156. This requires the representative to hold a letter of authority from the member, entitling him so to act and signed by or on behalf of the committee member (r 6.156(2)) .

The creditors' committee must consist of at least three and not more than five creditors.

The creditors' committee does not come into being until the trustee has issued a certificate of its due constitution (r 6.151) and his certificate must not be issued until he has received the written consent to act from at least three members of the committee (r 6.151(3) and (3A)). A proxy holder of a creditor can give consent for the creditor unless the proxy states otherwise (r 6.151(3)).

3 Functions and rights of the committee

The role of the creditors' committee is primarily supervisory although it is also a function of the committee to determine the trustee's remuneration (r 6.138(3)). It can determine that the trustee should be paid a percentage of the value of the assets realised and/or distributed, or by reference to the time spent by the trustee and his staff; and must have regard to the complexity or otherwise of the matter, any exceptional responsibility falling on the trustee, the trustee's effectiveness and the value and nature of the assets dealt with by the trustee. If the committee resolves that a trustee who has used improper solicitation to obtain proxies or to procure his appointment as trustee should none the less receive remuneration for acting as trustee, the court can override this resolution (r 6.148(2)). A distinction must therefore be drawn between proper solicitation and improper solicitation since it is only the latter which disentitles the trustee from his remuneration. Improper solicitation would include offering financial inducements to a creditor to secure his vote in favour of a particular person as trustee.

Schedule 5 to the Act sets out a number of powers which a trustee can only exercise with sanction. Where there is a committee, it is that committee from whom sanction must be sought in the first instance (see Chapter 23).

It is the duty of the committee to review the adequacy of the trustee's security (r 12.8).

It is the duty of the trustee to report to the committee all such matters as appear to him or as the committee have indicated to him to be of concern to them with respect to the administration of the estate (r 6.152(1)). The trustee need not comply with any request for information where it appears to him that the request is frivolous or unreasonable or the cost of complying would be excessive or there are not sufficient assets to meet the cost of complying (r 6.152(1)). The trustee must send a report to every member of the committee setting out the position generally regarding the progress of his administration. Such reports must be sent not less than once every six months or as and when directed by the committee but not more often than once every two months (r 6.163).

4 Meetings of the committee

The first meeting of the committee must take place within three months of its establishment and thereafter within 21 days of a request for a meeting by a member of the committee or on the date previously resolved by the committee for a further meeting (r 6.153(2)). Meetings are to be held otherwise when and where determined by the trustee (r 6.153(1)).

The trustee is to chair meetings of the committee but he may nominate someone else to stand in for him and that person must either be an employee of his, be experienced in insolvency matters, or be another qualified insolvency practitioner (r 6.154).

The quorum for meetings of the committee is two (r 6.155). A member of the committee can be represented by someone else provided that person is holding a letter of authority duly signed by the member and a proxy holder is treated as being authorised unless his proxy states otherwise (r 6.156).

5 Resolutions by post

The trustee can seek to obtain the agreement of members of the committee to a resolution by sending to every member a copy of the proposed resolution (r 6.162(1)). If there is more than one resolution for consideration, they must be set out in such a way that the committee member can signify his assent or dissent to each one separately. Any members of the committee can within seven business days of the resolution being sent out require the trustee to summon a meeting to consider the matters raised by the resolution (r 6.162(3)) . In the absence of such a request, the resolution is deemed to have been passed if and when the trustee is notified in writing by a majority of the members that they concur (r 6.162(4)).

6 Termination of membership and vacancies

A committee member may resign by notice in writing to the trustee (r 6.157).
A person's membership of the committee is automatically terminated:
(a) if he becomes bankrupt (his trustee replaces him) or he compounds with his creditors;
(b) if he is not present or represented at three consecutive meetings (unless at the third meeting it is resolved that this rule will not apply); and
(c) if he ceases to be or is found never to have been a creditor (r 6.158).

A committee member may be removed by resolution of the creditors at a meeting of which 14 days' notice has been given.

If a vacancy on the committee exists, then:
(a) it need not be filled if the trustee and a majority of the remaining members so agree;
(b) the trustee may appoint some other creditor to be a member if the majority of the remaining members so agree; or
(c) a meeting of creditors should be convened so that another creditor can be appointed and 14 days' notice of such meeting must be given (r 6.160) .

7 Dealings with committee members

No member of the committee, his representative or associate of his, nor any person who was a member of the committee in the last 12 months may enter into any transaction whereby he receives out of the estate any payment for services given or goods supplied in connection with the administration, or obtains any profit from the administration or acquires any asset forming part of the estate (r 6.155(2)) except with leave of the court, with prior sanction of the committee where full value for the transaction is given and in cases of urgency or by way of performance of a contract in existence at the date of the bankruptcy order, where leave of the court is sought subsequently without delay (r 6.153(3)) .

No member of the committee, his representative or associate must vote on any resolution to sanction any such transactions (r 6.165(4)).

8 Expenses of members

Members of the committee are entitled to receive any travelling or other out-of-pocket expenses directly incurred by them or their representatives in attending at committee meetings or otherwise on the committee's business (r 6.164). These expenses are payable out of the estate in the order of priority prescribed in r 6.224. Members of the committee cannot be paid a fee for performing their duties.

9 No committee

Where there is no committee and the trustee is other than the official receiver, the functions of such a committee are vested in the Secretary of State (in the person of the official receiver) except to the extent that the Rules otherwise provide (s 302(2)).

Chapter 13

Administration by the Trustee

1 General functions of the trustee

The function of the trustee (whether he is the official receiver or a qualified insolvency practitioner) is to get in, realise and distribute the bankrupt's estate. In carrying out this function and in the management of the bankrupt's estate, the trustee is entitled to use his own discretion (s 305(2)).

It is the duty of the trustee, if he is not the official receiver, to furnish the official receiver with such information, to produce such books, papers and records and to give such other assistance as the official receiver may reasonably require for the purpose of enabling him to carry out his functions in relation to the bankruptcy (s 305(3)).

2 Vesting of bankrupt's estate

Immediately on the trustee's appointment taking effect, the bankrupt's estate vests in the trustee. Until, therefore, there is a trustee appointed, the bankrupt's estate is in limbo and even though the official receiver automatically becomes receiver and manager of the estate on the making of a bankruptcy order, his powers as receiver and manager are limited. Vesting takes effect without any conveyance, assignment or transfer (s 306(2)). For the purposes of any law in force in any part of the British Commonwealth which requires registration, enrolment or recording of conveyances or assignments of property, the trustee's certificate of appointment is deemed to be a conveyance or assignment of property and may be registered, enrolled or recorded accordingly.

A bankrupt's estate comprises all property belonging to or vested in him at the commencement of the bankruptcy and any property which by virtue of the Act is to be treated as falling within the preceding definition (s 283(1)). Excluded from the definition of the bankrupt's estate are such tools, books, vehicles and other items of equipment as are to the bankrupt for use personally by him in employment, business or vocation and such clothing, bedding, furniture, household equipment and provisions as are necessary for satisfying the basic domestic needs of the bankrupt and his family (s 283(2)). Occupational pension schemes do not form part of the bankrupt's estate but see

5 below as to income payment orders. Personal pension plans do not form part of the bankrupt's estate even though expressed to be non-assignable even by operation of law. This will change with s 342A in 1997 when the Pensions Act 1995 comes into force.

Included in the definition of property is any entitlement incidental to property (*Re Rae* [1995] BCC 102). Monies ordered to be paid to a husband's solicitor as ancilliary relief for the purpose of protecting his wife's interests were not property comprised in the husband's estate when he was made bankrupt (*Re Mordant Mordant and Halls* [1995] BCC 209.

3 After-acquired property

Unlike under the old law, after-acquired property of the bankrupt does not now automatically vest in his trustee for the benefit of the estate. However, the trustee may claim for the bankrupt's estate any property which has been acquired by or has devolved upon the bankrupt since the commencement of the bankruptcy. To exercise this right, the trustee must give the bankrupt notice within 42 days of the trustee first obtaining knowledge that the property in question had been acquired by or had devolved upon the bankrupt (ss 307 and 308). The court can extend the period of time for serving this notice. The bankrupt is under an obligation to inform his trustee within 21 days of his acquiring any property, and once his trustee has served a notice on him, the bankrupt must not dispose of that property without leave of his trustee within the period of 42 days after giving the trustee notice, but if he does dispose of property in contravention of this rule or before receiving notice from his trustee, the bankrupt must inform his trustee of the name and address of the disponee (s 333 and r 6.200(1) and (2)). The trustee can then serve notice on the disponee claiming the property as part of the estate but such notice must be served within 28 days of the trustee becoming aware of the disponee's identity and an address at which he can be served (r 6.201).

Certain property is excluded from the trustee's rights to claim. The personal tools and domestic effects protected by s 283(2) from being comprised in the bankrupt's estate cannot be claimed by the trustee as after-acquired property. The income of the bankrupt cannot be claimed as after-acquired property but can be the subject of an income payments order under s 310 (see below).

No particular form of notice is required to be given by the trustee except that it must be in writing and takes effect only when served on the bankrupt. The effect of giving notice is to vest the property in the trustee and the trustee's title relates back to the time when the bankrupt himself acquired title to that property. Protection is, however, given to those who have dealt with the bankrupt either before or after his trustee has given notice to him of a claim to after-acquired property. Under s 307(4), where a person acquires property from the bankrupt in good faith, for value and without notice of the bankruptcy or where a banker enters into a transaction in good faith and without notice of the bankruptcy, the trustee would have no remedy against that person or anyone whose title derives from that person or banker.

A bankrupt can continue in business after his bankruptcy. He is of course under an obligation to inform anyone from whom he seeks credit of more than £250 (fixed by the Insolvency Proceedings (Monetary Limits) Order 1986 (SI No 1996)) that he is an undischarged bankrupt but any business assets built up by the bankrupt are not necessarily liable to be taken by his trustee as after-acquired assets. The bankrupt is entitled under s 283(2) to retain such tools, books, vehicles and other items of equipment as are necessary for his use personally by him in his employment, business or vocation. Under r 6.200(4), the obligation of the bankrupt to inform his trustee of any property acquired by him does not apply to property acquired in the ordinary course of a business carried on by the bankrupt but by r 6.200(5) the bankrupt is obliged to furnish his trustee, not less than once every six months, with information relating to any business carried on by him including details of goods bought and sold and the profit or loss made.

4 Vesting of items of excess value

Where property is excluded from the bankrupt's estate because it comprises tools of trade or household effects under s 283(2) and the trustee is of the opinion that the realisable value of any of these items exceeds the value of a reasonable replacement, then he can, by notice in writing to the bankrupt, claim that property for the estate (s 308(1)). A replacement is regarded as reasonable if it is reasonably adequate for meeting the needs that the property it replaces met (s 308(4)).

The trustee can apply funds in the estate for the purchase of the replacement in priority to his obligation to distribute such funds to the bankrupt's creditors (s 308(3)). The trustee is under no obligation to apply funds to the purchase of a replacement of property vested in him unless and until he has sufficient funds in the estate for that purpose (r 6.187(2)). The trustee may accept an offer from a third party so as to allow the bankrupt to remain in possession of the property which would otherwise vest in his trustee under s 308 provided that he is satisfied that the offer is a reasonable one and that the estate will benefit to the extent of the value of the property in question less the cost of a reasonable replacement (r 6.188).

The property to which a notice relates vests in the trustee upon service of the notice claiming it and the trustee's title to that property relates back to the commencement of the bankruptcy except against a purchaser in good faith, for value and without notice of the bankruptcy (s 308(2)).

A notice under s 308 cannot be served more than 42 days after the property in question first came to the knowledge of the trustee unless the court gives leave (s 309).

5 Income payments orders

The court can, on the application of the trustee, make an order, called an income payments order, claiming for the estate so much of the bankrupt's income and for such period as the court thinks fit (s 310(1)). The court must not, however, require the bankrupt to make such payments from his income as would reduce his remaining income below what appears to the court necessary for meeting the reasonable domestic needs of himself and his family (s 310(2)). The court order can be directed to the bankrupt requiring him to make payments to his trustee or can be directed to the person making payments to the bankrupt requiring him to make payments instead to the trustee, that is, in effect an attachment of earnings order, and if there was in force an attachment of earnings order against the bankrupt's income, the court can vary or discharge that order (s 310(3) and (4)). The court can order an employer, under s 366, to attend court and provide information as to the bankrupt's earnings so as to enable an income payments order to be made.

Income, for the purposes of an income payments order, is widely interpreted and is not confined to wages or salary. It includes every payment in the nature of income to which the bankrupt becomes entitled including any payment in respect of the carrying on of any business (s 310(7)). Therefore, income under a trust and pension income under an occupational scheme would be caught under s 310 but would not be subject to the automatic vesting of assets rules. Personal pension plans are dealt with in **2** above.

Where the trustee wishes to apply for an income payments order, the court must fix a time and date for the hearing and the bankrupt must be given at least 28 days' notice of the hearing by the trustee together with a copy of the application and a short statement of the grounds on which it is made (r 6.189(2)). The notice of the application must inform the bankrupt that unless he consents, at least seven days before the hearing in writing to the court and the trustee, to an order being made in the terms of the application, he must attend court on the date fixed and if he attends he will be given an opportunity to show cause why the order should not be made in the form applied for by the trustee. There is no set form for the trustee's statement but it must identify the income which is sought to be attached, indicate what the bankrupt's reasonable domestic needs are and what they are likely to be during the currency of the order and identify any known attachment of earnings orders which may need to be varied or discharged.

An income payments order cannot be made after the bankrupt has obtained his discharge and, even if obtained before discharge, cannot be effective after discharge unless its making was a condition of discharge being granted by order of the court or, if discharge was obtained by effluxion of time, the court making the order directed it was to continue after discharge but in such cases the maximum duration of the order is three years (s 310(6)).

When an income payments order is made, a sealed copy of the order must be sent by the court to the bankrupt or to the person who is required to make payments to the trustee (r 6.190). If the bankrupt does not comply with the order made against him, the trustee can apply to the court *ex parte* for the order to be varied so as to be directed to the payer of the relevant income (r 6.191).

The payer of income who is required to make payments under an income payments order direct to the trustee can deduct the appropriate fee towards the clerical and administrative costs of compliance in the same way as an employer whose employee is subject to an attachment of earnings order (r 6.192).

Under r 6.193 either the bankrupt or his trustee can apply to the court for an income payments order to be varied or discharged on the grounds of changed circumstances. If the bankrupt makes the application, it must be accompanied by a short statement of the grounds upon which it is made. If the court thinks the application is without merit, it can dismiss the application without a full hearing but only after the bankrupt has been given the opportunity of attending an *ex parte* hearing before the court. If the application is allowed to proceed, at least 28 days' notice must be given to the trustee and the trustee may file a report in answer to the application at least seven days before the hearing whether he intends to appear at the hearing. A sealed copy of the order made must be served by the court on the trustee, the bankrupt and the payer (if other than the bankrupt).

6 Acquisition of control

The trustee is empowered by s 311 to take possession of all books, papers and other records which relate to the bankrupt's estate or affairs and which belong to him, or are in his possession or under his control. The trustee for these purposes is in the same position as a receiver of property appointed by the High Court and the court can enforce his powers accordingly.

The trustee can exercise the right to transfer stocks, shares or any property in the books of a company, office or person in the same way as the bankrupt might have (s 311(3)). Any chose in action is deemed to have been assigned to the trustee and notice of assignment is not necessary except in so far as it is necessary for protecting the priority of the trustee (s 311(4)).

Where goods comprised in the estate are held by any person by way of pledge, pawn or other security and no notice has been served by the official receiver under s 285 (restriction on realising security), the trustee may serve such a notice and may exercise the bankrupt's right of redemption (s 311(5)).

The bankrupt is under an obligation to deliver up to his trustee all his property, books, papers or other records of which he has possession or control and of which the trustee is required to take possession. If he fails to comply with this obligation without reasonable excuse, he is guilty of contempt of court (s 312).

7 Charge on bankrupt's home

Where a bankrupt's estate includes an interest in a dwelling-house occupied by the bankrupt or his spouse or former spouse and the trustee is unable, for any reason, to realise that property, he may apply to the court for an order imposing a charge on the property for the benefit of the estate (s 313(1)). The amount of the charge to be imposed is, in effect, the total of the liabilities of the bankrupt together with interest and the costs of the bankruptcy less the value of any other assets which the trustee has realised. Any surplus equity would, as a result of an order imposing a charge being made, vest in the bankrupt and not in his trustee (s 313(3)).

This procedure will be used where the trustee is unable to realise the bankrupt's interest in the property because of ss 336 and 337 (see Chapter 18) or where he does not yet have sufficient funds to litigate with the occupier.

The provisions of certain subsections of s 3 of the Charging Orders Act 1979 are incorporated into bankruptcy law by s 313(4). The court is given flexible discretionary powers both at the time when the charge is made and subsequently. The charge can be made subject to a condition of notification of those interested, presumably in these cases the spouse or former spouse, and as to the time when the charge can be enforced. The charge can be registered under the Land Charges Act 1972 and the Land Registration Act 1925 as appropriate. Under s 3(5) of the Charging Orders Act 1979, any person interested in the property can apply for the order to be discharged or varied.

8 Powers of the trustee

The trustee may with the permission of the creditors' committee or the court exercise the following powers (s 314 and Sched 5, Part I):
- (1) Carry on the business of the bankrupt so far as is necessary for winding it up beneficially.
- (2) Bring, institute or defend any legal actions relating to the bankrupt's property.
- (3) Accept deferred payment on the sale of any of the bankrupt's property.
- (4) Mortgage the bankrupt's property for the purpose of raising money for the payment of his debts.
- (5) Make payments to secure any property subject to a right, power or option.
- (6) Compromise or refer to arbitration any claim of the bankrupt against a third party.
- (7) Compromise any dispute with the bankrupt's creditors.

The trustee may without the permission of the creditors' committee or the court exercise the following powers (s 314 and Sched 5, Part II):
- (a) sell the bankrupt's property;
- (b) give receipts in full and final satisfaction for money received;
- (c) prove for such debts as are due to the bankrupt;
- (d) exercise the rights and duties given to a trustee under the Act;
- (e) deal with any property in which the bankrupt was entitled to a beneficial interest in the same manner as the bankrupt might have dealt with it.

With the permission of the creditors' committee or the court, the trustee can appoint the bankrupt to carry on his business for the benefit of his creditors or assist in administering the estate (s 314(2)).

If the trustee does anything for which permission is required without getting that permission, he may ask the court or the creditors' committee to ratify what he has done so as to enable him to meet his expenses out of the estate but the committee must not ratify his actions unless it is satisfied that he acted in a case of urgency and has sought ratification without undue delay (s 314(4)).

If the trustee disposes of property of the bankrupt to an associate of the bankrupt, he does not require sanction, but must give notice to the committee (if there is one); likewise, with regard to the employment by the trustee of a solicitor (s 314(6)).

The trustee may summon a general meeting of creditors at any time that he thinks fit and must if requested to do so by a creditor acting with the concurrence of one-tenth in value of all the creditors (s 314(7)).

9 Priority of payment of expenses

If there are insufficient assets in the bankruptcy estate, the available assets are used to meet expenses in the following order of priority (r 6.224 as amended as from 1 April 1995):
- (a) expenses incurred by the official receiver in realising any of the assets and running the business and his remuneration for the work done by him;
- (b) any deposits paid by the petitioner (either when presenting the petition or as required by the official receiver to perform certain duties);
- (c) the remuneration and expenses of any interim receiver;
- (d) the petitioning creditor's costs;
- (e) the remuneration and expenses of any special manager appointed;
- (f) the remuneration and expenses of the trustee up to the scale laid down by the official receiver;
- (g) any capital gains tax payable on the disposal of any of the debtor's assets after the bankruptcy order;
- (h) the balance of the trustee's remuneration.

In the case of those bankruptcies which commenced before 1 April 1995, the remuneration of the official receiver ranks after any deposit paid by the petitioner.

Chapter 14

Disclaimer

1 General power

The trustee may, under s 315, disclaim property of the bankrupt which is onerous. Onerous property is defined by s 315(2) as any unprofitable contract and any other property which is unsaleable or not readily saleable, or is such that it may give rise to a liability to pay money or perform any other act on the part of the trustee. The unsaleability or lack of value need not be connected with the fact that property gives rise to a liability to pay money or perform any other onerous covenant. The trustee may disclaim notwithstanding that he had endeavoured to sell or had taken possession of the property or had exercised any act of ownership in relation to it.

There is no right to disclaim a contract affecting land belonging to the estate simply because that contract is not beneficial to the estate without disclaiming the property itself.

2 Exercise of power

The decision whether or not to disclaim is entirely within the discretion of the trustee and the court will not interfere with his decision unless it can be shown that he has acted *male fides* or perversely in relation to the disclaimer; it matters not that one creditor, the landlord, suffers from the trustee's decision (*Re Hans Place* [1992] 4 EG 143).

In order to disclaim any property, the trustee must give a notice in the prescribed form (Form 6.61 in Sched 4 to the Rules; see Appendix 3, form 34). The notice and a copy must be filed at court and the copy notice, once sealed and endorsed with the date of filing, is returned to the trustee. The notice must contain sufficient particulars of the property so as to enable it to be identified and the notice must be signed by the trustee. If the original notice was handed in, the court file must be endorsed with a note to this effect and the fact that the copy notice was handed back. If the notice was lodged by post, then the copy will be sent back by post and the court file endorsed accordingly (r 6.178).

The effective date of disclaimer is the date endorsed on the copy notice by the court.

Notice of disclaimer cannot be given in respect of any property that has been claimed for the bankrupt's estate under s 307 (after-acquired property) or s 308 (personal property of the bankrupt exceeding reasonable replacement value) except with leave of the court.

If the trustee wishes to make application for leave to disclaim, r 6.182 requires him to file a report with the application giving particulars of the property proposed to be disclaimed, setting out the reasons why, the property having been claimed for the estate, disclaimer is now desired and specifying who has been informed of his intentions. Provision is made in the rule for leave to be granted *ex p* but there is also reference to all persons who might be entitled to apply for a vesting order (see below) being given notice of the application and presumably being entitled to attend an *inter partes* hearing.

If it appears to the trustee that there is some person who may claim to have an interest in property which the trustee wishes to disclaim, he may give notice to that person calling upon him to declare within 14 days whether he claims any such interest and if so, the nature and extent of it. Failing compliance with the notice, the trustee is entitled to assume that the person concerned has no such interest in the property as would prevent its disclaimer (r 6.184).

3 Time limits

There is no time limit within which the trustee must give notice to the court of his intention to disclaim, unless an application has been made in writing by a person interested in the property requiring him to make a decision. Under s 316, notice of disclaimer cannot be given if a person interested in the property has applied in writing to the trustee or one of his predecessors to decide whether he will disclaim or not and 28 days have elapsed since the application was received by the trustee without a notice of disclaimer being given.

A subsequent trustee cannot give a notice of disclaimer where his predecessor received an application from a person interested and did not make up his mind whether to disclaim within the 28-day period. That trustee is therefore tied with the neglect or omission of his predecessor.

There is no provision for the 28-day period to be extended but similarly there is no provision in this section saying that the time limit cannot be extended as was the case under the old law. It would, therefore, seem to be the case that the court could extend the period for the trustee to disclaim notwithstanding the receipt of an application by him to make up his mind and the passage of more than 28 days, since under s 376 the court is given a general power to extend time in relation to any time limits provided for in the Act or the Rules. The official receiver when acting as trustee is bound by exactly the same provisions as any other trustee, again contrary to the provisions of the old law.

4 Communication of disclaimer

Within seven days of the trustee receiving a copy of the notice of disclaimer sealed and endorsed from the court the trustee must send a copy or give a copy to the following persons:
- (a) in the case of a leasehold property, any underlessee or mortgagee;
- (b) in the case of a dwelling-house, every person in occupation or who claims the right to occupy;
- (c) in the case of an unprofitable contract, all parties to the contract or who have interests under it;
- (d) in every case, any person claiming an interest in the disclaimed property or who is under any liability in respect of the property, not being a liability discharged by the disclaimer (r 6.179).

If it subsequently comes to the trustee's notice that someone else is interested in the property disclaimed then he must give notice of disclaimer to that person unless he is satisfied that that person is already aware of the disclaimer or the court orders otherwise (r 6.179(6)).

The trustee must notify the court from time to time of the names and addresses of the persons to whom he has given notice of disclaimer pursuant to r 6.179 (r 6.180).

Any disclaimer of property is presumed valid and effective unless it is proved that the trustee has been in breach of his duty as to the giving of notice of disclaimer or otherwise under ss 315 to 319 or under the Rules (r 6.185).

5 Disclaimer of leaseholds

Disclaimer of any leasehold property does not take effect unless a copy of the disclaimer has been served (so far as the trustee is aware of their addresses) on every underlessee or mortgagee of the lease and either no application under s 320 for a vesting order has been made (see below) within 14 days of service of the disclaimer notice or, where such an application has been made, the court none the less directs that disclaimer is to take effect (s 317). A copy of the notice of disclaimer must be served on the landlord pursuant to r 6.179 but it takes effect from the date endorsed on it by the court, not the date it is served on the landlord.

Where the court directs that disclaimer is to take effect, irrespective of whether the court also makes a vesting order under s 320, the court may make such order with respect to fixtures and tenant's improvements arising out of the lease as it thinks fit (s 317(2)). The court will provide either for these items to be vested in the landlord or the holder of the new lease pursuant to a vesting order or that they are to be retained by the trustee for the benefit of the estate.

6 Disclaimer of dwelling-house

Disclaimer of a dwelling-house is not to take effect unless a copy of the notice of disclaimer has been served (so far as the trustee is aware of their addresses) on every person in occupation of, or claiming a right to occupy the dwelling-house and either no application for a vesting order has been made within 14 days of service of the notice or such application has been made but none the less the court has directed that the disclaimer is to take effect (s 318). The bankrupt and his family are given special rights to occupy the family home under ss 336 and 337 and these are dealt with in Chapter 18.

7 Disclaimer of land subject to rentcharge

Where land subject to a rentcharge is disclaimed and that land is vested in the Crown or any other person by operation of law, then no liability for pre-disclaimer sums due under the rentcharge falls on the Crown or that other person (s 319).

8 Vesting order

There are three categories of person who can apply for an order vesting the property which has been disclaimed by the trustee in them. They are:
  (a) any person claiming an interest in the disclaimed property;
  (b) any person who is under any liability in respect of the property, not being a liability discharged by the disclaimer; or
  (c) where the disclaimed property is a dwelling-house, any person who at the time the bankruptcy petition was presented was in occupation of or entitled to occupy the dwelling-house (s 320(2)).

On an application for a vesting order, the court can vest the disclaimed property in one of the categories of persons mentioned, subject to any liability not otherwise discharged by disclaimer or, where the property is a dwelling-house, in the person or persons in occupation etc as referred to above (s 320(3)).

The court must not make a vesting order except where it appears to the court that it would be just to do so for the purpose of compensating the person subject to the liability in respect of the disclaimer (s 320(4)).

The court must not make a vesting order in respect of leasehold property except on terms that the person obtaining the property is subject to the same liabilities and obligations as the bankrupt was subject to on the day the bankruptcy petition was presented or, if the court thinks fit, subject to the same liabilities as an assignee of the lease to whom the lease was assigned on that day (s 321(1)). Where no one is willing to accept a vesting of leasehold property on these terms, the court may order that the property be vested in someone who is already liable to perform the lessee's covenants in the lease, freed from all encumbrances created by the bankrupt (s 321(3)).

It is not necessary for there to be any conveyance, assignment or transfer to complete the vesting of the property (s 329(6)).

An application for a vesting order must be made within three months of the applicant becoming aware of the disclaimer or of his receiving a copy of the trustee's notice of disclaimer, whichever is the earlier (r 6.186), subject to the power of the court to extend the time limit under s 376. The application must be supported by an affidavit stating whether the application is made by a person claiming an interest in the property, a person subject to a liability in respect of the disclaimed property or a person in occupation of a dwelling-house, specifying the date on which he became aware that the notice of disclaimer had been received and specifying the grounds of the application and the order desired (r 6.186(3)) . The court must fix a date for the application to be heard and not less than seven days' notice must be given to the trustee. On the hearing, the court can give directions as to other persons who should be given notice of the application.

9 Effect of disclaimer

A disclaimer operates, as from the date of disclaimer, so as to determine the rights, interests and liabilities of the bankrupt and his estate in respect of the disclaimed property and discharges the trustee from all personal liability in respect of the disclaimed property as from the commencement of his trusteeship (s 315(3)).

Disclaimer does not affect the rights and liabilities of third parties, except so far as is necessary for the purpose of releasing the bankrupt's estate and the trustee from any liability. Thus, the guarantor of a lease in the name of the bankrupt would not be released from liability from the date of disclaimer (*Hindcastle v Barbara Attenborough Associates* [1996] 1 All ER 737, overruling *Stacey v Hill* [1901] 1 KB 660).

Any person sustaining loss or damage as a result of disclaimer is deemed to be a creditor of the bankrupt to the extent of the loss or damage suffered and can prove for the loss or damage sustained (s 315(5)).

Chapter 15

Debts and Dividends

1 Classes of debts

There are four classes of debts, secured, preferential, unsecured and deferred.

Secured debts have no special priority afforded to them by the Act or the Rules but the holders of them have those rights given to them by virtue of their security. As to how a secured creditor values his security for voting purposes and for the purposes of proving for any shortfall, see below.

Preferential debts are defined in s 386 and Sched 6 to the Act. As their name implies, they are given priority over the general body of debts owed by the bankrupt to his creditors. They consist primarily of various taxes owed to the government and are as follows:

(1) Arrears of PAYE for the 12 months prior to the making of the bankruptcy order or the appointment of an interim receiver.

(2) Arrears of VAT for the six-month period prior to the making of the bankruptcy order or the appointment of an interim receiver.

(3) Arrears of social security contributions (of employees) for the 12 months prior to the making of the bankruptcy order or the appointment of an interim receiver.

(4) Arrears of social security contributions of the bankrupt himself as a self-employed person limited to a sum not exceeding one year's contributions and which are assessed for up to 5 April next before the date of the making of the bankruptcy order or the appointment of an interim receiver.

(5) Arrears of contributions to occupational pensions schemes (under Sched 3 to the Social Security Pensions Act 1975) without limit as to time.

(6) Amounts due to employees for wages for the four months prior to the making of the bankruptcy order or the appointment of an interim receiver but not exceeding for each employee the prescribed sum, currently £800, together with all arrears of holiday pay. If money has been advanced by a third party to pay wages and holiday pay which would, if not paid, have been preferential debts, then the person who advanced the money becomes a preferential creditor for the amount

advanced. The claims of such persons to be treated as preferential creditors are construed strictly (see *Re Baker, ex p Eastbourne Waterworks & Co* [1954] 1 WLR 1144). If someone has advanced money to pay any other debt which, if unpaid, would have been preferential (eg, VAT), the lender does not obtain the preferential status enjoyed by the original creditor.

Unsecured debts are the ordinary debts of the bankrupt which are neither secured nor preferential.

Deferred debts are those owed by the bankrupt to his or her spouse (spouse being defined at the date of the bankruptcy order not the giving of credit). These debts rank in priority after the preferential and ordinary unsecured debts (and any interest thereon) and are payable with interest thereon in the same way as other debts (s 329).

As to the provisions for the payment of interest on debts, see below.

2 Mode and form of proof

Every person claiming to be a creditor of the bankrupt must submit his claim in writing to the official receiver acting as receiver and manager, or to the trustee (r 6.96). This is called proving a debt and the document by which the creditor seeks to establish his claim is his proof (r 6.96(2)). A proof must be in the form known as 'proof of debt' (whether the form prescribed by the Rules and set out in Sched 4 to the Rules as Form 6.37 or a substantially similar form; see Appendix 3, form 28) and must be signed by the creditor or someone authorised on his behalf (r 6.96(3)). Government departments do not have to use this form provided they give all the information required.

Proof of debt forms must be sent out by the official receiver or trustee to every creditor who is known to him or identified in the statement of affairs (r 6.97). If the official receiver decides not to summon a meeting of creditors, he must none the less send out proofs of debt with the notice of his decision. If he decides to call a meeting, then the proofs of debt must be sent with the notice convening the meeting. If the trustee is appointed by the court, he must send out proofs of debt with notice of his appointment (r 6.97(2)).

The trustee may require a proof of debt to be verified by affidavit in the form set out in Sched 4 to the Rules or a substantially similar form (Form 6.39; see Appendix 3, form 29). Such an affidavit can be sworn by the creditor before his own solicitor (r 7.57).

3 Provable debts

All claims by creditors are provable as debts against the bankrupt whether they are present or future, certain or contingent, ascertained or sounding only in damages (r 12.3). Formerly unliquidated damages in tort were not provable debts but they are now covered by the wide nature of r 12.3. However, fines or obligations under family or domestic court proceedings are not provable (r 12.3(7)). The bankrupt is under an obligation to continue these payments notwithstanding his bankruptcy (*Re Linton* (1885) 15 QBD 239). Neither arrears which became due prior to the bankruptcy order (*Kerr v Kerr* [1897] 2 QB 439) nor arrears accruing after the making of the bankruptcy order (*Re Hawkins, ex p Hawkins* [1894] 1 QB 25) are provable debts. In the case of a separation deed or agreement between a husband and wife, the sums due from the husband to the wife are provable debts—they are a contractual liability. The trustee must assess the value of the contractual liability and the discharge of the husband releases him from the liability to make further payments under the deed or agreement (*Victor v Victor* [1912] 1 KB 247). The wife would, however, be able to apply to the family court for financial provision if the husband used his bankruptcy as a means of circumventing his obligation to maintain his wife or children. A lump sum order in divorce proceedings is a provable debt (*Curtis v Curtis* [1969] 1 WLR 422).

4 Contents of proof

The following must be stated in a proof of debt (r 6.98(1)):
  (a) the creditor's name and address;
  (b) the total amount of the debt as at the date of the bankruptcy order;
  (c) whether interest is included;
  (d) whether VAT is included;
  (e) whether any part of the debt is a preferential debt as defined in s 386 and Sched 6 to the Act;
  (f) particulars of how and when the debt was incurred;
  (g) particulars of any security held and if so, its value;
  (h) the name, address and authority of person signing if not the creditor himself;
  (i) any documents which can substantiate the claim though these need not be sent unless the trustee requests them (r 6.98(3)); and
  (j) if the debt was incurred in a foreign currency, the sterling equivalent at the date of the bankruptcy order must be calculated and stated (r 6.111) and the rate of exchange must be the official rate, ie, that fixed by the Bank of England or by the court.

5 Debt payable at a future date and of a periodic nature

If a creditor is owed a debt not payable at the date of the bankruptcy order, he may none the less prove for the same (r 6.114) but subject to an adjustment of his dividend where payment of dividend is made before the time when the debt would have become payable. See r 11.13 for the method of calculation of the adjustment.

In the case of rent and other payments of a periodic nature, the creditor may prove for any amounts due and unpaid up to the date of the bankruptcy order (r 6.112(1)). Where at that date any payment was accruing due, that is, where payment in arrears was stipulated, the creditor may prove for the amount which would have fallen due if the debt had accrued from day to day (r 6.112(2)).

6 Bills of exchange and promissory notes

Unless the trustee allows otherwise, a proof in respect of money owed on a bill of exchange, promissory note or other negotiable instrument or security upon which the debtor is liable cannot be admitted for any purpose, unless the document or a certified copy is produced (r 6.108).

7 Time for proofs

There is no time limit for the submission of proofs but a creditor who has not proved his debt cannot benefit from any distribution of the bankrupt's assets. Also until such time as a creditor has lodged a proof of debt, he cannot vote at meetings of creditors.

Before declaring a dividend, the trustee must give notice of his intention to do so to all creditors of whom he is aware or who are identified in the statement of affairs who have not proved their debts (r 11.2(1)). The notice must specify the last date for proving which must be not less than 21 days after the date of the notice (r 11.2(2)). The notice must also state the trustee's intention to declare a dividend (specified as interim or final) within the period of four months from the last date for proving (r 11.2(3)) and unless he has already invited creditors by advertisement to prove their debts, he must advertise his intention to declare a dividend (r 11.2(1A)).

8 Admission and rejection of proofs

The trustee must examine every proof of debt and admit it wholly or in part for dividend. If he rejects a proof in whole or in part, he must give his reasons in writing and inform the creditor concerned (r 6.104). The trustee must within seven days of the last date for proving (see **7** above) deal with every creditor's proof by admitting it or rejecting it in whole or in part or by making such provision as he thinks fit in respect of it (r 11.3(1)) . He is not obliged to deal with proofs lodged after the last date for proving but may do so if he thinks fit (r 11.3(2)).

Acceptance of a proof of debt for voting purposes at the first meeting is not the same as acceptance by the trustee of a proof for dividend and the trustee is not bound by the earlier decision of the official receiver.

If a creditor is dissatisfied with the decision of the trustee, the court may on the application of the creditor reverse or vary the trustee's decision (r 6.105). However, subject to the power of the court to extend the time under s 376, no application to reverse or vary the decision of the trustee rejecting a proof will be entertained unless notice of the application is given before the expiration of 21 days from the date of service of the notice of rejection (r 6.105) . If the creditor makes application for time to be extended, the trustee would be entitled to be heard. For form of notice of rejection, see Appendix 3, form 30. For forms of summons or notice of motion, affidavit in support and order, see Appendix 3, forms 31 to 33. It is not open to the bankrupt to apply to have a pre-bankruptcy judgment against him set aside—only the trustee can do this (*Heath v Tang* (1993) *The Times*, 11 August).

9 Expunging proofs

The court may expunge or vary a proof which has been admitted either upon the application of the trustee or of a creditor if the trustee declines to interfere (r 6.107).

10 Interest

Up to the date of the bankruptcy order

Where a debt proved in a bankruptcy bears interest (be it contractual or statutory), interest up to the date of the bankruptcy order can also be proved for (r 6.113)) . Even if the proved debt did not include the right to interest, interest can be claimed up to the date of the bankruptcy order:
  (a) by virtue of a written instrument and in respect of a debt payable at a certain time, then from that time (r 6.113(2)) at judgment rate (r 6.113(4));
  (b) otherwise, after demand for repayment has been made stating that interest will thereafter be charged (r 6.113(3)) at the rate specified in the notice provided that it does not exceed judgment rate (r 6.113(4)) .

Interest due on debts which are preferential under s 386 and Sched 6 to the Act would not appear also to be preferential.

After the date of the bankruptcy order

If there is a surplus remaining after paying all proved debts (including interest on them up to the date of the bankruptcy order), it must be applied to the payment of interest on all proved debts (including any interest thereon up to the date of the bankruptcy order (s 328(4))). All debts for the purpose of entitlement to interest under this section rank equally, ie, preferential debts do not have preferential rights to interest. The rate of interest allowable is the greater of contractual and judgment rate of interest.

As from 1 April 1993 the judgment rate of interest was reduced from 15 per cent to 8 per cent. However, this reduced rate of interest only applies to those bankruptcies commenced on or after that date. For all purposes, the rate of interest applicable to pre 1 April 1993 bankruptcies remains at 15 per cent.

11 VAT

A creditor whose claim includes an element of VAT can either prove for the whole amount of the claim (and pay to HM Customs and Excise the VAT element irrespective of whether or not he receives any dividend) or prove for the amount of his claim net of VAT and reclaim the VAT (Finance Act 1983, s 22(5)). In connection with the supply of goods or services on or after 1 April 1989, VAT Bad Debt Relief can be claimed by the creditor simply by entering the VAT as an input in his return for the period one year after the debt was incurred provided that the creditor has written the debt off in his books (though this does not prevent the creditor from proving for his debt in a bankruptcy). It is therefore no longer necessary for the creditor to seek and for the trustee to supply a VAT Bad Debt Relief certificate. If the trustee is able to pay 100p in the pound to creditors and still has funds available, creditors are not under any duty then to seek to claim, in addition, the VAT so as to pay it over to HM Customs and Excise (*Re T H Knitwear (Wholesale) Ltd* [1988] 4 BCC 102).

12 Secured creditors

A secured creditor may, with the agreement of the trustee or leave of the court, at any time alter the value which he has, in his proof of debt, placed upon his security but if he is the petitioner for the bankruptcy order or has voted in respect of his unsecured balance, he may revalue his security only with the leave of the court (r 6.115) .

If a secured creditor omits to disclose his security in his proof of debt, he must surrender it for the general benefit of creditors unless the court relieves him on the ground that omission was inadvertent or the result of honest mistake (r 6.116).

The trustee may at any time give notice to a secured creditor that he proposes at the end of 28 days to redeem the security at the value placed upon it by the creditor in his proof. The creditor then has 21 days in which, if he so wishes, to revalue his security (subject to r 6.115). The secured creditor has the right to call upon the trustee to elect whether or not to exercise his power to redeem and the trustee then has six months in which to exercise the power or decide not to exercise it (r 6.117(4)).

If the trustee is dissatisfied with the value placed on the security, he can call upon the creditor to offer the security for sale (r 6.118). When the security is ultimately realised, the net proceeds must be substituted for any value previously put upon it (r 6.119).

13 Dividends

The trustee must give notice of a dividend to all creditors who have proved their debts (r 11.6(1)). The notice, which can be sent out with the dividend itself, must include the following particulars:
   (a) amounts realised from the sale of assets;
   (b) payments made by the trustee in the administration of the estate;
   (c) provision for unsettled claims and funds retained for particular purposes;
   (d) the total amount to be distributed and the rate of dividend; and
   (e) whether, and if so when, any further dividend is expected to be declared (r 11.6(2)).

Dividends may be sent by post, held for collection or paid in some other way (r 11.6(4)). A creditor can assign his right to a dividend and give notice to the trustee of this whereupon the trustee must pay the dividend to the assignee (r 11.11). For a precedent of such an authority, see Appendix 3, form 35.

The trustee must not, except with the leave of the court, proceed to declare a dividend whilst there is pending any application to the court, to reverse or vary a decision of his on a proof or to expunge a proof or to reduce the amount claimed (r 11.5(2)). If the court gives leave, the trustee must make provision in respect of the proof in question as the court directs.

If the trustee is unable to declare any, or any further dividend, he must give notice to this effect to creditors and the notice must also contain a statement to the effect that no funds have been realised or that all funds realised have been distributed or used to meet the expenses of the administration (r 11.7).

A creditor who failed to lodge his proof before an interim dividend was declared is not entitled to disturb that interim distribution but is entitled to receive a payment in priority to other creditors from further funds as available; similarly a creditor whose proof is increased after an interim dividend has been declared.

A partially secured creditor is entitled to receive a dividend on the unsecured part of his claim having valued his security. If revaluation of his security is necessary, resulting in a greater shortfall, he is to be treated like the creditors referred to in the previous paragraph.

The trustee cannot be sued for a dividend but if he refuses to pay a dividend, the court may order him to pay it together with, out of his own funds, interest at judgment rate and costs (s 325(2)).

The trustee when declaring a dividend must give notice stating how the dividend is proposed to be distributed and containing the prescribed particulars of the bankrupt's estate (s 324(3)).

On a final distribution, the trustee can ignore any creditors who have not lodged proofs of debt, after receiving notice of the trustee's intention to declare a final dividend on a specified date (s 330).

Chapter 16

Mutual Credit and Set-off

1 The general law

Parties who have claims which can be ascertained with certainty at the time of leading can set off their claims one against the other and claim or tender the difference (see *Hanak v Green* [1958] 2 QB 9 and *British Anzani (Felixstowe) Ltd v International Marine Management (UK) Ltd* [1980] QB 637).

2 Application of bankruptcy law

Under s 323, an account must be taken of what sum is due from each party to the other where there have been mutual credits, mutual debts or other mutual dealings between the bankrupt and any creditor of the bankrupt proving or claiming to prove for a bankruptcy debt. The sum due from one party must be set off against the sum due from the other and only the balance of the account is provable as a bankruptcy debt or is to be paid to the trustee as part of the bankrupt's estate. However, sums due from the bankrupt to another party must not be included in the account if that other party had notice at the time they became due that a bankruptcy petition relating to the bankrupt was pending. It will be seen that s 323 extends the right of set-off to situations where there have been mutual dealings between the bankrupt and another. The object of the rule is not simply to avoid cross-claims (as under the general law) but 'to do substantial justice between the parties where a debt is really due from the bankrupt to a debtor to his estate' (*per* Parke B in *Forster v Wilson* (1843) 12 M & W 191).

Section 323 is mandatory and will include liabilities which may be due but not yet payable, or may be unascertained or subject to a contingency. Bankruptcy law treats the debts of the bankrupt as having been ascertained and his assets simultaneously distributed amongst his creditors at the date of his bankruptcy. The consequence of this is that it is not possible to assign a claim separate from a cross-claim because it has no separate existence. A trustee can assign a right of the bankrupt subject to a cross-claim like any other right of action (*Stein v Blake* [1995] BCC 543).

3 Definitions

'Mutual debts' occur where each party owes the other a liquidated sum, whether due now or in the future. 'Mutual credits' occur where each party allows the other to pay what is owing at some future time or on the happening of a certain event. 'Mutual dealings' occur where there are transactions giving rise to rights or liabilities between them.

4 Where set-off allowed

For set-off to be allowed in bankruptcy there must be obligations on both sides giving rise to pecuniary liabilities so that an account can be taken and a balance struck. If the obligation on one side is to deliver goods *in specie* and the obligation on the other side is to pay a sum of money, there can be no set-off (see *Eberle's Hotel Co v Jonas* (1887) 18 QBD 459). But in *Rolls Razor v Cox* [1967] 1 QB 552 set-off was allowed by salesmen of a company who had not been paid their sales commission against monies received by them for the sale of the company's goods and the value of such goods in their possession but unsold at the date of their employer's insolvency. The salesmen had the right to turn their employer's goods into money and this fact gave them the right of set-off.

Set-off is mandatory and no contracting out of its provisions is possible (*National Westminster Bank v Halesowen Presswork and Assemblies Ltd* [1972] AC 785 and *British Eagle International Air Lines Ltd v Compagnie Nationale Air France* [1975] 1 WLR 758).

All provable claims, provided there is mutuality, may be the subject of set-off. Thus unliquidated damages in tort which are now a provable debt can be set off against a liquidated sum due in respect of a debt. But for mutual liabilities to be set off against each other they must both have arisen prior to the making of the bankruptcy order. It is not necessary for the debts to be set off against each other for both to be immediately due and enforceable at that time. Thus a debt payable at a future time after the making of a bankruptcy order can be set off against a debt due at the time of the order (see, eg, *Re Daintrey ex p Mant* [1900] 1 QB 546).

5 Where set-off not allowed

The provisions as to mutual credit only apply as between the bankrupt and his creditor and not an assignee of his creditor where the assignment takes place after the making of the bankruptcy order (see, eg, *Re City Life Assurance Company Ltd* [1926] Ch 191). Unless there is specific agreement allowing the right of set-off, there can be no set-off between joint debts and separate debts. Thus, if a bankrupt is owed a sum by an individual, there can be no set-off against that liability of any sums due from the bankrupt to a partnership of which that individual is a partner. For there to be a right of set-off, the debts must be due in the same right. Debts due to or from the trustee in bankruptcy cannot be set off against debts due from or to the bankrupt (*Lister v Hooson* [1908] 1 KB 174). Thus, if the trustee sells the bankrupt's property to a person who had dealt with the bankrupt prior to the bankruptcy and was owed money by him, there can be no set-off of the sum due for the property bought from the trustee against the debt due from the bankrupt to that person, though that debt can, of course, be proved for in the bankruptcy.

If a creditor receives money after the bankruptcy has begun in circumstances requiring him to repay it to the trustee where, eg, the money was received by mistake or if a creditor is required to repay money to the trustee because his receipt of it constituted a preference, then that creditor cannot set off against the sum he is required to repay any sum due to him from the bankrupt (see *Elgood v Harris* [1896] 2 QB 419 and *Re a Debtor (No 82 of 1926)* [1927] 1 Ch 410).

No right of set-off is allowed where property has been entrusted to a creditor for a specific purpose in such circumstances that it would be a misappropriation for it to be applied for any other purpose (see, eg, *National Westminster Bank v Halesowen Presswork and Assemblies Ltd* [1972] AC 785, *Carreras Rothman Ltd v Freeman Matthews Treasure Ltd* [1985] Ch 207 and *Re Charge Card Services Ltd* [1986] 3 WLR 697).

6 Different classes of debt

A right to set-off may exist even though one of the debts is secured (see *Re Deveze* (1874) 9 Ch App 293 and *McKinnon v Armstrong Brothers & Co* (1887) 2 App Cas 531).

Where a creditor has both a preferential and a non-preferential claim in the bankruptcy, the amount due from him to the bankrupt must be set off rateably against the preferential and non-preferential debts (see *Re Unit 2 Windows Ltd* [1985] 1 WLR 1383).

7 Contingent debts

There has been some disagreement between the judges as to whether it is possible to set off against a debt due from one party a contingent liability of the other. In *Carreras Rothman Ltd v Freeman Matthews Treasure Ltd* [1985] Ch 207, Gibson J held that an obligation contingent at the date of the making of the bankruptcy order was not a debt due capable of being set off against a debt due from the other party. However, in *Re Charge Card Services Ltd* [1986] 3 WLR 697 Millett J held that an obligation which at the date of the making of the bankruptcy order was certain but the amount of which was unascertainable until the happening of future events was none the less capable of being set off against a sum due from the other party.

Both judges referred to the case of *Re a Debtor (No 66 of 1955)* [1956] 1 WLR 1226 which concerned the right to set off against a sum due to the estate a sum due in respect of a guarantee liability. The Court of Appeal held that as, at the date of the making of the bankruptcy order, the guarantor had not been called upon to pay and had not paid, there was no sum which could be set off against his liability to the bankrupt. If prior to the bankruptcy demand had been made, then perhaps, even if payment had not been made, there would have been a liability due to the guarantor which could be set off by him against any liability which he had to the bankrupt or more precisely to his estate.

8 Crown set-off

A Crown department can set off against a debt due by it any debt owed by the bankrupt to another Crown department (*Re Cushla Ltd* [1979] 3 All ER 415 and *Re D H Curtis (Builders) Ltd* [1978] Ch 162).

Chapter 17

Discharge

1 Automatic discharge

A person against whom a bankruptcy order has been made remains a bankrupt (unless that order is subsequently annulled) until such time as he is discharged. Discharge is automatic in the case of a person who has not at any time in the previous 15 years prior to the making of the bankruptcy order against him been bankrupt or, has not been made bankrupt as a result of a criminal bankruptcy order at the expiry of three years after the making of the bankruptcy order discharge occurs or, in the case of a bankruptcy where a certificate of summary administration is in force, at the expiry of two years after the making of the bankruptcy order (s 279 (1) and (2)).

However, if the court is satisfied, on the application of the official receiver, that the bankrupt has failed to comply with any of his obligations under the Act, it may order that the period, after which discharge is to be automatically granted, ceases to run until the bankrupt has fulfilled certain conditions or until after a certain time has passed (s 279(3)).

Where a person was adjudged bankrupt before the new law came into force, he was entitled to an automatic discharge on 29 December 1989, or, if he was adjudged bankrupt after 29 December 1986 on a petition presented under the old law, three years after his adjudication. This provision is subject to the bankrupt not having been previously bankrupt within the 15 years prior to the adjudication (Sched 11 to the Act, para 13(1) and (2)) and to an application by the official receiver under the equivalent of s 279(3).

2 Suspension of discharge (rr 6.215 and 216)

Where the official receiver applies to the court for the automatic discharge of the bankrupt to be suspended, he must file a report setting out his reasons and upon receipt of the application, the court will fix a time and date for the hearing of the application and give notice of the hearing to the official receiver, the trustee and the bankrupt. Copies of the official receiver's report must be sent by him to the trustee and the bankrupt so as to reach them at least 21 days before the hearing and the bankrupt can, not later than seven days before the hearing, file in court a notice specifying any statements in the report which he intends to deny or dispute. Copies of this notice must be sent by the bankrupt to the official receiver and the trustee not less than four days before the hearing (r 6.215). It is essential that circumstances giving rise to the possibility of an application to suspend the automatic discharge be notified to the official receiver as soon as possible by the trustee or the creditors. Failure to do so may make it impossible for an application to be made in sufficient time to prevent the automatic discharge being granted.

The application (if opposed), in the High Court, is heard by the registrar in open court unless he refers it to the judge. Under r 6.176(4), the official receiver is empowered to make this application without observing the requirements as to reports and notice if and when the court adjourns the bankrupt's public examination generally.

If the court makes an order suspending the bankrupt's discharge, a copy of the order must be sent by the court to the official receiver, the trustee and the bankrupt. It is open to the bankrupt to make an application to the court for the suspension to be lifted. On receipt of such an application, the court must fix a hearing date and the bankrupt must give 28 days' notice of his application to the official receiver and the trustee. The official receiver may serve a report (not less than 14 days before the hearing) on any matters which he considers ought to be drawn to the court's attention whether or not he intends to appear at the hearing. If the bankrupt wishes to reply to the matters contained in the report, he may do so not less than seven days before the hearing by filing a notice at court and serving a copy of the notice on the official receiver and the trustee not less than four days before the hearing. A district judge or registrar has jurisdiction to adjourn the bankrupt's public examination on short notice and to suspend his automatic discharge pending the happening of the first of the conclusion of his public examination or the period of nine months elapsing (*Holmes v Official Receiver* (1995) unreported, 7 July).

If the court had previously ordered the bankrupt's discharge to be suspended until the fulfilment of certain conditions, the court may request a report from the official receiver as to whether those conditions have or have not been fulfilled.

If the court lifts the suspension, it must issue to the bankrupt a certificate that it has done so and with effect from what date.

3 Application for discharge

Provision is made by s 280 for those who, in the last 15 years, have previously been bankrupt and those who have been made bankrupt as a result of a criminal bankruptcy order to apply to the court for their discharge. There is no other way in which such persons can obtain their discharge. No such application can be made until five years have elapsed since the making of the bankruptcy order and there are no means whereby this period can be shortened. Application to the court for discharge cannot be made by those entitled to an automatic discharge who wish to obtain their discharge earlier than at the end of three years (or two years as the case may be).

On making an application for discharge, the bankrupt must give notice of it to the official receiver and deposit with him such a sum of money as he requires to cover his costs of the application. Once the court is satisfied that this requirement has been fulfilled, a hearing date will be fixed and the court must give at least 42 days' notice of it to the bankrupt and the official receiver, who in turn must give notice to the trustee and every creditor remaining unpaid not later than 14 days before the hearing (r 6.217).

At least 21 days before the hearing, the official receiver must file at court a report containing information of any failures of the bankrupt to comply with obligations imposed upon him by the Act, the circumstances surrounding the present bankruptcy and any previous ones, the extent of the deficiency in all cases and particulars of any dividend paid or likely to be paid together with any other matters which the official receiver is of the opinion ought to be brought to the court's attention. This report must be sent by the official receiver to the bankrupt and the trustee so as to reach them at least 14 days before the hearing. The bankrupt can respond to the report by filing a notice not less than seven days before the hearing and sending a copy of it to the official receiver and the trustee not less than four days before the hearing. The official receiver, the trustee and any creditor may appear on the hearing of the application, make representations and put to the bankrupt such questions as the court allows (r 6.218).

On the hearing of the application, the court may refuse to order a discharge, make an order discharging the bankrupt absolutely or make an order discharging the bankrupt subject to conditions as to payment to his estate from his future income or property and may order that discharge is only to have effect at a specified date in the future or on fulfilment of specified conditions (s 280(2) and (3)).

If the court makes an order granting discharge, it takes effect only when it is drawn up by the court and then has retrospective effect back to the date on which it was made (r 6.219). Copies of the order must be sent by the court to the bankrupt, the official receiver and the trustee. An order granting a discharge must not be drawn or gazetted until the time allowed for appealing has expired or, if an appeal has been entered, until after the appeal has been determined (r 6.221).

4 Certificate of discharge

When a bankrupt has been discharged, whether it be under the automatic provisions by passage of time or as a result of an application to the court, the court must, at the request of the bankrupt, issue to him a certificate of his discharge and the date from which it was effective. The bankrupt can also require the Secretary of State in writing to advertise the discharge in the *London Gazette* and/or any newspaper in which the bankruptcy was advertised provided that the bankrupt pays the costs of the advertisements in advance (r 6.220).

5 Effect of discharge

When a bankrupt is discharged, he is released from all obligations in respect of his pre-bankruptcy liabilities except the following:
- (a) obligations incurred by fraud or fraudulent breach of trust;
- (b) fines except with the consent of the Treasury if they relate to revenue offences;
- (c) unless the court orders otherwise, damages for negligence, nuisance or breach of a statutory, contractual or other duty being in respect of personal injuries;
- (d) unless the court orders otherwise, obligations arising under any order made in family proceedings;
- (e) non-provable debts (s 281).

Chapter 18

The Home

1 Rights of occupation of the spouse

By s 1(1) of the Matrimonial Homes Act 1983, where one spouse has an interest in the home or is otherwise entitled to remain in occupation and the other spouse is not so entitled, then the other spouse has the right not to be evicted or excluded from the home except with leave of the court. This right of occupation is a charge on the spouse's interest in the property. This section of the 1983 Act was amended by Sched 10 of the Insolvency Act 1985.

In this section, it will be presumed for the sake of simplicity that the bankrupt is the husband and therefore the non-bankrupt spouse is the wife.

A wife cannot acquire such rights of occupation by any act done by her in the period between the presentation of the petition and the making of a bankruptcy order against her husband (s 336(1)). The wife's rights, which under s 1(1) of the 1983 Act constitute a charge on the husband's interest in the property, continue to subsist notwithstanding his bankruptcy. Any application for an order under the 1983 Act for leave to evict the wife must be made to the court having jurisdiction over the bankruptcy (s 336(2)). Likewise any application for an order for sale under s 30 of the Law of Property Act 1925 where the husband and wife are joint owners of the property must also be made to the bankruptcy court.

On the hearing of an application by the trustee in bankruptcy of the husband for an order under s 1 of the 1983 Act or s 30 of the 1925 Act, the court can make any order it thinks just and reasonable having regard to:
  (a) the interests of the creditors;
  (b) the conduct of the wife so far as contributing to her husband's bankruptcy;
  (c) the needs and financial resources of the wife;
  (d) the needs of any of the children; and
  (e) all the circumstances of the case, except the needs of the husband (s 336(5)).

If the trustee makes such an application before the end of one year after his appointment as trustee, then the interests of the wife (and the children) are presumed to outweigh the interests of the creditors. If the trustee makes the application after the end of the year after his appointment, the interests of the creditors are presumed to outweigh all other considerations, unless the circumstances of the case are exceptional (s 336(5)). No guidance as to what might constitute exceptional circumstances is to be found in the Act or the Rules. The mere fact that the wife and children of the debtor are faced with eviction and will be unable to buy a comparable home in the same area is not regarded as exceptional circumstances (*Re Lowrie* [1981] 3 All ER 353 and *Re Citro* [1990] 3 All ER 952). In *Re Holliday* [1981] Ch 405, the court held that there were exceptional circumstances because the husband had petitioned for his own bankruptcy to defeat the rights of his wife and children to a transfer of property order and there were no creditors pressing. Assistance to the bankrupt and his family might be obtained from the case of *Abbey National v Moss* (1993) *The Times*, 30 November where it was held that the collateral purpose for which the property was being held should not be overriden even where the beneficial interest of one of the parties had passed to a mortgagee. Whether this decision would override the clear words of s 336(5) remains to be tested.

Under s 1 of the 1983 Act the court can order the occupying spouse to make periodical payments to the other spouse (and therefore to his trustee) akin to rent and impose on the occupying spouse obligations as to the repair and maintenance of the property and the discharge of any liabilities (such as rates) in respect of it.

2 Rights of the bankrupt

Where the bankrupt has no spouse or children living with him, he has no rights to remain in the property as against his trustee. However, if the bankrupt was living in his home at the time of the making of the bankruptcy order against him with a person under the age of 18 years, then s 337(2) gives the bankrupt the right not to be evicted from his home or, if he is not in occupation, then the right with the leave of the court to return to the home. These rights are a charge on the trustee's interest in the property. The bankrupt is then put in much the same position as a spouse with rights of occupation under the 1983 Act.

If the trustee wishes to obtain possession of the bankrupt's home in these circumstances, he must make application to the court. The court which has jurisdiction to deal with such an application is the bankruptcy court. The court, on such an application, must make its order having regard to the interests of the creditors, the bankrupt's financial resources, the needs of the children and all the circumstances of the case except the needs of the bankrupt (s 337(5)). If the trustee's application is made after one year from the date of his appointment as trustee, the court must presume, unless the circumstances are exceptional, that the interests of the creditors outweigh all other considerations. Guidance as to what might constitute exceptional circumstances is not given but if, for example, the bankrupt had a handicapped child and the home was specially adapted for that child, then this might be enough to enable the bankrupt and the child to remain in the property. The court can, under s 1(3) of the 1983 Act, make an order requiring payments to be made akin to rent, and for the discharge of liabilities, such as mortgage instalments or rates, in respect of the property.

Where the court orders the bankrupt to make a payment towards the liabilities in respect of the property, such as mortgage instalments or rates, the bankrupt does not acquire any interest in the property as a result of these payments being made (s 338).

3 Charge on the bankrupt's home (s 313)

Where the bankrupt or his spouse, or former spouse, continue to occupy the home and the trustee is, therefore, unable to realise his interest in that property, he cannot conclude his administration and call a final meeting of creditors without the court first considering whether it is appropriate to impose a charge on the bankrupt's property (unless the Secretary of State issues a certificate that it is inappropriate or inexpedient to do so) (s 332).

The trustee may apply to the court for an order imposing a charge on the property for the benefit of the estate. The charge must be for the equivalent of the shortfall in the bankrupt's estate, that is, the difference between the bankrupt's other assets and all his liabilities (including the costs of the administration). The charge can also extend to interest on this sum at the prescribed rate, namely, the judgment rate, currently 15 per cent. The charge cannot create any liability beyond the value of the property for the time being.

The procedure for an application by the trustee is set out in r 6.237. The bankrupt's spouse or former spouse is made respondent to the trustee's application and the court has power to direct other persons to be made respondents also. The trustee must make a report to the court specifying the shortfall as regards creditors at the date of the application and if the terms of the charge cannot be agreed between the bankrupt and the trustee, the court will settle the terms. The order must specify the rate of interest together with a description of the property to be charged, whether the title is registered or not and if so, the title number, the interest of the bankrupt in the property, the amount of the charge and the terms of the charge. The order must also provide that when the charge has been satisfied, the property will vest once again in the bankrupt (and not his trustee). The charging order under s 313 is in Form 6.79A in Sched 4 to the Rules. The trustee as holder of a charging order against the interest of a joint owner of the property can apply for and hope to obtain an order for sale without undue difficulty (*Midland Bank v Pike* [1988] 2 All ER 434). The charge can be registered at the Land Registry or Land Charges Registry in the same manner as a charging order is registered.

4 Determining the extent of the bankrupt's interest

Where a property is conveyed into the joint names of the spouses as joint tenants and the conveyance or transfer recites the spouses' respective beneficial interests, then that recital, in the absence of fraud or mistake, will be binding on them (*Leake v Bruzzi* [1974] 1 WLR 1528). As the trustee, for this purpose, is in no better position than the bankrupt spouse, he is also bound by the recital unless he can set aside the conveyance, for example, under s 339 (transaction at an undervalue) or s 423 (transactions defrauding creditors); see Chapter 19. The trustee may be required to give credit for any mortgage repayments made by the other spouse (see *Leake v Bruzzi* and also *Suttill v Graham* [1977] 1 WLR 819 for a general statement of the principles applicable). Where property is jointly owned by the bankrupt and his wife, the trustee may be entitled after a sale of the property takes place to be credited with half of the proper occupation rent for the period from the date of the bankruptcy order to the date of sale and debited with half of any mortgage instalments paid by the other joint owner together with half of any sums spent in improving the value of the property (*Re Gorman* [1990] 1 All ER 717).

Where a property is conveyed into the sole name of one of the spouses, the extent to which the other spouse may claim a beneficial interest therein (which will be binding on the trustee) is determined by the principles laid down by the House of Lords in *Gissing v Gissing* [1971] AC 886 and subsequent decisions on s 17 of the Married Women's Property Act 1882. See also *Re Densham (a Bankrupt)* [1975] 1 WLR 1519.

Chapter 19

Adjustment of Prior Transactions

1 Transactions at an undervalue (ss 339 and 423)

Where the bankrupt entered into a transaction at an undervalue at the relevant time (for a definition of which see **3** below), the trustee may apply to the court for an order, for the terms of which see **4** below (s 339(1)). A transaction is at an undervalue if it is a gift or for no consideration, if it is in consideration of marriage or the consideration for it is significantly less than the value of the consideration provided by the bankrupt (s 339(3)).

A prerequisite under this section is that the bankrupt has 'entered into a transaction'. A positive act is required by the bankrupt. A passive act is not sufficient under this section but it may constitute a preference under s 340 (see **2** below). What amounts to consideration 'significantly less than the value received' is not defined in the Act. The court has to fix the invalidity point (from no consideration to full value) in respect of each transaction and has been left with a fairly wide discretion. In *Re Abbott (a Bankrupt)* [1983] Ch 45 the court held that the invalidity point was above the level of 'nominal or insignificant' consideration but below the level of equality.

Property adjustment orders in matrimonial proceedings can be 'transactions entered into' by the bankrupt (Matrimonial Causes Act 1973, s 39). It is suggested that an order made by consent will be a transaction which can be caught by s 339 whereas an order made by the court after argument and a hearing will not be caught. However, s 39 includes a provision that anything required to be done pursuant to a court order (eg the actual transfer or conveyance of a property) can still be caught by s 339. It is unlikely that a property adjustment order, whether made by consent or otherwise, will be for no consideration. The common type of order is one where the wife gives up her right to maintenance in return for an interest in or the whole of the former matrimonial home. Whatever the value of the wife's right to maintenance, it is of some value and more than 'nominal or insignificant' value. It is for the trustee to prove that the monetary value of the rights given up by the wife is of significantly less value than the property given up by the (now bankrupt) husband. This will be very difficult for the trustee to prove or even to evaluate. A transfer by a husband to his wife of his half share of the matrimonial home with equity of £110,000 when they became estranged only in return for the wife taking over sole responsibility for the mortgage was set aside as a transaction at an undervalue (*Re Kumar* [1993] 1 WLR 224).

In *Re Abbott* (above) the court held that the giving up of rights by the wife made her a purchaser for valuable consideration and the rights abandoned need not be of commensurate monetary value. Even where a consent order is safe from attack under s 339 (transaction at an undervalue), it may still be caught by s 340 (voidable preference).

Section 423 sets out almost identical provisions to s 339 under the heading 'transactions defrauding creditors' (akin to the provisions of s 172 of the Law of Property Act 1925) but it is not a prerequisite of an application under s 423 that the person entering into the transaction at an undervalue or to defraud creditors is bankrupt. What must be shown is that the transaction was entered into and that a dominant purpose of it was to put the asset beyond the reach of or otherwise to prejudice the interests of the creditor (*Chohan v Saggar* (1991) *The Times*, 16 October). Where the transferor has mixed motives, the court will have regard to the dominant motive when deciding if the requirements of s 423 have been satisfied. However, when a person has been adjudged bankrupt, the victim of the transaction can only make application under s 423 with leave of the court.

It has been held to be a transaction at an undervalue where an asset (immediately realisable) was sold to an associated entity in return for an income stream rather than a cash sum where it was clear that the sale was intended to keep the benefit of the assets within 'the family' (*Arbuthnot v Havelet* [1990] BCC 636). Likewise, a lease created by the debtor over his property in favour of himself and a partner was held to be a transaction at an undervalue (*AMC v Woodward* [1994] BCC 688).

Even if the transferor in a transaction attacked under s 423 is not bankrupt, communications between him and his solicitor will have to be disclosed on discovery of documents and his solicitor cannot plead professional privilege as a reason not to disclose such documents (*Barclays Bank v Eustice* [1995] 1 WLR 1238).

2 Voidable preference (s 340)

A preference is given when the bankrupt, at the relevant time (for a definition of which see below), does anything or allows anything to be done which has the effect of putting the recipient into a better position than he would have been had the thing not been done and the recipient is one of the bankrupt's creditors or a guarantor of one of his debts or liabilities (s 340(3)). The court must not make an order against the recipient requiring him to give back what he received from the bankrupt unless the bankrupt was influenced in deciding to make the transfer or payment to the recipient by a desire to prefer him (s 340(4)). The court can find that there has been a preference even if only one of the bankrupt's motives in making a payment to a creditor was a desire to prefer with the dominant motive being something else. In *Re M C Bacon* [1990] BCC 78 the court distinguished between 'intention' and 'desire' and whilst there was an intention to put the recipient in a better position than other creditors, there was no desire to do so, only a desire to stay in business. Accordingly there was no preference.

If the recipient was an associate of the bankrupt, then it is presumed, unless the contrary is proved, that the bankrupt was influenced by a desire to prefer the recipient (s 340(5)). The onus of proof is, therefore, shifted on to the recipient from the trustee as a result of this provision. An associate is defined by s 435 as including a close relative, a former spouse, a partner or employer. The fact that something is done pursuant to a court order does not prevent it being a preference (s 340(6)).

3 The relevant time (s 341)

The relevant time for transactions to be impeached as transactions at an undervalue or constituting voidable preferences is as follows:
  (a) transactions at an undervalue—any time in the period of five years before the presentation of the bankruptcy petition;
  (b) voidable preferences—any time in the period of six months before the presentation of the bankruptcy petition, unless the recipient is an associate in which case the period is two years.

If a transaction is both a transaction at an undervalue and a preference, the period for impeaching transactions at an undervalue applies.

If a transaction at an undervalue is entered into between two and five years before the presentation of the bankruptcy petition or a preference is made in the period of six months or two years (as the case may be) prior to the presentation of the bankruptcy petition, it is deemed not to have been made at a 'relevant time' unless the individual entering into the transaction or giving the preference was at that time insolvent or became insolvent in consequence of the transaction or preference (s 341(2)). In the case of a transaction at an undervalue entered into with an associate (other than an employee), it is presumed, unless the contrary is proved, that these requirements have been satisfied.

An individual is insolvent for the purposes of subs (2) if he is unable to pay his debts as they fall due (the cash-flow test) or the amount of his liabilities exceeds the value of his assets taking into account prospective and contingent liabilities (the balance sheet test) (s 341(3)).

4 Orders under ss 339 and 340

By s 339(2) and s 340(2), the court may, on an application to set aside a transaction at an undervalue or a voidable preference, make such order as it thinks fit for restoring the position to what it would have been if the transaction had not been entered into or the preference made. Under s 342, the court is given powers to require any property transferred or the proceeds of sale of it to be vested in the trustee, to release or discharge any security given or to reimpose the obligation of any guarantor released as a result of a payment to the creditor now reclaimed (s 342(1)). These orders can be made against any person whether he is the person with whom the now bankrupt individual entered into any transaction. However, a purchaser for value in good faith would not be affected, but if he had notice of the 'relevant circumstances and proceedings' or was a connected party, there is a presumption that the purchaser did not act in good faith (s 342(2A)). The 'relevant circumstances' referred to are the inability of the individual to meet his debts as they fall due or the fact that his liabilities exceed his assets (see s 341(3)). An application under s 339 can even be made after the bankrupt's discharge subject to protection of bona fide purchasers prior to the trustee's application *(Re Dent* (1993) EGCS 190).

5 Extortionate credit transactions (s 343)

Where a person has been adjudged bankrupt and has been a party to a transaction involving the provision of credit to him, the court may, on the application of the trustee, set aside a transaction if it was extortionate provided that it was entered into within three years of the presentation of the bankruptcy petition. A transaction is to be regarded as extortionate if the terms of it were such as to require grossly extortionate payments to be made or it otherwise grossly contravened ordinary principles of dealing, having regard to the risk accepted by the person giving the credit (s 343(3)). The onus of proving that the transaction was not extortionate is on the person who gave the credit. In *Woodstead Finance v Petrou* (1986) NL Rep 188 the court held that interest of 42 per cent per annum was not extortionate.

If the court makes an order that a transaction was an extortionate credit transaction, it may make an order setting aside the whole of the transaction, vary the terms of the transaction, require any security given to the released or require the recipient of any money under the transaction to repay it.

This section applies in place of and not in addition to remedies under the Consumer Credit Act 1974.

6 Avoidance of general assignment (s 344)

Where a person engaged in business entered into a general assignment of the book debts due to him and was subsequently adjudged bankrupt, the assignment is void against his trustee as regards any book debts which had not been paid at the date of the commencement of his bankruptcy unless the assignment was registered under the Bills of Sale Act 1878 (s 344(2)).

There is excluded from this provision the assignment of specific debts, present or future, and the assignment of debts included in a transfer of a business made in good faith and for value. A deed of assignment is a general assignment of book debts but as it is for the benefit of creditors generally it is specifically excluded from the effect of s 344(2) by s 344(3)(*b*).

7 Enforcement procedures (s 346)

Where a creditor has, before the commencement of the bankruptcy, issued execution against the goods or land of the bankrupt or attached a debt due to the bankrupt from another person, he cannot retain the benefit of his actions as against the official receiver or trustee unless the execution or attachment was completed or the sums due were paid before the bankruptcy order was made (s 346(1)).

Execution is completed by seizure and sale. Execution against land is completed by seizure, the appointment of a receiver or the making of charging order *nisi* under s 1 of the Charging Orders Act 1979. However, if only a charging order *nisi* (not absolute) was obtained prior to the commencement of the bankruptcy, the court may refuse in its discretion to make the order *nisi* absolute because the effect of doing so would be to put one creditor in a better position than all of the others and in such a case the order *nisi* is likely to be discharged. Accordingly, only a charging order absolute obtained prior to the commencement of the bankruptcy would give the creditor absolute protection. Attachment of a debt is completed by the receipt of the debt by the garnishor (s 346(5)).

Where goods have been seized by the sheriff or a bailiff but execution has not been completed by sale and notice has been given to the sheriff or bailiff that the debtor has been adjudged bankrupt, the sheriff or bailiff must deliver the proceeds of sale of them to the official receiver or trustee but has a first charge on those goods or their proceeds for his costs (s 346(2)).

Where the sheriff or bailiff has sold goods or received money from the debtor to avoid a sale and the judgment executed is more than the prescribed sum (currently £500 as provided by the Insolvency Proceedings (Monetary Limits) Order 1986 (SI No 1996)), the sheriff or bailiff must retain the money obtained for 14 days and if notice is given during that period that the debtor has been adjudged bankrupt, then the sheriff or bailiff must hand over the money to the official receiver or trustee subject to a retention sufficient to cover his costs of execution (s 346(3) and (4)). The court can set aside the rights conferred by subss (1) to (3) in favour of the creditor to the extent and on such terms as it thinks fit (s 346(6)). There are, however, no reported cases of this power (similarly contained in the old law) ever having been exercised in favour of a creditor.

8 Distress (s 347)

Section 285(3) restricts the right of a creditor to any remedy against the property of the bankrupt in respect of a debt which is provable in the bankruptcy. However, a landlord can continue to distrain against the goods of an undischarged bankrupt (that is, against goods under the control of his trustee if on the demised premises) even after the making of a bankruptcy order for up to six months' rent accrued due before the commencement of the bankruptcy (s 347(1)). If the landlord distrained prior to the making of the bankruptcy order but the distraint was not completed (by seizure and sale) before the making of the bankruptcy order, the excess over the rent due for the six-month period referred to must be handed over to the trustee for the benefit of the bankrupt's estate (s 347(2)).

The restrictions on distraints and the benefits of them only apply to distraints for rent and not to the other kinds of distraint. These other kinds of distraint can even be levied after the bankruptcy has commenced but only as regards post-bankruptcy accruals (s 347(8)). A landlord cannot distrain for rent on the goods comprised in the bankrupt's estate after the bankrupt has been discharged (s 347(5)).

Where there has been a distraint (whether by a landlord for rent, or government departments for various kinds of taxes) in the three months prior to the making of a bankruptcy order, the proceeds of that distraint are charged for the benefit of the bankrupt's estate with the preferential debts of the bankrupt to the extent that the bankrupt's estate is not sufficient to meet them (s 347(3)). If the distraining creditor surrenders the goods distrained upon for the benefit of the preferential creditors, then he becomes a preferential creditor in their place to the extent of the value of the goods surrendered (s 347(4)).

9 Liens on books and papers (s 349)

Any lien or other right to possession of any books, papers or other records of a bankrupt (other than documents which give a title to property) is unenforceable against the official receiver or trustee.

A solicitor may be entitled to exercise a lien over the files of the bankrupt in his possession but the value of that lien will be destroyed if the solicitor is obliged to attend court and answer questions relating to his dealings with the bankrupt and is also required to produce his file under s 366(1). Also see *Re Wells* [1892] Ch 116 and *Re Aveling Barford* [1988] 3 All ER 1019.

Chapter 20

Bankruptcy Offences

1 Liability to prosecution

Whilst bankruptcy itself is not a crime, once a bankruptcy order has been made, the bankrupt is liable to prosecution if he has committed any of the offences set out below by reason of his conduct both before bankruptcy proceedings were begun against him and during the currency of those proceedings. Even if the bankruptcy order is annulled, criminal proceedings, once begun, can be continued but new proceedings cannot be brought. Likewise, after discharge, proceedings cannot be commenced but proceedings already begun can be continued in relation to offences committed prior to discharge. It is not a defence to say that the acts complained of were committed outside England and Wales (s 350).

Only the Secretary of State or the Director of Public Prosecutions can bring criminal proceedings. The trustee's duty is to report to the official receiver any matters which would assist the official receiver in carrying out his duties. The duties of the official receiver include a duty to investigate the conduct of the bankrupt and to report to the court on his findings as he thinks fit. Presumably when the court receives a report from an official receiver that the bankrupt's conduct is such that a criminal offence may have been committed, the court will direct that the facts be brought to the attention of the appropriate authorities.

Schedule 10 to the Act sets out the maximum punishment for each offence under the Act. There is a different maximum depending on whether the offender is prosecuted summarily in the magistrates' court or on indictment in the Crown Court. The statutory maximum fine on conviction in the magistrates' court is prescribed by s 32 of the Magistrates' Courts Act 1980 and is currently £1000.

2 Defence of innocent intention

A bankrupt is not guilty of one of the bankruptcy offences if he proves that at the time of the conduct constituting the offence, he did not have intent to defraud or did not intend to conceal the true state of his affairs (s 352). However, s 352 is only a defence in connection with the following offences:

(a) non-disclosure of information (s 353);
(b) concealment of property (s 354(1) and (2));
(c) concealment or falsification of books and papers (s 355);
(d) material omission (s 356(1));
(e) fraudulent disposal of property (s 357);
(f) absconding from the country (s 358);
(g) disposal of goods on credit (s 359(1)).

A description of each of these offences is set out below.

3 Non-disclosure (s 353)

An offence is committed by a bankrupt if he does not, to the best of his knowledge and belief, disclose all his assets to the official receiver or his trustee or if he fails to inform the official receiver or trustee of any disposal of property which might be set aside and which would therefore result in further assets being comprised in his estate. This latter requirement does not extend to any disposal in the ordinary course of business nor to any payment of the ordinary expenses of the bankrupt or his family. Section 352 is available as a defence to a prosecution under this section.

The maximum punishment for an offence under this section is seven years' imprisonment or a fine or both (on indictment) or six months' imprisonment or a fine of £1000 or both (summary).

4 Concealment of property (s 354)

An offence is committed by a bankrupt if he fails to deliver to the official receiver or his trustee all the assets in his estate which he is required to deliver up, if he conceals any debt due to or from him or if he conceals any property the value of which is not less than the minimum prescribed value (currently £500 under the Insolvency Proceedings (Monetary Limits) Order 1986). The section also applies to the concealment of any debt due to or from the bankrupt or property of not less than the minimum prescribed value in the 12 months prior to the presentation of the petition. An offence is also committed if the bankrupt removes or, in the period between the presentation of the petition and the bankruptcy order, removed any property of not less than the minimum prescribed value which he would have been required to deliver up to the official receiver or trustee. Section 352 is available as a defence to a prosecution under this section.

The maximum punishment for offences under this section is seven years' imprisonment or a fine or both (on indictment) or six months' imprisonment or a fine of £1000 or both (summary).

5 Explanations (s 354(3))

An offence is committed if the bankrupt fails without reasonable excuse to account for the loss of any substantial part of his property incurred in the 12 months before the petition was presented or to give a satisfactory explanation of how much loss was incurred. Section 352 does not provide a defence to proceedings under this section.

The maximum punishment for an offence under this section is two years' imprisonment or a fine or both (on indictment) or six months' imprisonment or a fine of £1000 or both (summary).

6 Books and papers (s 355)

It is an offence for the bankrupt not to deliver up all books, papers and other records relating to his affairs and also if the bankrupt prevents the production of any books, papers and other records or conceals, destroys, mutilates or falsifies such documents. Likewise, an offence is committed if the bankrupt causes or permits the concealment, destruction, mutilation or falsification of any such documents. If any of these actions have been done within the 12 months prior to the presentation of the petition, an offence is likewise committed. Section 352 is available as a defence to a prosecution for all offences under s 355.

The maximum punishment for offences under this section is seven years' imprisonment or a fine or both (on indictment) or six months' imprisonment or a fine of £1000 or both (summary).

7 False statements (s 356)

If a bankrupt makes any material omission in any statement required to be made by him under the Act, then he commits an offence unless s 352 is available as a defence. If he fails to inform his trustee that a false debt has been proved or attempts to account for any part of his assets by fictitious losses or expenses, he is guilty of an offence. If he makes, or has made at any time, any false representation or other fraud with the object of procuring creditors to agree to some arrangement regarding his affairs, he is also guilty of an offence. Section 352 is not available as a defence to a prosecution for these offences.

The maximum punishment for offences under this section is seven years' imprisonment or a fine or both (on indictment) or six months' imprisonment or a fine of £1000 or both (summary).

8 Fraudulent disposal of property (s 357)

If the bankrupt makes any gift or transfer of, or any charge on, his property within five years of the presentation of the petition, an offence is committed. Similarly, if the bankrupt has concealed or removed any part of his property within five months before or after any judgment has been obtained against him, an offence is committed. Section 352 is available as a defence to a prosecution for either of these offences.

The maximum punishment for offences under this section is two years' imprisonment or a fine or both (on indictment) or six months' imprisonment or a fine of £1000 or both (summary).

9 Absconding (s 358)

A bankrupt commits an offence if he leaves, attempts to leave or makes preparation to leave England and Wales with any property of not less than the prescribed minimum value. The offence is committed if these actions were taken at any time in the six months prior to the presentation of the petition.

Section 352 is available as a defence to a prosecution under this section. The object of this section is to punish someone who knows that he is liable to be made bankrupt and decides, with knowledge of the likely bankruptcy proceedings against him, to leave the country and takes all his valuable assets with him.

The maximum punishment for these offences is two years' imprisonment or a fine or both (on indictment) or six months' imprisonment or a fine of £1000 or both (summary).

10 Fraudulent dealing with property obtained on credit (s 359)

The bankrupt is guilty of an offence if, in the 12 months before the presentation of the petition or subsequently before his property vested in his trustee, he disposed of any property which had been obtained on credit and in respect of which money was still owing. Section 352 is available as a defence to a prosecution under this section.

It is also an offence for a person to acquire or receive property from the bankrupt in the same period knowing that the bankrupt owed money in respect of that property and that the bankrupt did not intend or was unlikely to be able to pay the money owed on the property. There is a defence available to such a person, namely, that the transaction was in the ordinary course of business, but regard will then be had to the price paid for the property so as to judge whether the transaction could have been in the ordinary course of business.

References to the disposal or receipt of property in this section include the pawning or pledging of property.

The maximum punishment for offences under this section is seven years' imprisonment or a fine or both (on indictment) or six months' imprisonment or a fine of £1000 or both (summary).

11 Obtaining credit or engaging in business (s 360)

An offence is committed by a bankrupt if he obtains credit of more than the prescribed amount (currently £250) without disclosing the fact that he is a bankrupt or if he engages (directly or indirectly) in business in a name other than the one under which he was made bankrupt without disclosing his true name to anyone from whom credit is obtained. Obtaining credit includes taking goods on hire-purchase or receiving money in advance for the supply of goods or services.

It is an offence in England and Wales for someone who has been made bankrupt (or the equivalent) in Scotland or Northern Ireland to obtain credit or engage in business in a different name in exactly the same way as if that person had been made bankrupt in England and Wales.

The renting of a furnished house by a bankrupt was held to be obtaining credit and so to avoid an offence being committed, the bankrupt must disclose his status to his landlord (*R v Smith* (1915) 11 Crim App R 81).

The offence is an absolute one. Accordingly, it is no defence to a prosecution that the bankrupt, before obtaining credit, instructed his agent to inform the person giving credit that he was a bankrupt and had reasonable grounds for believing that the agent had done so (*R v Duke of Leinster* [1924] 1 KB 311). As to what the Crown must prove, see *R v Hayat* (1976) 63 Cr App R 181.

The maximum punishment for offences under this section is two years' imprisonment or a fine or both (on indictment) or six months' imprisonment or a fine of £1000 or both (summary).

12 Failure to keep proper accounts (s 361)

An offence is committed if a bankrupt has been engaged in business in any part of the two-year period prior to the presentation of the petition and he has not kept proper accounting records for his business or has not preserved those records. Proper accounting records mean records containing details of all cash received and paid out, statements of annual stock-taking and details of all stock purchased and sold with such detail of buyers and sellers so as to enable them to be identified (unless retail sale is involved).

Section 355 also makes it an offence if any books or records are concealed from the official receiver or trustee or any books or records are falsified (see above).

No offence is committed under this section when proper books of account are not kept if the total of the bankrupt's unsecured liabilities at the commencement of the bankruptcy does not exceed the limit for small bankruptcies (currently £20,000) or if the bankrupt proves that in the circumstances in which he carried on business, the omission to keep proper accounts was honest and excusable.

The maximum punishment for an offence under this section is two years' imprisonment or a fine or both (on indictment) or six months' imprisonment or a fine of £1000 or both (summary).

13 Gambling (s 362)

The bankrupt is guilty of an offence if, in the two years prior to the presentation of the petition or before the vesting of his property in a trustee, he materially contributed to or increased the extent of his insolvency by gambling or by rash and hazardous speculations. In determining whether or not any speculations were rash and hazardous, his financial position at the time must be considered.

This is an absolute offence (*R v Salter* [1968] 2 QB 793). The maximum punishment for an offence under this section is two years' imprisonment or a fine or both (on indictment) or six months' imprisonment or a fine of £1000 or both (summary).

14 Being a director of a limited company

It is an offence under s 11 of the Company Directors Disqualification Act 1986 for an undischarged bankrupt to act as a director of, or directly or indirectly to take part in or be concerned in the management of, a company without leave of the court by which he was made bankrupt. Being concerned in the management of a company is a very wide phrase and was deliberately widely cast. It virtually makes it impossible for a person to be part of a management team which directs in any way the affairs of a company. The prohibition extends to being a consultant, not being involved in the day-to-day management of the company but merely giving advice to the directors (*Re Campbell* [1984] BCLC 83).

The maximum punishment for an offence under this section is two years' imprisonment or a fine or both (on indictment) or six months' imprisonment or a fine of £1000 or both (summary).

It is also an offence for an undischarged bankrupt to act as a receiver or manager of a company on the appointment of a debenture holder except with leave of the court (s 31).

15 Contempt of court

In addition to the offences listed in this chapter, the bankrupt is also liable to be arrested and punished for contempt of court if he fails to do as he was directed by the court (see Chapter 21).

16 Evidence

The transcript of the bankrupt's public examination may be used against him in criminal proceedings. Admissions made by the bankrupt at his preliminary examination in the presence of the official receiver or his examiner may also be used in evidence against him (*R v Tuttle* (1929) 140 LT 701; see also *R v Maywhort* [1955] 1 WLR 848). However, neither the transcript nor any statements made at an examination in court can be used as evidence in proceedings against the maker of the statements or spouse in proceedings under the Theft Act 1968.

17 Criminal court action

Until 1988, the court had power after the conviction of an offender for an offence involving £15,000 or more of loss or damage to make a criminal bankruptcy order against that offender. The Director of Public Prosecutions could then petition for the bankruptcy of the offender (Powers of the Criminal Courts Act 1973). There is no longer any such power though the criminal courts do have analogous powers to make a confiscation order or a restraint order under ss 71 and 77 of the Administration of Justice Act 1988. The court can make a restraint order to prevent an accused from disposing of his property prior to the conclusion of the criminal proceedings.

The court can appoint a receiver to realise the property of the offender in such manner as it directs and can impose a charge on that property until payment is obtained (s 80 above).

If the offender is adjudged bankrupt, any property subject to a restraint order and any proceeds of sale of property realised by a receiver are excluded from the bankrupt's estate (s 84(1)). If the offender is adjudged bankrupt before the making of the restraint order or the appointment of a receiver, then s 84(1) does not apply. No order can be made under s 339 or s 423 (avoidance of transactions at an undervalue or transactions defrauding creditors) while criminal proceedings which might result in a confiscation order, restraint or charging order are pending (s 84(6)). If a trustee in bankruptcy sells property which unbeknown to him is subject to a restraint or charging order, he will not be liable for any loss resulting from its disposal (unless he was negligent) and he is also entitled to a lien on the proceeds of sale for his expenses in connection with its disposal (s 87).

Chapter 21

Powers of the Court

1 General powers of the court

Every bankruptcy is under the general control of the court and the court has full power to decide all questions of priorities and all other questions arising in any bankruptcy (s 363(1)).

A bankrupt must do everything he is directed to do by the court for the purposes of his bankruptcy and the administration of his estate (s 363(2)). If he fails to do so, he is guilty of contempt of court and is liable to be punished accordingly (s 363(4)). The official receiver and trustee can apply to the court for a direction requiring the bankrupt to comply with their instructions (s 363(3)).

2 Power of arrest (s 364)

The court can issue a warrant for the arrest of a debtor against whom a bankruptcy petition has been presented, an undischarged bankrupt or a discharged bankrupt whose estate is still being administered in the following circumstances:

(1) Where there are reasonable grounds for believing that he has absconded or is about to abscond with a view to avoiding or delaying payment of his debts, to avoiding his appearance to a bankruptcy petition or to disrupting, delaying or avoiding any proceedings in his bankruptcy.
(2) Where he is about to remove any of his property with a view to preventing his trustee taking possession of it.
(3) Where there are reasonable grounds for believing that he has concealed or destroyed or is about to conceal or destroy any of his goods or books and records which might be of use to his creditors or in connection with the administration of his estate.
(4) Where he has removed any goods in his possession of more than the prescribed value (currently £500) without the leave of his trustee.
(5) Where he has failed, without reasonable excuse, to attend any examination ordered by the court.

A warrant under this section can be issued by the High Court or county court. In the case of the High Court the warrant is issued to the tipstaff and in the case of the county court to the district judge and the bailiffs (r 7.21).

When arrested, the debtor or bankrupt is taken into custody and kept there until such time as the court otherwise orders and must be produced to the court as it from time to time directs (r 7.22).

3 Seizure of the bankrupt's property (s 365)

At any time after a bankruptcy order has been made, the court can, on the application of the official receiver or trustee, issue a warrant for the seizure of any property comprised in the bankrupt's estate still in his possession or in the possession of any other person and for the seizure of any books or records relating to the bankrupt's estate.

For the purpose of executing such a warrant, any premises where it is suspected such property or books and records are situated or where the bankrupt is, can be broken into. Likewise, a search warrant can be issued directed to a constable or proper officer of the court (tipstaff or bailiff) where the court is satisfied that any property comprised in the bankrupt's estate or any books and records relating to it have been concealed in any premises not belonging to the bankrupt. It is provided in s 365(4) that such a warrant must not be executed except in the prescribed manner but no manner of execution is set out in the Act or the Rules. But before the warrant is issued, the court will have to be satisfied, presumably by affidavit evidence, that such a warrant is necessary in the circumstances.

4 Inquiry into the bankrupt's dealings and property

At any time after the making of a bankruptcy order, on the application of the official receiver or trustee, the court can summon to appear before it the bankrupt, his spouse or former spouse and any person believed to have any property belonging to the bankrupt or to be indebted to the bankrupt and any person appearing to the court to have any information concerning the bankrupt, his dealings, affairs or property. The court may require any such person to submit an affidavit concerning his dealings with the bankrupt and to produce any documents in his possession or under his control relating to the bankrupt, his dealings, affairs or property. It would appear that the preparation of an affidavit can be required before the first attendance at court by the examinee rather than as a result of the first attendance (s 366).

Under r 9.6(4), a reasonable sum for travelling expenses must be tendered to the examinee to enable him to get to court for the examination. It is not necessary for any other sums, for example, witness allowance, to be tendered. These are dealt with by the court at the examination in its discretion.

The court can order that such an examination be held in any part of the United Kingdom where he may be for the time being or in any place outside the United Kingdom (s 367(3)). Notwithstanding the provision for the examination to be held abroad, it has been doubted whether such orders are valid and enforceable. In *Re Tucker* [1990] 1 All ER 603 it was held that an order for the examination in England of the bankrupt's brother who, though English, lived abroad, could not be served abroad. This dictum has been criticised and in the light of the decision in *Re Seagull* [1991] 4 All ER 257 may not be good law. The examinee is not entitled to invoke the privilege against self-incrimination (*Bishopsgate Investment Managers v Maxwell* [1992] 2 All ER 856. In May 1993 The Law Society issued a revision to its guide on professional conduct as to the position of a solicitor who had acted for a client who subsequently became bankrupt and the handing over to the official receiver or trustee of information and files relating to that client. The Law Society has concluded that a solicitor is under a duty by virtue of ss 311 and 312 to deliver up to the official receiver or trustee papers belonging to the bankrupt and this includes privileged communications. Even if the solicitor has not been paid his fees for advice given, the solicitor's lien on the papers will be of no use to him because of the provisions of s 366 and the effect of *Re Aveling Barford* ([1988] 3 All ER 1019).

Where a transaction is being attacked under s 423 (see Chapter 9, **1** above) a solicitor acting for the transferor, whether bankrupt or not, will have to give discovery of communications between the transferor and himself and cannot claim professional privilege (*Barclays Bank v Eustice* [1995] 1 WLR 1238).

If the proposed examinee fails to attend court to be examined without reasonable excuse, or there are reasonable grounds for believing that he has absconded or is about to abscond with a view to avoiding his appearance at court, then he can be arrested and kept in custody until brought before the court. Any relevant property, books or records can also be seized.

If, at an examination, it appears to the court that the examinee is indebted to the bankrupt or has any property belonging to the bankrupt, the court can order that the debt be paid or the property handed over to the trustee (s 367).

There are special rules relating to information which the Inland Revenue can give regarding the bankrupt's affairs. An Inland Revenue official can be summoned to appear in court and s 369 and rr 6.194 to 196 set out the applicable law and practice.

When an interim receiver has been appointed under s 286, the powers conferred by ss 366 and 367 can be exercised by the interim receiver in the same way as they can be exercised by the official receiver or trustee after the making of a bankruptcy order (s 369).

5 Special manager (s 370)

The court may, on the application of the official receiver or trustee, appoint any person to be the special manager of the estate or business of a bankrupt, or the special manager of the property or business of a debtor where an interim receiver has been appointed. Such an order will be made where it appears to the court that the nature of the estate, property or business, or the interests of creditors, require the appointment.

The special manager's powers are only those which the court gives him but the court can direct that his powers are to be the same as those of the official receiver, trustee or interim receiver (s 370(3) and (4)). The special manager must give security and produce accounts of his dealings with the bankrupt's property.

6 Redirection of mail (s 371)

After a bankruptcy order has been made, the court may, on the application of the official receiver or trustee, order the Post Office to redirect the bankrupt's mail to the official receiver or trustee. The order cannot be for a longer period than three months but can be renewed from time to time.

Chapter 22

Appeals

1 General

Every court having jurisdiction in bankruptcy can review, rescind or vary any order made by it (s 375(1)). However, this rule does not give jurisdiction for an order made by a county court district judge to be reviewed, rescinded or varied by the judge (*Re Maugham, ex p Maugham* (1888) 21 QBD 21). The correct remedy is for the order complained of to be appealed against.

An appeal from a decision of either the county court district or circuit judge or from a decision of a registrar in bankruptcy of the High Court lies to a single judge of the High Court and an appeal from a decision of that judge lies, with the leave of the judge or of the Court of Appeal, to the Court of Appeal (s 375(2)). The appeal is not a hearing *de novo* at which the judge exercises his own discretion. It is necessary to show that there has been an error of principle or law in the way the registrar or district judge exercised his discretion (*Re Gilmartin* (1988) *The Independent*, 21 November). An appeal from a judge of the High Court sitting in bankruptcy at first instance lies to the Court of Appeal pursuant to s 16 of the Supreme Court Act 1981.

An appeal from the Court of Appeal to the House of Lords is now possible either with the leave of the Court of Appeal or of the House of Lords itself.

Appeals can also be brought against certain decisions of the Secretary of State and the official receiver. Such appeals must be made within 28 days of the notification of the decision complained of (r 7.50) and are treated as applications to the registrar in bankruptcy in the High Court or the county court.

In the North and North-eastern Circuits, appeals normally go to the Vice Chancellor of the County Palatine Court of Lancaster sitting in Liverpool, Manchester, Preston, Leeds or Newcastle. In areas covered by the Birmingham, Bristol and Cardiff Chancery District Registries, appeals are heard in those cities. But appeals from these areas can be set down in London. A Practice Direction deals with the procedure for appeals including what documents are required, time limits and where to lodge documents (*Practice Direction, No 1 of 1995 (Insolvency Appeals: Individuals)* [1995] BCC 1129).

Decisions of the Secretary of State and the official receiver which can be appealed against include the following:

(1) A decision of the official receiver not to refer the need for the appointment of a trustee to the Secretary of State or the Secretary of State's decision not to appoint (s 295(3) and r 6.122).
(2) A decision of the Secretary of State to appoint or not to appoint an outside trustee (s 296(2) and r 6.122).
(3) A decision of the Secretary of State to remove a trustee appointed by him (s 298(5)).
(4) A decision by the Secretary of State not to release a trustee removed by creditors or one who had vacated office (s 299).
(5) A decision by the Secretary of State to appoint or not to appoint a trustee in a summary administration case (s 300(6)).
(6) A decision of the Secretary of State acting as a creditors' committee (acting through the official receiver) (r 6.166(2)).
(7) A decision by the Secretary of State to remove the trustee (r 6.133).
(8) A decision by the Secretary of State refusing the trustee his release (r 6.135(4)).
(9) A decision of the official receiver as chairman of a meeting of creditors in relation to a creditor's right to vote or proof of debt.

2 Who may appeal

Appeals against decisions by courts exercising bankruptcy jurisdiction can be made by:
(a) the debtor or bankrupt;
(b) the petitioning creditor in the case of the refusal to make a bankruptcy order;
(c) any creditor against decisions affecting his proof of debt or the decision of the chairman of any meeting as to his right to vote at that meeting and against any decision relating to the rescission or annulment of a bankruptcy order and the granting to the bankrupt of his discharge;
(d) the Secretary of State in relation to orders for the rescission or annulment of a bankruptcy order or the bankrupt's discharge (r 7.48(1));
(e) the trustee or official receiver acting as trustee in respect of any matter affecting the administration of the estate or his remuneration.

3 Rehearing

A court having bankruptcy jurisdiction can review, rescind or vary its own order (s 375). This section confers on the court the power of rehearing but proceedings under it are not by way of appeal. No time limit is fixed in the Act or Rules for bringing the application for review, but as a general rule a rehearing after the expiry of the time limited for appealing from an order will be approached by the court by reference to the principles governing applications for leave to appeal out of time.

On a rehearing, the court is not bound simply to reconsider the evidence adduced at the original hearing but may, in an appropriate case, entertain fresh evidence (*Re Cohen* [1950] 2 All ER 36). The court may, however, take the view that if the 'fresh' evidence was available at the time of the original hearing, it should view it now with more scepticism and even if the original order is reversed, may decide to deprive the party who failed to adduce that evidence originally of the costs which otherwise he would have been entitled to.

Rehearing is an indulgence and the power is exercised with caution; otherwise parties would gain by indirect means the benefit of an appeal after the time for appealing had expired (*Re Jeavons, ex p Brown* (1874) 9 Ch App 304).

An application for a rehearing should be supported by an affidavit. Such an application should never be made *ex parte*.

4 Time limits

There is no time limit provided in the Act or the Rules for application for the review, rescission or variation of an order under s 375. However, see above for the attitude of the court to such an application made after the time for appealing had expired.

Appeals both from the county court to a judge of the Chancery Division and appeals from the High Court to the Court of Appeal are regulated by Ord 59 of the RSC. Order 59 provides that the notice of appeal must be served within four weeks from the date on which the judgment or order of the court below was signed, entered or otherwise perfected, or in the case of the refusal of an application, from the date of the refusal. The appeal must then be set down within seven days by producing to the court the required documents.

The time for appealing against the order runs from the date the order is perfected, so that if an order is perfected on the signature of the registrar, the time for appealing runs from the date of the signature (*Re Helsby, ex p Trustee* [1894] 1 QB 742).

The court is given a very general power in s 376, to extend the time, either before or after it has expired, for doing anything required by the Act or the Rules. The court can extend time on such terms as it thinks fit. The effect of this section is not to enable all the time limits to be ignored with impunity but to give the court power to extend time in appropriate cases. On an application for leave to appeal out of time, that is, for the time limit within which to appeal to be disregarded, the court is likely to have regard to the following factors:

(a) whether there is a reasonable excuse for the delay;
(b) whether there is any substance in the proposed appeal;
(c) whether the applicant will obtain any real benefit if the appeal succeeds;
(d) whether it would be a hardship or an injustice to other parties if the application were granted; and
(e) whether the applicant's conduct has been such as to forfeit any claim to favourable consideration of the exercise of the court's discretion (*per* Cairns LJ in *Re Benson* (*a Debtor*) (1971) 8 March, unreported)).

The Court of Appeal has refused to extend time for appealing against a bankruptcy order (then a receiving order) which had been wrongly made because the applicant was hopelessly insolvent and no useful purpose would therefore have been served by allowing an appeal against the order to proceed (*Re Noble (a Bankrupt*) [1965] Ch 129). When considering an application for leave to appeal out of time against a bankruptcy order, the registrar of bankruptcy appeals was not entitled to consider and deal with the application as if on a mini-trial but had to satisfy himself that the appeal was unarguable or doomed to failure, the onus being on the respondent to the application (*Re a Debtor (No 799 of 1994*) [1995] 3 All ER 723).

5 Procedure

The procedure for appeals from the county court to a judge of the Chancery Division and from the High Court to the Court of Appeal are now the same, both governed by Ord 59 of the RSC. Reference should also be made to the *Practice Direction* referred to in **1** above.

The notice of appeal

The notice of appeal (for a precedent of which, see Supreme Court Practice 1995) is the document used to commence an appeal. It must state whether the whole or part only of the order is complained of and if only part, then which part of the order must be specified. The grounds of appeal should be stated but the court can allow a notice of appeal to be amended and a ground not specified in the notice of appeal to be relied upon. The order which the appellant proposes to ask the court to make in place of the order appealed against should also be stated.

Service of the notice of appeal

The notice of appeal must be served on all parties directly affected by the appeal. The court can direct that notice of appeal be served on any party and in the meantime may postpone or adjourn the hearing of the appeal on such terms as may be just. If the appeal is against the making of a bankruptcy order, the official receiver as well as the petitioning creditor must be served with the appeal. He is an essential party to such an appeal but he ought not to appear at the hearing of the appeal unless there are material circumstances which he desires to bring before the court (*Re Webber, ex p Webber* (1889) 24 QBD 313). Likewise, if the appeal against the bankruptcy order is made after a trustee has been appointed, he should be served with the notice of appeal but should not appear at the hearing of the appeal unless he can assist the court (*Re Arden, ex p Arden* (1884) 14 QBD 121).

The notice of appeal need not be served personally, it can be sent by post or if solicitors are acting and are on the record, via the document exchange.

Respondent's notice

If the respondent to an appeal wishes to contend that the order appealed against should be varied, either in any event or in the event of the appeal being allowed in whole or in part, or that the decision of the court below should be affirmed on grounds other than those relied on by that court, he should serve a respondent's notice within 21 days after service on him of the notice of appeal (and lodge copies of his notice with the court within two days thereafter).

Setting down

Within seven days after the service of the notice of appeal (or such further time as the court may allow), the appellant must set down the appeal and within two days after setting down give notice of the setting down to all other parties to the appeal.

To set down an appeal, the appellant will require copies of the notice of appeal, the order appealed from and a copy of any list of exhibits used at the original hearing. A fee will also have to be paid which is currently £25 (if to a single judge of the High Court) or £120 (if to the Court of Appeal).

Documents

Not more than 14 days after the appeal first appears in the list of forthcoming appeals, the appellant must lodge with the court copies of all the necessary documents, including the notice of appeal and any amendments to it, the respondent's notice (if any), the order appealed against, all documents used at the original hearing, all originating process and affidavits in the case, such parts of the transcript of the original hearing as are relevant to the issue in the appeal and the registrar's or judge's notes. In the case of an appeal to the Court of Appeal, three sets of all the documents must be provided for the court, otherwise only one set is required. All the documents must be paginated and placed in some suitable form of binding, and an index must be provided. All transcripts lodged must be originals, not unofficial copies. Where no official transcript of the judgment was taken and the registrar or judge did not make a note of his own judgment, counsel or solicitors who appeared at the original hearing must prepare an agreed note of the judgment and submit it to the registrar or judge for approval and this should be included in the bundle of documents lodged with the court. As it may take some time to get the note of judgment prepared, agreed and approved, the process should be started as soon as possible after the appeal has been entered.

Security for costs

The court can, in special circumstances, order that security for the costs of an appeal be given as may be just (Ord 59, r 10(5)). For the considerations to be applied in application for security for costs, see Ord 23.

Stay of execution

An appeal does not operate as a stay of execution of the order appealed against and if a stay pending hearing of the appeal is desired and the respondent to the appeal is not prepared to consent to a stay, an application for such a stay must be made, either to the court which made the order the subject of the appeal or to the appellate court.

Hearing

The appeal is by way of rehearing and the court has power to receive further evidence on questions of fact, either orally or by affidavit. But fresh evidence will only be admitted on special grounds and the court will not normally allow fresh evidence to be used if the party tendering it had the opportunity of adducing it in the court below but elected not to do so (*Re Wike, ex p Keighley* (1874) 9 Ch App 667).

The court has power to draw inferences of fact, to give any judgment and make any order which ought to have been made and to make any further order which the case may require. These powers may be exercised notwithstanding that the appeal is against part only of the decision or that the respondent or party in whose favour they are exercised has not appealed from or complained of the decision.

Chapter 23

Control of the Trustee

1 Control by the creditors

General

The creditors have a general control over the administration of the bankrupt's estate and its distribution. It is with the creditors that the choice of trustee lies. The creditors have the power to apply to the court for the trustee's removal (see Chapter 11). The creditors can also appoint a creditors' committee and Sched 5 to the Act sets out those powers which the trustee can only exercise with the sanction of the creditors' committee, if there is one, or if there is no committee with the sanction of a general meeting of creditors. See Chapter 13, **8**. Only the power to sell any of the assets of the bankrupt or to prove in the bankruptcy or liquidation of one of the bankrupt's debtors can be exercised by the trustee without sanction.

If the trustee does anything requiring sanction without having obtained prior sanction, the creditors' committee can ratify his actions retrospectively to enable him to meet his expenses out of the estate but only if satisfied that he acted in a case of urgency and sought ratification without undue delay (s 314(4)). Formerly the trustee needed sanction even to employ a solicitor or agent to act on his behalf. Now, the trustee need only inform the creditors' committee of the fact that he has employed a solicitor or disposed of any of the bankrupt's assets to an associate of the bankrupt after he has done those acts (s 314(6)).

Where there is no creditors' committee and the trustee is someone other than the official receiver, the functions of the committee are exercised by the Secretary of State of the Department of Trade and Industry (s 302(2)).

Remuneration

It is the creditors' committee which fixes the remuneration of the trustee. The committee can decide to allow the trustee to charge a fee based on the value of the assets of the estate or based on the time spent. If the trustee's fee is to be based on the value of the assets, the committee can decide what percentage of the value of the assets the trustee is to receive by way of fee. The percentage can be applied to the value of assets realised or distributed or both. If there is no creditors' committee, the trustee's remuneration can be fixed by a resolution of a general meeting of creditors. If the trustee's remuneration is not fixed by the methods referred to above, then his fees are to be calculated on the scale laid down for the official receiver when he is the trustee (r 6.138). If the trustee is not satisfied with the decision of the committee, then he can request that it be increased by a resolution of the creditors (r 6.140). If still not satisfied, the trustee can apply to the court (r 6.141). Any creditor can apply to the court, provided that 25 per cent in value of all creditors are party to the application, for the trustee's remuneration to be reduced on the grounds that it is excessive (r 6.142).

Notwithstanding that the trustee is satisfied that the fees and disbursements of the solicitors he has employed are reasonable, the creditors' committee can resolve that those fees and disbursements be taxed by the court (r 7.34(2)).

Any creditor can apply to the court for the decision of the trustee on any matter to be reversed or modified if dissatisfied by the act, omission or decision of the trustee (s 303(1)). The trustee can himself apply to the court for directions in relation to any matter arising in the bankruptcy administration (s 303(2)).

On the request of any creditor the trustee must send a copy of an account of his receipts and payments for any period free of charge (Insolvency Regulations 1986, para 13).

2 Control by the court

As mentioned above, any creditor dissatisfied with the acts, omissions or decision of the trustee can apply to the court. The court on such application can confirm, reverse or modify the act or decision of the trustee and may give him directions or make any other order as it thinks fit (s 303(1)). The bankrupt and any other person (not being a creditor) also have this right though it has been held that unless there was a surplus after the payment of all creditors and costs or a real probability of a surplus which the trustee's actions might diminish or eliminate, the bankrupt himself could not challenge the trustee's actions (*Ex p Lloyd* (1882) 47 LT 64 and *Re a Debtor (No 400 of 1940)* [1940] Ch 236). In *Re a Debtor* (above) it was also held that the court would not, in the absence of fraud, interfere on the application of a bankrupt in the day-to-day administration of the estate or hold the trustee liable for an error of judgment made in good faith in respect of a matter within his discretion.

The trustee's decisions on proofs of debt are subject to appeal to the court under r 6.105 (see Chapter 15).

3 Control by the Department of Trade and Industry

The trustee is subject to control by the Department of Trade and Industry as a result of regulations made by the Secretary of State affecting monetary aspects of the trustee's administration. Under the Insolvency Rules 1986, the trustee is obliged to pay all monies received by him into the Insolvency Services Account kept by the Secretary of State with the Bank of England. Monies must be remitted every 14 days or if £5000 or more is received, then it must be remitted immediately. Monies can be drawn out of the account to meet the proper expenses of the administration and dividends but proper vouchers evidencing all expenses have to be produced before a cheque will be drawn. The main drawback to using this account is the fee which is charged on all sums paid into the account. These fees are based on a sliding scale starting at 15 per cent and reducing to 2 per cent. In addition, no interest is paid on the balance deposited. The trustee can apply for authorisation to operate a local bank account where he intends to carry on the bankrupt's business and the Secretary of State can authorise this where some administrative advantage will be derived. If the trustee fails to pay money into the Insolvency Services Account as required, he is required to pay interest on the monies withheld at the rate of 20 per cent per annum plus any expenses incurred as a result of his default.

The trustee must keep proper records of his administration, that is, minutes of all creditors' or creditors' committee meetings and all appropriate financial records. He must send to the Secretary of State an account of all his receipts and payments every year. An account must also be submitted when the administration comes to an end. If so required by the Secretary of State, the trustee must send all vouchers and books so that the accounts submitted can be audited.

4 The rule in *ex p James*

This principle, first enunciated in *Re Condon, ex p James* (1874) 9 Ch App 609, is that a court in bankruptcy will not allow its officer, the trustee in bankruptcy, to retain or claim monies for distribution amongst the creditors when it would be inconsistent with natural justice to do so and something which an honest man would not do. The leading modern authority on the application of the rule is *Re Clark (a Bankrupt)* [1975] 1 WLR 559 where all the earlier cases were considered. In that case, Walton J laid down the following principles:

(1) There must be some form of enrichment of the assets of the bankrupt by the person seeking to have the rule applied.
(2) Except in the most unusual cases, the claimant must not be in a position to submit an ordinary proof of debt.
(3) The crucial test is whether in all the circumstances of the case an honest man personally affected by the result would nevertheless be bound to admit that it would be unfair that he should keep the money and that his claim had no merits.
(4) When the rule does apply, it applies only to the extent necessary to nullify the enrichment of the estate.

Where the rule operates in favour of a party who would otherwise suffer injustice, it derogates from the rights of other parties interested in the assets available for distribution in the bankruptcy (*Re T H Knitwear (Wholesale) Ltd* (1988) 4 BCC 102).

5 Maintenance and Champerty

It has been established for 100 years that the principles of maintenance and champerty do not apply to trustees in bankruptcy such that they can sell causes of action on terms that some part of the fruits of success come back to the estate for division among the creditors. This was reaffirmed in the case of *Ramsey v Hartley* [1977] 1 WLR 686.

Trustees still face difficulty in funding legal actions where there are insufficient assets within the estate to meet the likely costs. Obtaining a fighting fund from creditors is the obvious answer if one can be set up. Legal aid for the estate is also possible if there is likely to be a surplus for the debtor as a result of the successful outcome of the legal action and the debtor can therefore be shown to benefit from it.

Trustees now also have available to them Conditional Fee Agreements. These have been introduced by the Conditional Fee Agreements Order 1995 (SI No 1674) which came into effect on 5 July 1995. Under such agreements, it is proper for a trustee to agree to pay his solicitors a percentage of the amount recovered as a result of successful legal action in addition to the basic time-based fee with the solicitors taking the risk that they will not receive any fee if the action is unsuccessful. Trustees can insure against the liability for the other side's costs if the action is unsuccessful.

Chapter 24

General Procedure

1 Title of proceedings

All proceedings relating to bankruptcy must be entitled 'IN BANKRUPTCY' (r 7.26(2)). See Appendix 3, forms 45 and 46 for the general title of proceedings in both the county court and the High Court.

2 Applications

Rules 7.2 to 7.4 set out the procedure and practice on the filing and service of originating and other applications. It is necessary for the respondent to an application to be served with a sealed copy of an application. Normally an application must be served at least 14 days before the hearing of it, though the court has power to extend or abridge time under s 376, and under r 7.4(6) the court may hear an application immediately, with or without the attendance of the other party, or authorise a shorter period of service. Where the Act or the Rules do not require service of an application, the court may hear it *ex parte* (r 7.5).

Originating applications must be in Form 7.1 in Sched 4 to the Rules. Other applications are to be in Form 7.2 in Sched 4 to the Rules. Both these forms can be found in Appendix 3, forms 36 and 37. An originating application is required when there is not yet a court file relating to the matter in existence. Thus, an application to set aside a statutory demand must be in Form 7.1 because there is no court file in being at the time the application is made. Certain orders if sought by consent can be made *ex parte* (see *Practice Note (Bankruptcy: consent orders) (No 2 of 1992)* ([1992] 1 WLR 379).

3 Hearing of applications

Unless allowed or authorised otherwise, every application before the registrar or district judge must be in chambers and every application before the circuit or High Court judge may be heard in chambers (r 7.6(1)).

All applications are to be made, in the first instance, to the registrar or district judge unless the circuit or High Court judge has given a general or special direction to the contrary or it is not within the registrar's or district judge's power to make the order sought (r 7.6(2)).

The registrar or district judge may refer any matter to the judge that he thinks should properly be decided by the circuit or High Court judge and he can either dispose of the matter or refer it back to the registrar or district judge (r 7.6(3)).

Nothing in r 7.6 precludes an application being made directly to a circuit or High Court judge in a proper case (r 7.6(4)).

4 Transfer of proceedings

Proceedings can be transferred to and from the High Court to the county court or from one county court to another (r 7.11). If proceedings are commenced in the wrong court, the court can transfer them to the right court, allow them to continue where they are or strike them out (r 7.12).

5 Evidence

Evidence may be given by affidavit but the court may order the attendance of the deponent for cross-examination and if he does not attend, his affidavit may only be used with leave of the court (r 7.7). Affidavits should be filed by the applicant at least 14 days before the hearing at which they are to be used so that the respondent can file his affidavit not later than seven days before the hearing (r 7.8). The court has power to extend or abridge time under s 376 as mentioned in **2** above.

A report may be filed instead of an affidavit by the official receiver or trustee (r 7.9). Such reports are to be treated as if they were affidavits.

6 Fee on issue

The fee on all applications to a registrar or district judge is £20. The fee on all applications to a circuit or High Court judge is £20. These fees apply unless there is express provision for some other fee to apply.

7 Enforcement

Orders in bankruptcy proceedings are enforced in the same manner as a judgment and one court can enforce the order of another court (r 7.19).

The court can make such orders as it thinks fit for the enforcement of the duty to submit a statement of affairs and similar duties (r 7.20).

Warrants, addressed to the High Court tipstaff or the county court registrar and bailiff, can be issued to arrest a bankrupt where there are reasonable grounds for believing that he may abscond with a view to avoiding or delaying payment of his debts or his appearance to a petition or to avoiding, delaying or disrupting any proceedings against him or any examination of his affairs (s 364(1) and r 7.21). Similarly warrants can be issued to arrest any person required to attend court and answer questions relating to the bankrupt under s 366 (r 7.23).

These warrants can also be addressed to any constable (r 7.21).

8 Computation of time

Where the last day for doing any act or taking a proceeding is a Sunday, Christmas Day, Good Friday or Monday or Tuesday in Easter week, or on a day on which the offices of the court are closed, the act or proceeding may be done or taken on the next day afterwards which is not one of the aforesaid days.

Where by the Act or the Rules the time limited for doing any act is less than seven days, Saturday, Sunday, Christmas Day, Good Friday, Monday and Tuesday in Easter week, Bank Holidays and any other day on which the offices of the court are closed must be excluded in computing such time. If served after 4 pm, the document is deemed served on the next day.

RSC Ord 3 (except rr 3 and 6) applies as regards the computation of time (r 12.9).

The court may extend or abridge the time appointed by the Rules for doing any act or taking any step in the proceedings either before or after the time has elapsed (s 376).

9 Service by post

Any document which is to be served by post is properly served if sent by ordinary prepaid post. Where first class post is used, the document is treated as served two days after it was posted. Where second class post is used, the document is treated as served four days after it was posted (r 12.10).

10 Access to court file

The trustee, the debtor and any person stating in writing that he is a creditor may, at all reasonable times, inspect the file of proceedings (r 7.31).

If the registrar or district judge of the court is not satisfied as to the propriety of the purpose of the inspection, he may refuse it. A circuit or High Court judge on an *ex parte* application can allow inspection (r 7.28(2)).

11 Paper, forms etc

RSC Ord 66, r 1 requires all documents for use in the High Court to be on ISO A4 size paper of durable quality. All the printed bankruptcy forms available from law stationers, whether for use in the High Court or county court, are A4 size and this size of paper should be used for all bankruptcy documents.

The forms set out in Sched 4 to the Rules must be used in bankruptcy proceedings with such variations, if any, as the circumstances require (r 12.7).

Old forms, even those which are substantially the same as the forms prescribed under the Rules, can no longer be used.

12 Costs rules

Subject to any provisions of inconsistent effect, RSC Ord 62 applies to bankruptcy proceedings in the High Court and CCR Ord 38 applies to bankruptcy proceedings in a county court (r 7.33).

There is no requirement for costs payable out of the bankrupt's estate to be taxed, be they the costs of the petitioning creditor or the costs of the solicitors acting for the trustee (r 7.34). The official receiver or trustee can agree costs though if there is a creditors' committee, it can require the trustee to ask for any costs payable out of the estate to be taxed.

In any proceedings before the court, including proceedings on a petition, the court may order costs to be taxed (r 7.34(4)). It would therefore seem desirable that the order for costs on the making of a bankruptcy order should be that the petitioning creditor's costs '*to be agreed or taxed*' be paid out of the estate.

If an order requiring taxation of costs is made and a bill is not lodged for taxation within three months or such further time as the court may allow, the right to costs is forfeited (r 7.35).

Unless otherwise directed or authorised, the costs of a trustee are to be allowed on the standard basis (r 7.34(5)).

There is no scale of costs in the Rules and reference should therefore be had to the fees and disbursements allowed in High Court and county court matters generally.

The official receiver or trustee can require the sheriff to tax his costs where the sheriff is entitled to costs as a result of insolvency overtaking an execution (r 7.36).

13 Review

The court has the unusual power to review, rescind or vary its own orders under s 375. See Chapter 9 for more on this subject.

Chapter 25

Insolvent Partnerships

1 Introduction

The rules relating to insolvent partnerships are set out in the Insolvent Partnerships Order 1994 (SI No 2421) (referred to in this chapter as the IPO) which came into force on 1 December 1994 and replaced the 1986 Order which was revoked from that date. The new Order introduced two new concepts into insolvent partnership law but otherwise continued the old rules of procedures albeit by insertion into the Act rather than in the IPO itself. There are three Schedules to the IPO.

Insolvent partnerships are treated as unregistered companies for the purpose of the insolvency legislation and can be wound up accordingly. Individual partners can also be made the subject of bankruptcy orders or, if they are corporate members of a partnership, the subject of winding up orders. A partnership can now propose a Partnership Voluntary Arrangement (PVA) in the same way as a company can propose a Company Voluntary Arrangement under Part I of the Act. Likewise, a partnership can apply to the court for a Partnership Administration Order (PAO) just as a company can under Part II of the Act. Any petition against the partnership for its winding up must be in the court having jurisdiction to wind up companies of that size and not the bankruptcy court, whereas the petition against the individual members must be in the appropriate bankruptcy court which may or may not be in the same town.

In accordance with s 175A (inserted by IPO), where a partnership is being wound up, the partnership assets are first to be used to meet the partnership liabilities, with any surplus then going to meet any shortfall in the personal liabilities of the partners. If there is a shortfall, it passes over to the separate estates of the partners where it ranks *pari passu* with the separate debts of the partners (s 175A(5)(*b*)).

Since a partnership, when wound up, is treated very much like a company, the partners are liable to disqualification from acting as directors of a company under the Company Directors Disqualification Act 1986 in the same way as directors of insolvent companies.

For the practice and procedure for winding up an insolvent partnership as an unregistered company after the presentation of a winding up petition, see

Steven A Frieze, *Compulsory Winding Up Procedure*, (Longman 3rd edn, 1991). This book will deal only with the procedure up to and including the petition. For more about PVAs and PAOs see *Insolvency* (FTLT).

From a creditor's point of view there are four alternative ways of dealing with an insolvent partnership. They are to:

(a) wind up the partnership;
(b) wind up the partnership and make the individual partners bankrupt (or in the case of a corporate partner, put it into compulsory liquidation, though for the purposes of these notes only the bankruptcy of non-corporate partners will be discussed);
(c) make the individual partners bankrupt without the making of any insolvency order against the partnership as such; or
(d) make one or more of the individual partners bankrupt without making all of them bankrupt and without making any insolvency order against the partnership.

The partnership and its partners can propose a PVA or apply for a PAO or the partners can present a petition to wind up the partnership with or without bankruptcy petitions against themselves or some of them.

2 Winding up of an insolvent partnership

A creditor may issue a winding up petition against the partnership in the same way as a creditor may present a petition for the compulsory winding up of a company. If a statutory demand has to be served to base such a petition, it must be in the prescribed form and served on the partnership and on one or more of the partners. The prescribed form of the statutory demand is Form 4.1 in Sched 9 to the IPO. The partnershp has no right to apply to have the statutory demand set aside but the individual partners (if not corporate entities) do have the right. There is no prescribed form of petition for a creditor to wind up a partnership as an unregistered company. A creditor's petition to wind up the partnership presented in conjunction with a petition against a corporate member is Form 6 in Sched 9 to the IPO and in conjunction with a bankruptcy petition against the individual members of the partnership is Form 6. The bankruptcy petition itself is Form 7 (see Appendix 3, form 39).

If the partners themselves wish to have the partnership wound up and if an individual partner, with or without the consent of the other partners, wishes to have the partnership wound up, a winding up petition can be presented provided that (s 221A):

(a) the partnership consists of eight or more partners; or
(b) in the case of a petition presented by one partner, he has obtained the leave of the court to petition having satisfied the court that he has obtained a judgment against the partnership for a debt not less than £750 owed by the partnership to him, the court is satisfied that all reasonable steps to enforce the judgment have been taken and he has served a statutory demand in Form 10 in Sched 9 to the IPO. If such a petition

is presented by a liquidator or trustee of an insolvent partnership, that petition must be in Form 3 in Sched 9 to the IPO.

A partnership is insolvent if, as an entity, it is unable to pay its debts as they fall due or if its assets when realised would be insufficient to discharge its liabilities. It will not be insolvent if one or more of its members is or are insolvent individually but the partnership itself is able to pay its debts or has assets which exceed its liabilities *(Re Hough* (1990) *The Independent,* 26 April).

3 Winding up the partnership and making the individual partners bankrupt

There will be at least three petitions if this alternative is chosen. One petition will be against the partnership itself—for its winding up (for the procedure, see above)—and the other petitions will be against the two or more individual partners. If the partners are corporate members, the petitions will be winding up petitions. Otherwise they will be petitions for bankruptcy orders. The only grounds for the petition against the partnership are that the partnership is unable to pay its debts as evidenced by the failure to pay a debt exceeding £750 and to comply with a statutory demand served on the partnership and the individual partners against whom it is desired to present bankruptcy petitions. The demand must be in the prescribed form, Form 4 in Sched 9 to the IPO (see Appendix 3, form 38). The petition must be in Form 5 in Sched 9 to the IPO together with a winding up petition against the corporate member (Form 6 in Sched 9 to the IPO) or a bankruptcy petition against each of the individual members (Form 7 in Sched 9 to the IPO).

The petition against a non-corporate partner must be in Form 7 in Sched 3 to the IPO (see Appendix 3, form 39). It too must be presented to the same court as the winding up petition against the partnership. There is a prerequisite that there be an outstanding debt of the partnership of at least £750 for which a statutory demand has been served which has not been complied with. It is open to a partner served with such a demand to apply for it to be set aside, unlike the partnership itself or a corporate partner. The demand must include details of the court to which an application to set aside can be made. This court will not necessarily be the closest court to the recipient of the demand since any proceedings relating to an insolvent partnership must be taken in the court for the area of the principal place of business of the partnership.

As regards the partnership, the demand can be served at the principal place of business of the partnership, on the individual member, or on any other partner or person having at the time of service control of the partnership business there, provided that:

(1) A judgment has been obtained against the individual partner or the partnership in respect of the debt.
(2) In the case of a demand served on someone other than the partner against whom it is desired to present a petition, the creditor was entitled to take enforcement action against that partner in respect of the partnership debt

under RSC Ord 81, r 5. The demand must also be served on at least two of the partners.

The provisions with regard to creditors with security (s 269) and expedited petitions (s 270) do not apply. Otherwise the procedure with such petitions is the same as with petitions against individuals' debtors. The petitions against the partners are not advertised even though the petition against the partnership is. Likewise, there is no requirement for a certificate of compliance with the Rules for the bankruptcy petition against the partners whereas there is such a requirement in relation to the winding up petition against the partnership.

The petition against the individual partners can only be heard after the hearing of the winding up petition against the partnership. If a winding up order is made against the partnership, a bankruptcy order does not have to be made in respect of the individual partner against whom a bankruptcy petition has been presented.

The court may also dismiss a bankruptcy petition against an individual partner if it considers it just to do so because of a change in circumstances since the making of the winding up order against the partnership (s 125A(6)).

Questions arise when considering the time limit for the trustee to investigate antecedent transactions entered into by the partnership under the provisions relating to preferences, transactions at an undervalue etc. If the partnership has entered into such a transaction, then the time limit specified by the Act will be determined by reference to the date when the partnership winding up petition was presented and not from the date or dates when the individual bankruptcy petition against each partner was presented.

The rationale behind this rule is that bankruptcy acts as an automatic dissolution of a partnership and the surviving solvent partners or those who have not been served with bankruptcy petitions are entitled to carry on the business of the partnership with a view to winding up its affairs and distributing its assets or apportioning its liabilities. As a result, any creditor who issues bankruptcy petitions against partners one by one and fails to present a petition to wind up the partnership will present the trustee or trustees with an enormous problem in identifying the relevant date for the purposes of assessing which transactions can be investigated.

An individual partner can present a petition for a bankruptcy order against himself because of his inability to meet the partnership debts but only if the partnership has petitioned for a winding up order against itself and all other partners have presented petitions for bankruptcy orders against themselves, except for those partners who are limited partners where there are rules for the provision of security equal to the extent of their liability to avoid their bankruptcy.

4 Partner's own petition for bankruptcy order

This is the equivalent of the debtor's petition in the case of a partnership. It is applicable where the partnership is insolvent but it is not desired to make a winding up order against the partnership. It will be used in the case of small partnerships. Under art 11 of the IPO all the partners must join in with the proceedings. The petition is in Form 10 in Sched 9 to the IPO. It need not be signed by all the partners but if it is not signed by them all, an affidavit by the signatory must be sworn showing that the consent of all the partners has been given. If such a petition is presented, the partners are not treated as directors for the purposes of the Company Directors Disqualification Act 1986 and are not liable to be disqualified from being directors under that Act. They will, however, become bankrupts and as such will not be able to act as directors of companies whilst undischarged.

The petition must be presented to the court which would have jurisdiction to wind up the partnership, namely, the court for the area where the partnership had its principal place of business. There is no requirement for the petition to be accompanied by a statement of affairs as is the case with an individual's debtor's petition. The statement of affairs is lodged at a later date.

There is no provision for the appointment of an insolvency practitioner by the court to consider the possibility of proposing a voluntary arrangement with creditors. No certificate of summary administration can be issued even if the assets and liabilities of the individual partners are within the limits. There is nothing to stop the partners, after a bankruptcy order has been made against them, proposing a voluntary arrangement to their creditors.

The court can transfer the proceedings to the 'home' court of the partners if this would be more convenient but the practice is to wait until the official receiver requests the transfer.

The effect of the bankruptcy order is that the trustees of the partners' individual estate wind up the partnership without a winding up order as such being made. There is an obvious saving in cost by avoiding a multiplicity of actions affecting, in essence, the same matters. As to consolidations of bankruptcy cases where a joint petition by the partners was not presented, see **6** below.

5 Petition against some of the partners

There is no need for a creditor owed money by a partnership to petition either for the winding up of the partnership or the bankruptcy of all the partners. He can simply make demand for payment of the debt owed by the partnership of one or more of the partners and if payment is not forthcoming, present a bankruptcy petition against that partner or those partners without joining the other partners or the partnership itself. If such action is taken, the normal rules of bankruptcy procedure apply.

A prerequisite of being able to make demand for payment against an individual partner is that the creditor was entitled to take enforcement action against that partner under the provisions of RSC Ord 81, r 5.

The disadvantage of using this alternative is that if the partnership has entered into transactions which may be reviewable by a trustee or liquidator, they will not be reviewable unless and until a winding up order is made against the partnership and the relevant date back from which the various time limits are calculated will be the date of presentation of the winding up petition only.

6 Consolidation

Utilising the consolidation provisions of the IPO has all the benefits of winding up the partnership as an unregistered company without presenting a petition under the IPO. Section 303(2A)–(C) provides that where at any time after a winding up or a bankruptcy petition has been presented against any insolvent member of a partnership, the court's attention is drawn to the fact that the person is a member of an insolvent partnership, the court may make an order as to the future conduct of the insolvency proceedings and any such order may apply any provisions of the IPO with any necessary modifications. Where a bankruptcy petition has been presented against more than one individual partner, the court may give directions as to consolidating the proceedings or any of them as it thinks just. Any order or directions consolidating the proceedings may be made or given on the application of the official receiver, any responsible insolvency practitioner or any other interested person and may include provisions as to the administration of the estate of the partnership and in particular as to the joint estate of the partnership and any separate estate of any member.

The effect of s 303(2A)–(C) is that the provisions of the IPO can be introduced into the estate by the 'back door' thereby providing the insolvency practitioner with the framework in which to administer the estates of the bankrupts and their partnership. Under s 303(2A)–(C) it is necessary to draw the court's attention to the fact that the person in question is a member of an insolvent partnership. Clearly if all the partners have bankruptcy petitions pending against them and the petitions are heard at the same time, this will cause little problem. Problems, however, arise where the petitions are given different hearing dates so that for a brief period there is a bankrupt partner with other partners who, although having outstanding petitions against them, will still be in power to wind up the affairs of the insolvent partnership under the terms of the automatic dissolution provisions of the Partnership Act 1890. In this case, and in the absence of any failure to comply with a statutory demand served in accordance with the provisions of the IPO, a creditor will only be able to show that the partnership itself is insolvent as and when the final bankruptcy order is made.

Having obtained a consolidation order, the trustees are then in a position to administer the estates of the individual partners and their joint estates for the purposes of paying all the classes of creditors in each estate. They can insist on the members of the partnership delivering up partnership property for the purposes of enabling them to exercise their functions as trustees pursuant to the provisions of s 303(2C). They can take advantage of Sched 4 (modifying Sched 4 to the Act) which confers upon them all the powers that a liquidator would have where the partnership was being wound up as an unregistered company.

The provisions of s 175 and s 175A (as modified or introduced by Sched 4 to the IPO) deal with priority of debts where insolvency orders are made in relation to insolvent partnerships. It will be useful for the trustees to take advantage of the consolidating provisions where all the partners are bankrupt and no order has been made in respect of the partnership since they will be able to have two estates in respect of each individual partner, one dealing with his personal affairs and the other dealing with the partnership. In addition, creditors will be able to assess their dividend prospects in the estate where they have proved their debts.

It is important to remember that transactions entered into by the partnership are reviewable for the period specified in the Act as if a petition to wind up the partnership as an unregistered company had been presented on the same day as the individual petitions against the partners. Problems will arise as to which date will be applicable where petitions against the individual partners were presented on different days. In such cases, logic dictates that the relevant periods for review will run back from the date when a petition was presented against the last partner. Until that time, the partnership still had at least one member who was not subject to bankruptcy proceedings and the trustees' power can only relate to his affairs as and when his petition is presented.

See **1** above as to the priority of personal and partnership debts against the personal or partnership assets where there is a shortfall.

7 Loss of rights

Whilst there is no doubt that creditors of a partnership can take legal action against the partnership and the individual partners at the same time, once insolvency procedures affect either or both of the partnership and the individual partners, creditors' rights can be restricted. Once a winding up order has been made against the partnership, it would appear that the rights of creditors against the individual partners whether it be for the entirety of the debt or just the shortfall likely to be suffered by creditors after realisation of all the partnership assets vest in the liquidator of the partnership and he alone can take action against the partners.

Chapter 26

Deceaseds' Insolvent Estates

1 Introduction

The Administration of Insolvent Estates of Deceased Persons Order 1986 (SI No 1999) governs the administration of the affairs of deceased debtors. In this chapter, all references to 'the Order' are to this order.

There are three situations where the insolvency of an estate occurs:
(a) where administration has begun and it is discovered that the estate is insolvent;
(b) where a bankruptcy petition against the deceased was pending at the time of his death; and
(c) where no administration has even been applied for when a creditor begins to press.

Each of these situations will be examined in turn together with the provisions applicable to all of them.

2 Where administration has begun

Where the estate of a deceased person is insolvent and is being administered by the executors or administrators, then that administration continues but the same provisions as are in force under the law of bankruptcy must be applied to the administration of the estate in the following areas:
(a) the rights of secured and unsecured creditors;
(b) the debts provable;
(c) the valuation of future and contingent liabilities;
(d) the priority of debts and other payments (art 4 of the Order).

There are two exceptions to this general rule. In the administration of the estate, the reasonable funeral, testamentary and administration expenses have priority over the preferential debts. Also, it is not necessary for the executors or administrators to be licensed insolvency practitioners as provided in s 292(2) (art 4(2) and (3) of the Order).

The provisions of art 4 of the Order also apply in the case where no grant of probate or administration has been obtained at the time when creditors begin to take action. No petition for the insolvency administration of a deceased's insolvent estate can even be presented after proceedings have been commenced for the administration of the estate (Sched 1, Part II, art 5(2) of the Order). The application for a grant of probate or administration is the equivalent of the commencement of proceedings in the High Court for the administration of the estate. However, where an application for the administration of the estate is pending, the court dealing with the application can, if satisfied that the estate is insolvent, transfer the proceedings to the court which would have had jurisdiction to receive a bankruptcy petition presented by or against the deceased debtor and when the proceedings have been transferred, the bankruptcy court can make an Insolvency Administration Order (art 5(3) and (4), Sched 1, Part II to the Order).

The executors or administrators are under the same duty as a debtor would have been under in regard to the submission of a statement of affairs. There is a form prescribed in Sched 3 to the Order, namely, Form 7 which is in substantially the same form as is required to be completed by a debtor against whom a bankruptcy order has been made as a result of a creditor's petition.

3 Petition pending at time of death

If a debtor by or against whom a bankruptcy petition had been presented died before the making of a bankruptcy order, the bankruptcy proceedings continue as if the debtor was still alive subject to certain modifications (art 5 of the Order). One modification is that the reasonable funeral and testamentary expenses have priority over the preferential debts. There is no provision for any administration expenses of the estate having like priority because there is no need for the normal administration of the estate by the executors or administrators as the estate will be administered in bankruptcy by the official receiver or a trustee.

If the petition has not been served at the date of death of the debtor, the court can order service on the personal representatives or such other person as it thinks fit (art 5(3) of the Order).

If a bankruptcy order is made as a result of a debtor's petition, after his death, the statement of affairs will have been lodged at the time of presentation of the petition, that is, before death. If the bankruptcy order is made as a result of a creditor's petition, no statement of affairs will have been sworn by the debtor. The personal representatives or such other persons as the court, on the application of the official receiver, may direct, must submit the statement of affairs on behalf of the estate. The form of the statement of affairs is Form 7 in Sched 3 to the Order and must be submitted within 56 days of the request by the official receiver or such longer period as the court may allow (art 1 of Sched 2 to the Order). There is no guidance in the Order as to what person other than the personal representative might be ordered to submit the statement of affairs.

4 Where no administration is pending

Where no grant of probate or administration has been applied for or obtained, a creditor can issue a petition for an Insolvency Administration Order against the estate. The form of the petition is prescribed and is Form 1 in Sched 3 to the Order.

The petition must be served on the personal representative of the deceased unless the court orders otherwise together with such other persons as the court may direct (art 2, Sched 1, Part II of the Order). The same minimum debt to ground a petition is required and the court may make an Insolvency Administration Order if it is satisfied, in the same way as under s 271, that the debt in respect of which the petition was presented is a debt which was payable at the date of the petition or has become due since that date and has neither been paid nor secured nor compounded for or there is no reasonable prospect of it being paid when it falls due and that there is a reasonable probability that the estate will be insolvent (art 5, above).

The ordinary creditor's petition for an Insolvency Administration Order is Form 1 in Sched 3 to the Order. If the petition is presented by the supervisor or creditor of an Individual Voluntary Arrangement, the petition is in Form 2. Where the personal representative of the deceased himself wishes to petition for an Insolvency Administration Order (that is, the equivalent of the debtor's own petition), the petition is in Form 6 (there would be a requirement for a statement of affairs to be submitted by the personal representative at that time). The Insolvency Administration Order is Form 4 in Sched 3 to the Order. If the Insolvency Administration Order is made as a result of the transfer of proceedings from the probate court to the bankruptcy court, the Insolvency Administration Order is in Form 5.

5 Modifications of the general law

Nothing in the Act will invalidate any payment made or any act or thing done in good faith by the personal representatives before the date of the Insolvency Administration Order (art 5(5), Sched 1, Part II of the Order).

The court will not appoint an insolvency practitioner to consider whether a voluntary arrangement could be proposed (under s 273) in the case of an insolvent estate.

For the purposes of ss 283 to 285, the petition *and* the Insolvency Administration Order are deemed to have been made on the date of the death of the deceased insolvent (art 12, Sched 1, Part II of the Order). This provision therefore catches any disposition made after the deceased's death subject to art 5(2) above, and the provisions of s 284(4) which protect the rights of any recipient of a disposition of property who receives it in good faith and for value and without notice of the presentation of the petition. But the making of such an order is not deemed to have occurred prior to the actual time of death with the result that the law of survivorship applicable to joint tenancies of property will not be displaced (*Re Palmer* [1994] Ch 316).

The same protection given to the family of a bankrupt as regards the home they occupy, which is owned by him, applies to the family of the deceased debtor (art 12 above).

The date for the calculation of preferential debts is the date of death (art 24 above). Reasonable funeral and testamentary expenses have priority over the preferential debts listed in Sched 6 to the Act.

Notwithstanding the death of the debtor, the same inquiry into his dealings and conduct can be made with the object of recovering further assets rather than ascertaining if the debtor ought to be the subject of prosecution for any bankruptcy offences since such prosecution, of course, cannot be brought against a deceased person.

Chapter 27

Individual Voluntary Arrangements

1 Introduction

An Individual Voluntary Arrangement (IVA) is an arrangement between an individual debtor and his creditors whereby the creditors agree to accept something less than 100p in the £ on their debts or agree to some deferment of the time for payment of their debts and also agree not to force the debtor into bankruptcy. It replaces the old concept of a composition with creditors after the making of a receiving order or even adjudication in bankruptcy under the Bankruptcy Acts and, because of the rules whereby dissenting minority creditors can be bound by the wishes of the majority, has advantages over the deed of arrangement or assignment under the Deeds of Arrangement Act 1914 (see Chapter 28) which it has largely replaced.

An IVA is essentially a private matter between the debtor and his creditors but there are provisions for applications to the court to give protection to the debtor while his proposals to creditors are being considered and provisions for the protection of creditors to ensure due regard for the requirements of the Rules regarding the information to be given to them, the way in which their wishes are taken into account and the opportunity for objection to be made.

An IVA envisages the close involvement of a nominee in the first instance and a supervisor (more often than not the same person) to act in a similar way to a trustee in bankruptcy or trustee under a deed of arrangement. The nominee or supervisor must be a qualified insolvency practitioner.

An application for an IVA involves the following steps:

(1) The debtor obtains the consent of a qualified insolvency practitioner to act as nominee.
(2) The debtor submits to the nominee his proposals in writing.
(3) The debtor applies to the court for an interim order to give him protection from his creditors while the nominee considers his proposals.
(4) The nominee considers the debtor's proposals and comments upon them.
(5) The court considers the proposals and the nominee's comments on them and directs whether or not a creditors' meeting should be held.

(6) The creditors' meeting takes place and the debtor's proposals are either accepted as made, or modified or rejected.
(7) The court is informed of the outcome of the meeting and, in the absence of any objections, makes an order approving the IVA.
(8) The proposals are implemented by the supervisor.

2 The proposal

If the debtor is an undischarged bankrupt, the proposal can be made by the debtor himself (after due notice has been given by him to the official receiver and his trustee), the official receiver or the trustee (s 253(2)). If the debtor is not an undischarged bankrupt, then only he can make a proposal.

Only an individual debtor can make a proposal for an IVA. Joint debtors, such as partners, cannot make a proposal for an IVA as such. They have to wait until bankruptcy orders have been made against them and then, as individuals, can make a proposal to their creditors so as to obtain an annulment of the bankruptcy orders against them. Alternatively, they can separately make a proposal with their own creditors and include the joint creditors as additional or contingent creditors (the contingency exists because those creditors are also creditors of another person and they might receive payment from the other person). Deceaseds' insolvent estates cannot make a proposal for an IVA. See also Chapter 25 for further alternatives available to partners by way of a Partnership Voluntary Arrangement or a Partnership Administration Order

The debtor must obtain the consent of a qualified insolvency practitioner to act as nominee in relation to the proposed IVA. The debtor must give written notice of his proposal to the intended nominee at the same time as seeking his consent to act and therefore it is incumbent on the debtor to formulate his proposal before the machinery for approval of an IVA can be set in motion.

The proposal must contain the following information:
(1) A short explanation as to why the debtor thinks an IVA is desirable and why the creditors may be expected to agree to it.
(2) Details of all his assets with an estimate of their values.
(3) The extent of any charges on those assets.
(4) Whether any assets are excluded from the IVA.
(5) Details of any third party assets which it is proposed be included in the IVA, the source of those assets and the terms upon which they are to be made available.
(6) Details of the debtor's liabilities.
(7) How secured and preferential creditors are to be dealt with.
(8) How associates of the debtor are to be dealt with.
(9) Whether there are any circumstances which could give rise to the possibility, in the event of the debtor's bankruptcy, to claims under:
 (i) s 339 (transactions at an undervalue),
 (ii) s 340 (preferences), or
 (iii) s 343 (extortionate credit transactions),
 and how such matters are to be dealt with under the proposed IVA.

INDIVIDUAL VOLUNTARY ARRANGEMENTS

(10) What guarantees have been given for any of the debtor's debts.
(11) The proposed duration of the IVA with likely dates for distributions to creditors.
(12) How much the nominee and supervisor are to be paid by way of remuneration and for expenses.
(13) What guarantee of payment to creditors is being offered, if any.
(14) How the debtor is to continue in business and who is to supervise him and what credit facilities he will need.
(15) The identity, qualifications and confirmation to act of the proposed supervisor (r 5.3).

The basic conditions (according to the Insolvency Service) regarding the debtor's proposal are;
   (a) is it feasible?
   (b) is it fair to creditors?
   (c) is it fair to the debtor?
   (d) is it an acceptable alternative to bankruptcy?
   (e) is it fit to be considered by creditors?

3 Application for an interim order

A debtor who wants to make a proposal to his creditors for a composition in satisfaction of his debts or a scheme of arrangement of his affairs (both of which are defined as being IVAs) must apply to the court for an interim order to give him protection from his creditors while that proposal is being formulated and considered (s 253). Even if such protection is not needed the interim order must be applied for. If the interim order is discharged (because of procedural problems or after rejection of the debtor's proposal by his creditors), no further application for an interim order can be made until 12 months have elapsed since the last application (s 255(1)(c)). The effect of an application for an interim order, that is, even before the application has been heard, is to give the court the jurisdiction to stay any action against the person or property of the debtor (s 254(1)). This means that no steps in bankruptcy proceedings commenced against the debtor can be taken and a secured creditor cannot take any action to enforce his security. However, an interim order does not prevent a landlord exercising the self help remedy of distress (*McMullen v Cerrone* [1994] BCC 25). Any court in which proceedings are pending may, on proof that an application for an interim order has been made, either stay the proceedings or allow them to continue on such terms as it thinks fit (s 254(2)).

Because it is necessary to exhibit to the application for an interim order the consent of the nominee to act and the notice to the nominee seeking his consent must contain the debtor's proposals (r 5.4), it follows that an application for an interim order cannot be made until the debtor has formulated his proposals and set them down in writing. The application for the interim order should be on Form 7.1 in Sched 4 to the Rules, being an originating application, suitably amended. If the application is made by or on behalf of an undischarged bankrupt, then it should be on Form 7.2 in the existing bankruptcy proceedings. The fee payable on the application is £20 (in the county court) or £130 (in the High Court).

The application must be accompanied by an affidavit setting out:
(a) the reasons for making the application;
(b) details of legal process or executions of which the debtor is aware;
(c) that the debtor is able to petition for his own bankruptcy or, as the case may be, that he is an undischarged bankrupt;
(d) that no previous application for an interim order has been made in the last twelve months;
(e) that the nominee is qualified to act and has consented to do so(r 5.5(1)).

For a precedent of the application for an interim order and the affidavit in support in non-bankruptcy cases see Appendix 3, forms 40 and 41, and in bankruptcy cases forms 42 and 43. A copy of the notice to the nominee endorsed with his consent and the debtor's proposals to the nominee must be exhibited (r 5.5(2)).

The court to which the application must be made is the court to which the debtor would be entitled to present his own bankruptcy petition (unless the debtor was already bankrupt in which case the application is made to the court dealing with that bankruptcy) (r 5.5A). The application is heard by the registrar or district judge in chambers.

The application must be served on the nominee, on any creditor who has presented a bankruptcy petition against the debtor or, if the debtor is already bankrupt, on the official receiver or trustee unless the official receiver or trustee is himself the applicant. The application must be served at least two clear days before the hearing (r 5.5(4)).

In cases where there are no bankruptcy proceedings pending or no bankruptcy order has been made against the debtor, all the steps necessary to obtain an interim order, extension of the same and a final order after the creditors' meeting has been held can be taken without any attendance before the registrar or district judge—all the orders are *ex parte* and without any attendance (*Practice Direction: Bankruptcy 1 of 1991* [1992] 1 All ER 678 and see **9** below).

4 Hearing of the application

The applicant for an interim order and any other person to whom notice has been given under r 5.5(4) is entitled to be heard.

If the debtor is an undischarged bankrupt, the court can stay the bankruptcy proceedings or modify or relax the rules for the administration of the bankruptcy but only if the court is satisfied that the modification or relaxation is unlikely to result in any significant diminution in the value of the debtor's estate (s 255(5)).

If the court is satisfied, after hearing all representations, that an interim order should be made so as to facilitate the obtaining of creditors' approval to an IVA, then it *may* make such an order. It is not a proper exercise of the court's discretion to refuse to make an interim order because it is felt that creditors will not approve the debtor's proposal. It is for the creditors to give their judgment on the debtor's proposal at a meeting of creditors (*Re Jones (VA 289 of 1994)* (1995) unreported, 24 March.

An interim order lasts only for 14 days but this can be extended if the nominee asks for more time to file his report (r 5.6(4)). This application can be made at the original hearing or at any time within the period of 14 days during which the interim order lasts. If the nominee fails to file his report, the debtor can also apply for the order to be extended to give him the opportunity of finding another qualified insolvency practitioner willing to act as nominee. Bearing in mind that the nominee's report has to be filed two days before the interim order is to cease to have effect, it is likely that the court will be asked for and will grant an extension of the interim order at the first hearing to avoid the almost invariable necessity of a further application at a later date being made.

The court, on the making of the interim order, must fix a date and venue for consideration of the nominee's report. This date will also be the date when the interim order ceases to have effect. The nominee's report must be filed two days before this second hearing (r 5.10).

5 Action following the interim order

The court draws up and seals two copies of the interim order, one of which is served on the applicant and the other on the nominee (r 5.7). The applicant must inform all those who were given notice of the hearing but were not present at it of the making of the order.

Within seven days of delivering his proposal to the nominee the debtor must deliver to the nominee a statement of his affairs (r 5.8). The statement of affairs must contain all the information set out in his proposal together with names, addresses and amount of each of his creditors and debtors. The statement of affairs must be made up to a date not earlier than two weeks before the debtor's original proposal though the nominee may allow the statement of affairs to be made up to an earlier date, not more than two months before the date of the debtor's original proposal (r 5.8(4)), though the nominee must report to the court his reasons for allowing this. The debtor must also supply to the nominee any further information which the nominee reasonably requires and must allow the nominee access to his books and records (r 5.9).

The nominee must prepare his report on the debtor's proposals and lodge it in court at least two days before the second hearing. With the report must be delivered a copy of the debtor's proposals and statement of affairs. The nominee must give his reasons for his opinion that a creditors' meeting should or should not be convened to consider the debtor's proposals. The nominee's report should bring a critical eye on the debtor's statement of assets and liabilities and should attempt to assess whether the proposal is in accordance with the Rules (*Re a Debtor* (*No 222 of 1990*) [1992] BCLC 137. The nominee must send a copy of his report, the debtor's proposals and statement of affairs to the official receiver and trustee, if the debtor is bankrupt, or to any person who has presented a bankruptcy petition against the debtor, if the debtor is not bankrupt (r 5.10). Any creditor of the debtor can inspect a copy of the report on the court file (r 5.10(4)).

6 The second hearing

At the second hearing, the court will have before it the nominee's report and the debtor's statement of affairs. The court has two alternatives open to it:
  (1) If the nominee has come to the conclusion that there is no point in pursuing the proposals or the debtor has himself failed to comply with any obligations imposed upon him, it may formally discharge the interim order.
  (2) If the court is satisfied that a meeting of creditors should be convened, it should direct that the period for which the interim order is to have effect be extended to enable the debtor's proposals to be considered by his creditors. The date to which the interim order should be extended will usually be seven to nine weeks after the date on which it is proposed to hold the creditors' meeting.

The order extending the effect of the interim order is Form 5.3 in Sched 4 to the Rules. This order is drawn up by the court and served on the same parties as above.

The meeting of creditors ordered by the court to be convened must be held not less than 14 nor more than 28 days after the second hearing (r 5.13).

The reason why the interim order is extended for 9 to 11 weeks is to cover the period until the meeting of creditors is held (14 to 28 days), a further 14 days for any adjournments, the time for the chairman to lodge his report of the meeting (four days) and the period for objections to be made (28 days)—the total of these periods is 60 to 74 days or about 9 to 11 weeks.

If the court is aware from what the petitioning creditor says that there is no likelihood of the debtor's proposals being approved, the petitioning creditor's vote being sufficient by itself to ensure the rejection of the debtor's proposals, it may refuse to extend the interim order since to do so would serve no practical use (*Re Cove* [1990] 1 All ER 949).

7 The creditors' meeting

Notices calling the meeting must be sent out by the nominee, at least 14 days before the meeting, to all creditors (secured and unsecured) specified in the statement of affairs or of whom the nominee is aware. For an IVA to be binding on a creditor, that creditor must have been given at least 14 days' notice of and been entitled to vote at the creditors' meeting. Where notice was sent to the wrong address for the creditor, the IVA was held not to be binding on the creditor concerned (*Re a Debtor (No 64 of 1992), Bradford and Bingley Building Society v a Debtor* [1994] BCC 55). Likewise, where insufficient notice of the (first) meeting was given, though sufficient notice of the adjourned meeting, the IVA held not to be binding on the creditor (*Myrtle v Reynolds*

(1995) unreported, 20 October). With the notice there must be a copy of the debtor's proposal, his statement of affairs and the nominee's comments on the proposal. With every notice, there must also be sent a form of proxy (in Form 8.1 in Sched 4 to the Rules; see Appendix 3, form 42) and an extract from the Rules relating to entitlement to vote and the requisite majorities at such meetings together with a proxy form (Form 8.1 in Sched 4 to the Rules; see Appendix 3, form 47). Whilst it is preferable for signed proxies to be returned to the nominee or handed in at the meeting, faxed proxies should be accepted by the nominee (*Re a Debtor (No 2021 of 1995)* (1995) unreported). The nominee must have regard to the convenience of creditors in fixing the venue of the meeting and it should be held between 10 am and 4 pm on business days (r 5.14). The nominee, an experienced employee of his, or another qualified insolvency practitioner should chair the meeting. The same rules apply as to the conduct of this meeting as apply to other meetings in connection with insolvency matters. These include (r 5.17):

(a) votes are calculated by reference to amount of the debt;
(b) no voting rights are accorded in respect of debts which are secured, or for unliquidated amounts, unless in the latter case the nominee is prepared to put an estimated value on the claim for voting purposes (*Saigol v Goldstein* [1994] BCC 576 and *Re a Debtor (No 162 of 1993) Doorbar v Alltime Securities No 1* [1995] BCC 1149).
(c) the chairman has power to reject a creditor's claim for voting purposes or to reduce the amount of a creditor's claim for voting purposes.

Legal costs if not the subject of a court cannot be included in a claim for voting purposes (*Re Wisepark* [1994] BCC 221) but can if subject to a court order even though not yet agreed or taxed (*Re Bradley Hole* [1995] BCC 418)).

Partially secured creditors (despite the somewhat ambiguous wording of r 5.18(3)(*b*) can vote for the unsecured element of their claim (*Calor Gas v Piercy* [1994] BCC 69). A creditor with the benefit of a charging order is to be treated as secured (*Calor Gas v Piercy* above), as is a creditor who has levied execution where the sheriff is in walking possession of some of the debtor's goods (*Re a Debtor (No 10 of 1992)* [1995] BCC 529). A secured creditor is defined as one holding security for his debt over an asset of the debtor not the assets of another party albeit for the same debt (*Re a Debtor (No 310 of 1988)* [1989] 2 All ER 42).

Landlords can vote for the amount of any arrears of rent and it has been held that the rent that will become due during the remainder of the term of the lease can be included (see *Burford Midland Properties v Marley Extrusions* [1994] BCC 604, *Re Cancol* (1995) [1996] 1 All ER 37 and *Re a Debtor (No 162 of 1993) Doorbar v Alltime Securities No 1* [1995] BCC 1149), but it depends on the wording of the proposal.

If the chairman is in doubt as to whether a vote should be allowed or not, he should mark it as objected to but allow the creditor to vote. There is an appeal against the chairman's decisions on these matters and if the chairman's decision is overturned by the court, a fresh meeting may be ordered if the court considers that unfair prejudice or material irregularity has been caused. However, no application to the court by way of appeal against the chairman's decision can be made 28 days after the chairman has filed his report with the court under s 259. See also **10** below.

For the proposal to be approved by the creditors, there must be in excess of 75 per cent in value of the creditors present in person or by proxy and voting on the resolution (r 5.18(1)). The same applies to any other resolution proposed to the meeting except that a simple majority only is required (r 5.18(2)) . To vote at the meeting, the creditor must have given notice of his claim either before or at the meeting and must not be secured unless he is willing to give up his security or values his security and votes only for the unsecured shortfall.

A resolution is not passed if, despite the majority of more than 75 per cent or 50 per cent in favour of it, those voting against the resolution include more than half in value of the creditors excluding the votes of associates of the debtor and the votes of those creditors who were not sent notice of the meeting (r 5.18(4) and (5)) . The object of these provisions is to avoid creditors suddenly appearing about whom the chairman may have no information and in respect of whom he cannot make a decision not to allow them to vote and who vote in favour of the proposals of the debtor contrary to the wishes of the majority of other creditors whose existence and amount of debt is not in any way in doubt. These provisions also exclude associates of the debtor from being able unduly to influence the decision to approve the debtor's proposals.

The meeting can be adjourned any number of times. But the final meeting can only be held on a date not later than 14 days after it was originally held (r 5.19(1) and (3)). If there is not the requisite majority in favour of the proposals, the chairman can adjourn the meeting for another attempt to obtain approval to be made. If the proposals are not approved of at the adjourned meeting, they are deemed rejected. The chairman must adjourn the meeting if a majority of those present require him to do so. If the meeting is adjourned, the chairman must report the fact to the court. An application to the court to extend this time limit can be made but it has been been doubted whether the court has power to extend an interim order in such circumstances.

The meeting can put forward to the debtor modifications to his proposals (s 258) and if these are accepted by the debtor, they become part of his proposals. If the debtor declines to agree to those modifications, then it is for the creditors to decide whether to approve the proposals as originally put by the debtor or reject them. It is very likely that one of the modifications which will be suggested by the creditors will be as to the choice of supervisor, with creditors or their representatives all seeking to have a supervisor of their choice appointed instead of the nominee. Two or more qualified insolvency practitioners can be appointed to act jointly as supervisor.

The meeting must not approve any proposals which would affect the right of a secured creditor to enforce his security or the rights of preferential creditors to be treated with the priority normally accorded to them without the concurrence of those classes of creditor.

After the conclusion of the meeting, the chairman must report the decision of the meeting to the court (s 259). The report states whether the debtor's proposals were approved or rejected and if approved, with what modifications if any, all the resolutions put to the meeting and the decision on each and a list of all the creditors who were present or represented at the meeting with details of the amounts of their debts and how they voted on each resolution. The report must be filed at court within four days of the meeting (r 5.22). The court has no jurisdiction to extend the interim order to enable a second meeting of creditors to be convened if the debtor's proposals were rejected at the first meeting (*Re a Debtor (No 1036 of 1995)* (1995) unreported, 28 July). The nominee in such a case should adjourn the meeting of creditors rather than allow it to be concluded with a rejection of the debtor's proposals.

8 The third hearing

At this hearing, the court considers the chairman's report of the creditors' meeting. If the meeting has declined the debtor's proposals, the court will discharge the interim order and the debtor is thereafter at the mercy of his creditors. If the meeting has approved the debtor's proposals with or without modifications, the court will recite this fact and make no further order. The interim order ceases to have effect, in any event, 28 days after the filing of the chairman's report of the creditors' meeting (s 260(4)).

If the debtor's proposals have been approved and there are bankruptcy proceedings pending against the debtor which have been stayed by the interim order, these are deemed dismissed (s 260(5)). The court dealing with the IVA, even if different from the court in which the bankruptcy proceedings are pending, can dismiss the bankruptcy proceedings. If the debtor was already bankrupt, the effect of the approval of his proposals for an IVA is that the bankruptcy order against him is annulled but only after the period during which an application to challenge the chairman's decision could be made has expired or any application has been dealt with by the court (s 261).

The form of order made by the court is Form 5.4 in Sched 4 to the Rules.

9 Procedure in non-bankruptcy cases

In a *Practice Direction (Bankruptcy No I of 1991)* [1992] 1 All ER 678, the procedure for handling applications for interim orders in connection with voluntary arrangements in cases where neither a bankruptcy order has been made nor (so far as is known) is a bankruptcy petition pending is set out. A 14-day interim order will be made where the papers are in order and the nominee's signed consent to act (including waiver of notice of the application for the interim order) or consent to the making of an interim order without the attendance of any of the parties. The application will then be adjourned for 14 days for consideration of the nominee's report.

When the nominee's report is lodged and has been considered, again an order will be made without attendance of any of the parties extending the interim order for seven weeks after the date of the proposed meeting of creditors, directing the meeting to be summoned (on a date not less than 14 nor more than 28 days after the date when the matter is being considered *ex parte* by the court) and adjourning the matter until about three weeks after the meeting.

A 'concertina order' combining both the procedures outlined above can be made, again without the attendance of any of the parties, if the nominee's report is lodged with the application for the interim order.

A final order will be made on consideration of the chairman's report of the creditors' meeting. Provided that the report complies with r 5.22(2), the order will record the effect of the chairman's report and discharge the interim order. This new procedure does not prevent parties from attending the court but merely avoids their obligatory attendance unless the court on consideration of the papers directs otherwise.

10 Challenge of meeting's decision

Any person affected by the voluntary arrangement can apply to the court within 28 days of the filing of the chairman's report for the decision at the meeting to be revoked on the ground that it is unfairly prejudicial to the interests of a creditor or that there has been some material irregularity at the meeting (s 262). It is not unfair for all creditors to be treated the same albeit in a way which the complaining creditor thinks unfair (*Re a Debtor (No 259 of 1990)* [1992] 1 All ER 641).

An example of material irregularity would be the allowance or disallowance of certain creditors' votes which caused the decision of the meeting to be affected. If the irregularity at the meeting had no material effect on the decision, the court will not intervene. The provision of false or misleading information by the debtor in his statement of affairs or proposal can also constitute a material irregularity (*Re a Debtor (No 87 of 1993) (No 2)* (1995) *The Times*, 7 August).

If the court is satisfied that it ought to intervene, it can revoke any approval given to the voluntary arrangement or give a direction for the convening of another meeting (s 262(4)).

If the challenge is based upon the decision to allow or not to allow a particular creditor's vote, then application should be made under r 5.17 and even if the court decides that the chairman's decision in relation to the particular creditor's vote was wrong, no order for costs should be made against him personally (r 5.17(9)) unless the personal conduct of the chairman/supervisor is open to question (*Re Naeem* [1990] 1 WLR 48). If the conduct of the chairman/supervisor falls so far below the standard of duty required of a professional licensed insolvency practitioner, then he is liable to be ordered to pay the costs of any successful application under s 262 (*Re a Debtor (No 222 of 1990)* [1992] BCLC 137.

11 Effect of approval

Where the debtor's proposals have been approved by his creditors, with or without modifications, the approved arrangement takes effect as if made by the debtor at the meeting of creditors and it binds every person who in accordance with the Rules had notice of the meeting and was entitled to vote at it (whether or not they were actually present or represented) as if he were a party to the arrangement (s 260(2)). The arrangement only binds creditors in their character as creditors. It does not affect proprietary rights such as those of a landlord to forfeit a lease for non-payment of rent but it would prevent a landlord from seeking to forfeit the lease for arrears which accrued prior to the voluntary arrangement (*Re Naeem* [1990] 1 WLR 48).

It follows that if a creditor was not given notice of the creditors' meeting when his existence and identity were known to the debtor and/or nominee then such creditor could initiate bankruptcy proceedings against the debtor in respect of the debt owing from the debtor. It is possible that the court would order a fresh meeting of creditors to be held rather than allow that creditor to succeed in a petition for the debtor's bankruptcy, particularly if that creditor's debt was such that the decision at the meeting would not have been materially affected by the inclusion of another creditor voting against the proposals.

12 Implementation of the arrangement

Once the debtor's proposals have been approved by creditors, the person charged with the task of supervising the implementation of the proposals is called the supervisor. Forthwith, the debtor (or the official receiver or trustee if the debtor is an undischarged bankrupt) must hand over his assets to the supervisor. The supervisor must discharge the amount due to the official receiver or trustee (of a bankrupt debtor) including any guarantees given by them for the benefit of the estate (r 5.21).

The supervisor's responsibility includes the realisation of those of the debtor's assets which it was proposed should be realised and the payment of the debtor's creditors, again in accordance with the proposals approved by the creditors, with due regard being had for the rights of secured and preferential creditors.

The supervisor must send a notice to the debtor and all his creditors once the arrangement has been fully implemented (not more than 28 days after the final completion of the IVA) and give the debtor and the creditors a summary of his receipts and payments with a comparison of the figures with those contained in the debtor's proposals as approved by the creditors. A copy of these documents must also be sent by the supervisor to the Secretary of State (r 5.29).

Any creditor or the debtor himself who is dissatisfied with anything done or omitted to be done by the supervisor can apply to the court to reverse or modify the supervisor's act or decision (s 263(3)). The supervisor himself can apply to the court for directions in relation to any matter arising under the IVA.

The court can also fill any vacancy in the post of supervisor from time to time (s 263(5)).

13 Offence

The debtor commits an offence if he makes any false representation or commits any other fraud for the purpose of obtaining the approval of his creditors to an IVA. The maximum punishment is seven years' imprisonment or a fine on indictment or six months' imprisonment and a fine on summary conviction (r 5.30).

14 Default by the debtor

If the debtor defaults on any of his obligations under the IVA, the supervisor or, possibly, any creditor bound by the IVA can petition for the debtor's bankruptcy. A bankruptcy order will also be made on the petition of the supervisor or a creditor if the debtor has provided false or misleading information in his statement of affairs or other documents supplied by him or if the debtor has failed to do all the things which the supervisor has reasonably requested him to do for the purposes of the IVA (s 276).

If the debtor is made bankrupt on the petition of the supervisor or a creditor bound by the terms of an IVA under s 264(1)(*c*), then the IVA comes to an end and any assets held by the supervisor would pass to the trustee in bankruptcy and form part of the estate available for distribution among all creditors. However, if the debtor was made bankrupt on the petition of any other type of creditor, then the IVA might continue at least to the extent that the assets of the debtor are held in trust for the benefit of the creditors bound by the IVA (see *Re Bradley Hole* [1995] 4 All ER 865, *Re Mckeen* [1995] BCC 412, *Re Leisure Study Group* [1994] 2 BCLC 65 and *Re Hussain* (1995) 8 *Insolvency Intelligence* 76).

Chapter 28

Deeds of Arrangement

(Except where otherwise stated, references in this chapter to sections are to the Deeds of Arrangement Act 1914 and those to Rules are to the Deeds of Arrangement Rules 1925 as amended.)

Whilst deeds of arrangement used to be quite rare because the execution of a deed itself constituted an act of bankruptcy upon which a creditor could petition for the debtor's bankruptcy and because any non-assenting creditor was not bound by it, the first of these reasons has been removed by the Insolvency Act which did not reproduce the concept of acts of bankruptcy as grounds for making a bankruptcy order and now the execution of the deed does not, of itself, give rise to any problems for the debtor. For those debtors who can hope to obtain the assent of all their creditors, a deed might be a preferable alternative to an Individual Voluntary Arrangement (see Chapter 27) since a deed does not require much formality, is essentially a private affair and no court attendances are necessary. However, deeds are now very rarely used and it remains to be seen how many deeds will be entered into in the future.

1 The nature of a deed

The nature of a deed of arrangement is the liquidation by arrangement between a debtor and his creditors, or some of them, of the affairs of the debtor outside the law of bankruptcy. The creditors agree to forgo the payment in full of their debts in consideration of the benefits to be obtained under what is essentially a private arrangement. This chapter is concerned only with deeds of arrangement to which the Deeds of Arrangement Act 1914 applies.

The essentials of a deed to which the Act applies are prescribed in s 1 and are the following:
(1) It must be an instrument, whether under seal or not, made by, for or in respect of the affairs of a debtor for the benefit of his creditors generally (ie all creditors who may assent to or take the benefit of it), or, if the debtor was insolvent at the date of the execution of the instrument, for the benefit of any three or more of his creditors.
(2) It must be made otherwise than in pursuance of the law for the time being in force relating to bankruptcy.

(3) It must be one of the classes of instruments specified in s 1(2), ie:
   (a) an assignment of property;
   (b) a deed of agreement for a composition;
   (c) a deed of inspectorship entered into for the purpose of carrying on or winding up a business;
   (d) a letter of licence authorising the debtor or any other person to manage, carry on, realise or dispose of a business with a view to the payment of debts; or
   (e) any agreement or instrument entered into for the purpose of carrying on or winding up the debtor's business, or authorising the debtor or any other person to arrange, carry on, realise or dispose of the debtor's business with a view to the payment of his debts.
   In respect of the classes of instrument in (c), (d) or (e), it is a prerequisite that the creditors obtain some control over the debtor's property or business.

For the purpose of determining the number of creditors for whose benefit a deed is made, two or more joint creditors are treated as a single creditor.

2 Avoidance for non-compliance with the statutory conditions

Any deed of arrangement to which the Act applies is void unless it is registered with the registrar appointed by the Department of Trade and Industry (the inspector-general of the insolvency service is now the registrar of deeds of arrangement) within seven clear days after its first execution by the debtor or any creditor, or, if executed out of England, within seven clear days of the date on which it would have arrived in England, if posted within a week of its execution. Further, the deed must bear the appropriate Inland Revenue duty (s 2).

In the case of a deed of arrangement which is for the benefit of creditors generally, the deed is void unless it has received the assent of a majority in number and value of the creditors within 21 days of the registration of the deed or within such extended time as may be allowed by the High Court or the court having bankruptcy jurisdiction in the district in which the debtor resided or carried on business at the date of the execution of the deed. In calculating a majority of creditors for this purpose, a creditor holding security on the debtor's property is reckoned as a creditor only in respect of the balance due to him after deducting the value of such security, and creditors whose debts amount to sums not exceeding £10 shall be reckoned only in ascertaining the majority in value, and not in number (s 3(1) and (5)). The deed must be registered with the registrar of deeds of arrangements and the local county court or the High Court in London as appropriate.

3 Registration of deeds of arrangement

The original deed must be produced to the registrar at the time of registration.

4 Effect of assent

As a rule, a creditor who has assented to a deed cannot present a bankruptcy petition.

A creditor who has acquiesced in the deed or recognised the title of the trustee under the deed is in a similar position because of the doctrine of estoppel (*Huddersfield Fine Worsteds Ltd v Todd* (1925) 134 LT 82).

5 Trustees

Appointment

The first trustee under a deed of arrangement is appointed by the deed itself. Should occasion arise for the appointment of a new trustee, power to do so is conferred by the Trustee Act 1925, s 41, which provides that a new trustee or trustees may be appointed by the court. The trustee must be a qualified insolvency practitioner. If the trustee ceased to be a qualified insolvency practitioner, he would have to cease to act as deed trustee.

Security

Section 11 provides that every trustee under a deed of arrangement is required to give security, within seven days from the date of filing the statutory declaration certifying the assent of creditors, to the court having jurisdiction in bankruptcy in the district in which the debtor resided or carried on business at the date of the execution of the deed.

Transmission of accounts to Department of Trade

Section 13 provides that a trustee must at the prescribed times transmit to the Department of Trade an account of his receipts and payments as trustee in the prescribed form and verified in the prescribed manner.

Transmission of accounts to creditors

A trustee is required by s 14, at the end of six months from the date of registration of the deed and thereafter at the end of every subsequent six months until the estate has been finally wound up, to send to each assenting creditor a statement in the prescribed form of the trustee's accounts and of the proceedings under the deed.

Audit of accounts

Section 15 provides for an audit by the Department of Trade of the trustee's accounts on an application in writing being made to the Department by a majority in number and value of the creditors who have assented to the deed, either during the course of administration of the estate or within 12 months from the date of the rendering of the final accounts to the Department.

Payment of undistributed money into court

Section 16 provides that after two years have expired from the date of the registration of a deed of arrangement, the court having jurisdiction in bankruptcy in the district in which the debtor resided or carried on business at the date of the execution of the deed may order that all monies representing unclaimed dividends and undistributed funds in the trustee's hands or under his control be paid into court.

Preferential payment to a creditor

It is an offence under s 17 if a trustee under a deed of arrangement for the benefit of creditors generally pays to any creditor out of the debtor's property a sum larger in proportion to the creditor's claim than that paid to other creditors, unless the deed authorises him to do so or unless such payments are either made to a creditor entitled to enforce his claim by distress or are such as would be lawful in a bankruptcy.

Provisions for protection of trustee under void deed

Section 19 protects a deed trustee where the deed is void by reason that the requisite majority of creditors has not assented thereto, or, in the case of a deed for the benefit of three or more creditors, by reason that the debtor was insolvent at the time of the execution and that the deed was not registered as required by the Act, but is not void for any other reason, *and* a bankruptcy order is made against the debtor upon a petition presented after a lapse of three months from the execution of the deed.

Appendix 1

County Court Areas and Bankruptcy Courts

County court	Court with bankruptcy jurisdiction
Aberdare	Aberdare
Aberystwyth	Aberystwyth
Accrington	Blackburn
Aldershot and Farnham	Guildford
Alfreton	Derby
Alnwick	Newcastle
Altrincham	Manchester
Ammanford	Carmarthen
Andover	Salisbury
Ashford	Canterbury
Aylesbury	Aylesbury
Banbury	Banbury
Bargoed	Blackwood
Barnet	High Court
Barnsley	Barnsley
Barnstaple	Barnstaple
Barrow in Furness and Ulverston	Barrow in Furness
Barry	Cardiff
Basingstoke	Reading
Bath	Bath
Bedford	Bedford
Berwick on Tweed	Newcastle
Birkenhead	Birkenhead
Birmingham	Birmingham
Bishop Auckland	Durham
Bishop's Stortford	Hertford
Blackburn	Blackburn
Blackpool	Blackpool
Blackwood	Blackwood
Blyth	Newcastle
Bodmin	Truro
Bolton	Bolton
Boston	Boston
Bournemouth	Bournemouth

159

APPENDIX 1

Bow	High Court
Bradford	Bradford
Braintree	Chelmsford
Brecknock	Merthyr Tydfil
Brentford	High Court
Brentwood	Southend
Bridgend	Bridgend
Bridgwater	Bridgwater
Bridlington	Scarborough
Brighton	Brighton
Bristol	Bristol
Bromley	Croydon
Burnley	Burnley
Burton upon Trent	Burton upon Trent
Bury	Bolton
Bury St Edmunds	Bury St Edmunds
Buxton	Stockport
Caernarfon	Caernarfon
Caerphilly	Pontypridd
Camborne and Redruth	Truro
Cambridge	Cambridge
Canterbury	Canterbury
Cardiff	Cardiff
Cardigan	Carmarthen
Carlisle	Carlisle
Carmarthen	Carmarthen
Central London	High Court
Chelmsford	Chelmsford
Cheltenham	Cheltenham
Chepstow	Newport (Gwent)
Chester	Chester
Chesterfield	Chesterfield
Chichester	Brighton
Chippenham	Bath
Chorley	Preston
Clerkenwell	High Court
Colchester	Colchester
Consett	Newcastle
Conwy and Colwyn	Caernarfon
Corby	Northampton
Coventry	Coventry
Crewe	Crewe
Croydon	Croydon
Darlington	Darlington
Dartford	Medway
Derby	Derby
Dewsbury	Dewsbury
Doncaster	Doncaster
Dover	Canterbury
Dudley	Dudley

Durham	Durham
Eastbourne	Eastbourne
Edmonton	High Court
Epsom	Croydon
Evesham	Worcester
Exeter	Exeter
Folkestone	Canterbury
Gateshead	Newcastle
Gloucester	Gloucester
Goole	Wakefield
Grantham	Lincoln
Gravesend	Medway
Grays Thurrock	Southend
Great Grimsby	Great Grimsby
Great Yarmouth	Great Yarmouth
Guildford	Guildford
Halifax	Halifax
Harlow	Hertford
Harrogate	Harrogate
Hartlepool	Teesside
Hastings	Hastings
Haverfordwest	Haverfordwest
Haywards Heath	Brighton
Hemel Hempstead	St Albans
Hereford	Hereford
Hertford	Hertford
High Wycombe	Aylesbury
Hitchin	Luton
Holywell	Rhyl
Horsham	Brighton
Huddersfield	Huddersfield
Huntingdon	Peterborough
Ilford	Romford
Ilkeston	Derby
Ipswich	Ipswich
Keighley	Bradford
Kendal	Kendal
Kettering	Northampton
Kidderminster	Kidderminster
King's Lynn	King's Lynn
Kingston upon Hull	Kingston upon Hull
Kingston upon Thames	Kingston upon Thames
Lambeth	High Court
Lancaster	Lancaster
Leeds	Leeds
Leicester	Leicester
Leigh	Wigan
Lewes	Brighton
Lichfield	Walsall
Lincoln	Lincoln

APPENDIX 1

Liverpool	Liverpool
Llandrindod Wells	Welshpool and Newtown
Llanelli	Swansea
Llangefni	Llangefni
Loughborough	Leicester
Lowestoft	Great Yarmouth
Ludlow	Hereford
Luton	Luton
Macclesfield	Macclesfield
Maidstone	Maidstone
Manchester	Manchester
Mansfield	Nottingham
Market Drayton	Shrewsbury
Matlock	Derby
Mayor's and City of London	High Court
Medway	Medway
Melton Mowbray	Leicester
Merthyr Tydfil	Merthyr Tydfil
Milton Keynes	Milton Keynes
Mold	Chester
Monmouth	Newport (Gwent)
Morpeth	Newcastle upon Tyne
Neath and Port Talbot	Neath
Nelson	Burnley
Newark	Nottingham
Newbury	Newbury
Newcastle upon Tyne	Newcastle upon Tyne
Newport (IoW)	Newport (IoW)
Newport (Gwent)	Newport (Gwent)
Newton Abbot	Torquay
Northampton	Northampton
North Shields	Newcastle upon Tyne
Northwich	Crewe
Norwich	Norwich
Nottingham	Nottingham
Nuneaton	Coventry
Oldham	Oldham
Oswestry	Wrexham
Oxford	Oxford
Penrith	Carlisle
Penzance	Truro
Peterborough	Peterborough
Plymouth	Plymouth
Pontefract	Wakefield
Pontypool	Newport (Gwent)
Pontypridd	Pontypridd
Poole	Bournemouth
Portsmouth	Portsmouth
Preston	Preston
Rawtenstall	Burnley

Reading	Reading
Redditch	Birmingham
Reigate	Croydon
Rhyl	Rhyl
Rochdale	Rochdale
Romford	Romford
Rotherham	Sheffield
Rugby	Coventry
Runcorn	Warrington
St Albans	St Albans
St Austell	Truro
St Helens	Liverpool
Salford	Salford
Salisbury	Salisbury
Scarborough	Scarborough
Scunthorpe	Scunthorpe
Sheffield	Sheffield
Shoreditch	High Court
Shrewsbury	Shrewsbury
Sittingbourne	Medway
Skegness and Spilsby	Boston
Skipton	Bradford
Sleaford	Boston
Slough	Slough
Southampton	Southampton
Southend	Southend
Southport	Liverpool
South Shields	Sunderland
Spalding	Peterborough
Stafford	Stafford
Staines	Slough
Stockport	Stockport
Stoke on Trent	Stoke on Trent
Stourbridge	Stourbridge
Stratford upon Avon	Warwick
Sunderland	Sunderland
Swansea	Swansea
Swindon	Swindon
Tameside	Tameside
Tamworth	Birmingham
Taunton	Taunton
Teesside	Teesside
Telford	Shrewsbury
Thanet	Canterbury
Torquay	Torquay
Trowbridge	Bath
Truro	Truro
Tunbridge Wells	Tunbridge Wells
Uxbridge	Slough
Wakefield	Wakefield

Walsall	Walsall
Wandsworth	High Court
Warrington	Warrington
Warwick	Warwick
Watford	St Albans
Wellingborough	Northampton
Welshpool and Newtown	Welshpool and Newtown
West Bromwich	West Bromwich
West London	High Court
West Midlands	Wolverhampton
Weston super Mare	Bristol
Weymouth	Weymouth
Whitehaven	Workington
Wigan	Wigan
Willesden	High Court
Winchester	Winchester
Wisbech	King's Lynn
Wolverhampton	Wolverhampton
Woolwich	Croydon
Worcester	Worcester
Workington	Workington
Worksop	Sheffield
Worthing	Brighton
Wrexham	Wrexham
Yeovil	Yeovil
York	York

Appendix 2

Alternative Courts for Debtors' Petitions in Bankruptcy

Debtor's own court	Nearest full-time court
Aberdare	Cardiff
Aberystwyth	Cardiff
Aylesbury	Luton
Banbury	Luton, Gloucester or Reading
Barnsley	Sheffield
Barnstaple	Exeter
Barrow in Furness	Blackpool
Bath	Bristol
Bedford	Luton
Blackburn	Preston
Blackwood	Cardiff
Boston	Nottingham
Bridgend	Cardiff
Bridgwater	Bristol
Burnley	Bolton or Preston
Burton on Trent	Derby, Leicester or Nottingham
Bury St Edmunds	Cambridge
Canterbury	Croydon or High Court
Carlisle	Blackpool or Preston
Carmarthen	Cardiff
Chelmsford	Southend or High Court
Cheltenham	Gloucester
Chester	Birkenhead
Chesterfield	Sheffield
Colchester	Southend
Coventry	Birmingham
Crewe	Chester or Stoke
Darlington	Middlesbrough
Derby	Nottingham
Dewsbury	Leeds
Doncaster	Sheffield
Dudley	Birmingham
Durham	Newcastle
Eastbourne	Brighton
Great Grimsby	Hull

APPENDIX 2

Great Yarmouth	Norwich
Guildford	Croydon
Halifax	Leeds
Harrogate	Leeds
Hastings	Brighton
Haverfordwest	Cardiff
Hereford	Gloucester
Hertford	Luton
Huddersfield	Leeds
Ipswich	Norwich or Southend
Kendal	Blackpool or Preston
Kidderminster	Birmingham
King's Lynn	Cambridge or Norwich
Lancaster	Blackpool or Preston
Lincoln	Nottingham
Macclesfield	Manchester or Stoke
Maidstone	Croydon or High Court
Medway	Croydon or High Court
Merthyr Tydfil	Cardiff
Milton Keynes	Luton
Neath	Cardiff
Newbury	Reading
Newport (Gwent)	Cardiff
Newport (IoW)	Portsmouth or Southampton
Northampton	Luton
Oxford	Reading
Peterborough	Cambridge
Pontypridd	Cardiff
Rhyl	Birkenhead or Chester
Rochdale	Manchester or Oldham
Salisbury	Bournemouth or Southampton
Scarborough	Hull, Middlesbrough or York
Scunthorpe	Hull or Sheffield
Shrewsbury	Stoke
St Albans	Luton
Stafford	Stoke
Stockport	Manchester
Stourbridge	Birmingham
Sunderland	Newcastle
Swansea	Cardiff
Swindon	Gloucester or Reading
Tameside	Manchester
Taunton	Bristol or Exeter
Torquay	Exeter
Truro	Plymouth
Tunbridge Wells	Croydon
Wakefield	Leeds
Warrington	Chester, Liverpool or Manchester
Warwick	Birmingham
Welshpool	Chester or Stoke

West Bromwich	Birmingham
Weymouth	Bournemouth
Wigan	Bolton, Manchester or Preston
Winchester	Southampton
Worcester	Gloucester
Workington	Blackpool or Preston
Wrexham	Birkenhead, Chester or Stoke
Yeovil	Bristol or Exeter

Appendix 3

Forms

The numbers which appear in brackets after the description of the forms are references to the numbers these forms are given in Schedule 4 to the Rules except where otherwise stated.

1. Statutory demand under section 268(1)(a) of the Insolvency Act 1986. Debt for liquidated sum payable immediately (6.1)
2. Statutory demand under section 268(1)(a) of the Insolvency Act 1986. Debt for liquidated sum payable immediately following a judgment or order of the court (6.2)
3. Statutory demand under section 268(2) of the Insolvency Act 1986. Debt payable at a future date (6.3)
4. Advertisement of statutory demand
5. Affidavit of personal service of statutory demand (6.11)
6. Affidavit of substituted service of statutory demand (6.12)
7. Application to set aside a statutory demand (6.4)
8. Affidavit in support of application to set aside statutory demand (6.5)
9. Additional paragraphs to Form 8 where extension of time sought
10. Order setting aside statutory demand (6.6)
11. Creditor's bankruptcy petition on failure to comply with a statutory demand for a liquidated sum payable immediately (6.7)
12. Creditor's bankruptcy petition on failure to comply with a statutory demand for a liquidated sum payable at a future date (6.8)
13. Creditor's bankruptcy petition where execution or other process on a judgment has been returned in whole or part (6.9)
14. Bankruptcy petition for default in connection with voluntary arrangement (6.10)
15. Affidavit of truth of statements in bankruptcy petition (6.13)
16. Order for substituted service of a bankruptcy petition (6.15)
17. Substituted service of bankruptcy petition—notice in Gazette (6.16)
18. Affidavit of personal service of bankruptcy petition (6.17)
19. Affidavit of substituted service of bankruptcy petition (6.18)
20. Notice by debtor of intention to oppose bankruptcy petition (6.19)
21. Notice of intention to appear on bankruptcy petition (6.20)
22. List of creditors intending to appear on the hearing of the bankruptcy petition (6.21)
23. Order of adjournment of bankruptcy petition (6.23)
24. Notice to debtor and creditors of order of adjournment of bankruptcy petition (6.24)
25. Debtor's statement of affairs (6.28)

26	Application to stay advertisement of bankruptcy order and to rescind or annul the bankruptcy order
27	Proxy (winding up by the court or bankruptcy) (8.4)
28	Proof of debt—general form (6.37)
29	Affidavit of debt (6.39)
30	Notice of rejection of proof of debt
31	Application to reverse or vary trustee's decision on proof
32	Affidavit in support of summons to reverse trustee's decision on proof
33	Order reversing or varying rejection of proof or giving leave to amend proof
34	Notice of disclaimer (6.61)
35	Authority to trustee to pay dividends to another person
36	Originating application (7.1)
37	Ordinary application (7.2)
38	Written/statutory demand by creditor (4 in IPO)
39	Bankruptcy petition against individual member (presented in conjunction with petition against partnership) (7 in IPO)
40	Application for interim order (non-bankruptcy case)
41	Affidavit in support of application for interim order (non-bankruptcy case)
42	Application for interim order (bankruptcy case)
43	Affidavit in support of application for interim order (bankruptcy case)
44	Proposals for voluntary arrangement
45	General title (High Court)
46	General title (county court)
47	Proxy (company or individual voluntary arrangements) (8.1)

APPENDIX 3

**Form 1
(prescribed form 6.1)**

Statutory Demand under section 268(1)(a) of the Insolvency Act 1986. Debt for Liquidated Sum Payable Immediately

Notes for Creditor
- If the creditor is entitled to the debt by way of assignment, details of the original creditor and any intermediary assignees should be given in part C on page 3.
- If the amount of debt includes interest not previously notified to the debtor as included in the debtor's liability, details should be given, including the grounds upon which interest is charged. The amount of interest must be shown separately.
- Any other charge accruing due from time to time may be claimed. The amount or rate of the charge must be identified and the grounds on which it is claimed must be stated.
- In either case the amount claimed must be limited to that which has accrued due at the date of the demand.
- If the creditor holds any security the amount of debt should be the sum the creditor is prepared to regard as unsecured for the purposes of this demand. Brief details of the total debt should be included and the nature of the security and the value put upon it by the creditor, as at the date of the demand, must be specified.
- If signatory of the demand is a solicitor or other agent of the creditor the name of his/her firm should be given.

*Delete if signed by the creditor himself

Warning
- This is an **important** document. You should refer to the notes entitled "How to comply with a statutory demand or have it set aside".
- If you wish to have this demand set aside you must make application to do so **within 18 days** from its service on you.
- If you do not apply to set aside **within 18 days** or otherwise deal with this demand as set out in the notes **within 21 days** after its service on you, you could be made bankrupt and your property and goods taken away from you.
- Please read the demand and notes carefully. If you are in any doubt about your position you should seek advice **immediately** from a solicitor or your nearest Citizens Advice Bureau.

Demand

To _____

Address _____

_____

This demand is served on you by the creditor:

Name _____

Address _____

_____

The creditor claims that you owe the sum of £_____ , full particulars of which are set out on page 2, and that it is payable immediately and, to the extent of the sum demanded, is unsecured.

The creditor demands that you pay the above debt or secure or compound for it to the creditor's satisfaction.

[The creditor making this demand is a Minister of the Crown or a Government Department, and it is intended to present a bankruptcy petition in the High Court in London.]
[Delete if inappropriate]

Signature of individual _____

Name _____
(BLOCK LETTERS)

Date _____

*Position with or relationship to creditor _____

_____

*I am authorised to make this demand on the creditor's behalf.
Address _____

_____

Tel. No._____ Ref. _____

N.B. The person making this demand must complete the whole of pages 1, 2 and parts A, B and C (as applicable) on page 3.

FORMS 171

Form 1 contd.

Particulars of Debt
(These particulars must include (a) when the debt was incurred, (b) the consideration for the debt (or if there is no consideration the way in which it arose) and (c) the amount due as at the date of this demand.)

Notes for Creditor
Please make sure that you have read the notes on page 1 before completing this page.

Note:
If space is insufficient continue on page 4 and clearly indicate on this page that you are doing so.

Form 1 contd.

Part A
Appropriate Court for Setting Aside Demand

Rule 6.4(2) of the Insolvency Rules 1986 states that the appropriate court is the court to which you would have to present your own bankruptcy petition in accordance with Rule 6.40(1) and 6.40(2). In accordance with those rules on present information the appropriate court is [the High Court of Justice] [County Court]
(address)

Any application by you to set aside this demand should be made to that court.

Part B
The individual or individuals to whom any communication regarding this demand may be addressed is/are:

Name _____
(BLOCK LETTERS)

Address _____

Telephone Number _____

Reference _____

Part C
For completion if the creditor is entitled to the debt by way of assignment

	Name	Date(s) of Assignment
Original creditor		
Assignees		

How to comply with a statutory demand or have it set aside (ACT WITHIN 18 DAYS)

If you wish to avoid a bankruptcy petition being presented against you, you must pay the debt shown on page 1, particulars of which are set out on page 2 of this notice, within the period of **21 days** after its service upon you. Alternatively, you can attempt to come to a settlement with the creditor. To do this you should:

- inform the individual (or one of the individuals) named in part B above immediately that you are willing and able to offer security for the debt to the creditor's satisfaction; or
- inform the individual (or one of the individuals) named in part B immediately that you are willing and able to compound for the debt to the creditor's satisfaction.

If you dispute the demand in whole or in part you should:

- contact the individual (or one of the individuals) named in part B immediately.

THERE ARE MORE IMPORTANT NOTES ON THE NEXT PAGE

Form 1 contd.

If you consider that you have grounds to have this demand set aside or if you do not quickly receive a satisfactory written reply from the individual named in part B whom you have contacted you should **apply within 18 days** from the date of service of this demand on you to the appropriate court shown in part A above to have the demand set aside.

Any application to set aside the demand (Form 6.4 in Schedule 4 to the Insolvency Rules 1986) should be made within 18 days from the date of service upon you and be supported by an affidavit (Form 6.5 in Schedule 4 to those Rules) stating the grounds on which the demand should be set aside. The forms may be obtained from the appropriate court when you attend to make the application.

Remember!—From the date of service on you of this document
    (a) you have only 18 days to apply to the court to have the demand set aside, and
    (b) you have only 21 days before the creditor may present a bankruptcy petition

Form 2
(prescribed form 6.2)

Statutory Demand under section 268(1)(a) of the Insolvency Act 1986. Debt for Liquidated Sum Payable Immediately Following a Judgment or Order of the Court

Notes for Creditor
- If the creditor is entitled to the debt by way of assignment, details of the original creditor and any intermediary assignees should be given in part C on page 3.
- If the amount of debt includes interest not previously notified to the debtor as included in the debtor's liability, details should be given, including the grounds upon which interest is charged. The amount of interest must be shown separately.
- Any other charge accruing due from time to time may be claimed. The amount or rate of the charge must be identified and the grounds on which it is claimed must be stated.
- In either case the amount claimed must be limited to that which has accrued due at the date of the demand.
- If the creditor holds any security the amount of debt should be the sum the creditor is prepared to regard as unsecured for the purposes of this demand. Brief details of the total debt should be included and the nature of the security and the value put upon it by the creditor, as at the date of the demand, must be specified.
- Details of the judgment or order should be inserted, including details of the Division of the Court or District Registry and court reference, where judgment is obtained in the High Court.
- If signatory of the demand is a solicitor or other agent of the creditor the name of his/her firm should be given.

*Delete if signed by the creditor himself

Warning
- This is an **important** document. You should refer to the notes entitled "How to comply with a statutory demand or have it set aside".
- If you wish to have this demand set aside you must make application to do so **within 18 days** from its service on you.
- If you do not apply to set aside **within 18 days** or otherwise deal with this demand as set out in the notes **within 21 days** after its service on you, you could be made bankrupt and your property and goods taken away from you.
- Please read the demand and notes carefully. If you are in any doubt about your position you should seek advice **immediately** from a solicitor or your nearest Citizens Advice Bureau.

Demand

To _____

Address _____

_____

This demand is served on you by the creditor:

Name _____

Address _____

_____

The creditor claims that you owe the sum of £_____ , full particulars of which are set out on page 2, and that it is payable immediately and, to the extent of the sum demanded, is unsecured.

By a Judgment/Order of the _____ court in proceedings entitled (Case) Number _____ between _____
Plaintiff and _____ Defendant it was adjudged/ordered that you pay to the creditor the sum of £_____ and £_____ for costs.

The creditor demands that you pay the above debt or secure or compound for it to the creditor's satisfaction.

[The creditor making this demand is a Minister of the Crown or a Government Department, and it is intended to present a bankruptcy petition in the High Court in London.]
[Delete if inappropriate]

Signature of individual _____

Name _____
(BLOCK LETTERS)

Date _____

*Position with or relationship to creditor _____

_____

*I am authorised to make this demand on the creditor's behalf.

Address _____

_____

Tel. No. _____   Ref. _____

N.B. The person making this demand must complete the whole of pages 1, 2 and parts A, B and C (as applicable) on page 3.

FORMS

Form 2 contd.

Particulars of Debt
(These particulars must include (a) when the debt was incurred, (b) the consideration for the debt (or if there is no consideration the way in which it arose) and (c) the amount due as at the date of this demand.)

Notes for Creditor
Please make sure that you have read the notes on page 1 before completing this page.

Note:
If space is insufficient continue on page 4 and clearly indicate on this page that you are doing so.

APPENDIX 3

Form 2 contd.

Part A

Appropriate Court for Setting Aside Demand

Rule 6.4(2) of the Insolvency Rules 1986 states that the appropriate court is the court to which you would have to present your own bankruptcy petition in accordance with Rule 6.40(1) and 6.40(2).

Any application by you to set aside this demand should be made to that court, or, if this demand is issued by a Minister of the Crown or a Government Department, you must apply to the High Court to set aside if it is intended to present a bankruptcy petition against you in the High Court (see page 1).

In accordance with those rules on present information the appropriate court is [the High Court of Justice] [County Court]
(address)

Part B

The individual or individuals to whom any communication regarding this demand may be addressed is/are:

Name _____
(BLOCK LETTERS)

Address _____

Telephone number _____

Reference _____

Part C

For completion if the creditor is entitled to the debt by way of assignment

	Name	Date(s) of Assignment
Original creditor		
Assignees		

THERE ARE IMPORTANT NOTES ON THE NEXT PAGE

Form 2 contd.

How to comply with a statutory demand or have it set aside (ACT WITHIN 18 DAYS)

If you wish to avoid a bankruptcy petition being presented against you, you must pay the debt shown on page 1, particulars of which are set out on page 2 of this notice, within the period of **21 days** after its service upon you. However, if the demand follows (includes) a judgment or order of a County Court, any payment must be made to that County Court (quoting the Case No.). Alternatively, you can attempt to come to a settlement with the creditor. To do this you should:

- inform the individual (or one of the individuals) named in part B above immediately that you are willing and able to offer security for the debt to the creditor's satisfaction; or
- inform the individual (or one of the individuals) named in part B immediately that you are willing and able to compound for the debt to the creditor's satisfaction.

If you dispute the demand in whole or in part you should:

- contact the individual (or one of the individuals) named in part B immediately.

If you consider that you have grounds to have this demand set aside or if you do not quickly receive a satisfactory written reply from the individual named in part B whom you have contacted you should **apply within 18 days** from the date of service of this demand on you to the appropriate court shown in part A above to have the demand set aside.

Any application to set aside the demand (Form 6.4 in Schedule 4 to the Insolvency Rules 1986) should be made within 18 days from the date of service upon you and be supported by an affidavit (Form 6.5 in Schedule 4 to those Rules) stating the grounds on which the demand should be set aside. The forms may be obtained from the appropriate court when you attend to make the application.

Remember!—From the date of service on you of this document
               (a) you have only 18 days to apply to the court to have the demand set aside, and
               (b) you have only 21 days before the creditor may present a bankruptcy petition.

Form 3
(prescribed form 6.3)

Statutory Demand under section 268(2) of the
Insolvency Act 1986. Debt Payable at Future Date.

Notes for Creditor
- If the creditor is entitled to the debt by way of assignment, details of the original creditor and any intermediary assignees should be given in part C on page 3.
- If the amount of debt when due includes interest not previously notified to the debtor as included in the debtor's liability, details should be given, including the grounds upon which interest is charged. The amount of interest must be shown separately.
- Any other charge accruing due from time to time may be claimed. The amount or rate of the charge must be identified and the grounds on which it is claimed must be stated.
- In either case the amount claimed must be limited to that which will have accrued due when payment falls due on the date specified.
- If the creditor holds any security the amount of debt should be the sum the creditor is prepared to regard as unsecured for the purposes of this demand. Brief details of the total debt should be included and the nature of the security and the value put upon it by the creditor, as at the date of the demand, must be specified.
- The grounds for the creditor's opinion that the debtor has no reasonable prospects of paying the debt when it falls due must be stated.
- If signatory of the demand is a solicitor or other agent of the creditor the name of his/her firm should be given.

*Delete if signed by the creditor himself

Warning
- This is an **important** document. You should refer to the notes entitled "How to comply with a statutory demand or have it set aside".
- If you wish to have this demand set aside you must make application to do so **within 18 days** from its service on you.
- If you do not apply to set aside **within 18 days** or otherwise deal with this demand as set out in the notes **within 21 days** after its service on you, you could be made bankrupt and your property and goods taken away from you.
- Please read the demand and notes carefully. If you are in any doubt about your position you should seek advice **immediately** from a solicitor or your nearest Citizens Advice Bureau.

Demand

To _____

Address _____

This demand is served on you by the creditor:

Name _____

Address _____
_____

The creditor claims that you will owe the sum of £_____ , full particulars of which are set out on page 2, when payment falls due on _____

The creditor is of the opinion that you have no reasonable prospect of paying this debt when it falls due because

[The creditor making this demand is a Minister of the Crown or Government Department, and it is intended to present a bankruptcy petition in the High Court in London.] [Delete if inappropriate]

Signature of individual _____

Name _____
(BLOCK LETTERS)

Date _____

*Position with or relationship to creditor _____
_____

*I am authorised to make this demand on the creditor's behalf.

Address _____
_____

Tel. No. _____   Ref. _____

N.B. The person making this demand must complete the whole of pages 1, 2 and parts A, B and C (as applicable) on page 3.

FORMS

Form 3 contd.

Particulars of Debt
(These particulars must include (a) when the debt was incurred, (b) the consideration for the debt (or if there is no consideration the way in which it will arise) and (c) the amount of future debt and the date payment is due.)

Notes for Creditor
Please make sure that you have read the notes on page 1 before completing this page.

Note:
If space is insufficient continue on page 4 and clearly indicate on this page that you are doing so.

Form 3 contd.

Part A

Appropriate Court for Setting Aside Demand

Rule 6.4(2) of the Insolvency Rules 1986 states that the appropriate court is the court to which you would have to present your own bankruptcy petition in accordance with Rule 6.40(1) and 6.40(2). In accordance with those rules on present information the appropriate court is [the High Court of Justice] [County Court]
(address)

Any application by you to set aside this demand should be made to that court.

Part B

The individual or individuals to whom any communication regarding this demand may be addressed is/are:

Name _____ | _____
(BLOCK LETTERS)

Address _____ | _____

_____ | _____

Telephone number _____ | _____

Reference _____ | _____

Part C

For completion if the creditor is entitled to the debt by way of assignment

	Name	Date(s) of Assignment
Original creditor		
Assignees		

How to comply with a statutory demand or have it set aside (ACT WITHIN 18 DAYS)

If you wish to avoid a bankruptcy petition being presented against you, you must within the period of **21 days** after its service upon you satisfy the creditor that you are able to meet the debt demanded when it is due.

If you dispute that the debt will be due in whole or in part or if you dispute the allegation that you will be unable to pay the debt when it falls due or if you consider that you may be able to offer security for the debt or to compound for it you should:

- contact the individual (or one of the individuals) named in part B immediately.

If you consider that you have grounds to have this demand set aside or if you do not quickly receive a satisfactory written reply from the individual named in part B whom you have contacted you should **apply within 18 days** from the date of service of this demand on you to the appropriate court shown in part A above to have the demand set aside.

THERE ARE MORE IMPORTANT NOTES ON THE NEXT PAGE

Form 3 contd.

Any application to set aside the demand (Form 6.4 in Schedule 4 to the Insolvency Rules 1986) should be made within 18 days from the date of service upon you and be supported by an affidavit (Form 6.5 in Schedule 4 to those Rules) stating the grounds on which the demand should be set aside. The forms may be obtained from the appropriate court when you attend to make the application.

Remember!—From the date of service on you of this document
  (a) you have only 18 days to apply to the court to have the demand set aside, and
  (b) you have only 21 days before the creditor may present a bankruptcy petition.

Form 4

Advertisement of Statutory Demand

(TITLE)

Statutory Demand

(Debt for liquidated sum payable immediately following a Judgment or Order of the Court)

To (*block letters*)
of

TAKE NOTICE that a statutory demand has been issued by
Name of creditor
Address

The creditor demands payment of £   the amount now due on a Judgment/Order of the (High Court of Justice   Division) (_____ County Court) dated the   day of   19

The statutory demand is an important document and it is deemed to have been served on you on the date of the first appearance of this advertisement. You *must* deal with this demand within 21 days of the service upon you or you could be made bankrupt and your property and goods taken away from you. If you are in any doubt as to your position, you should seek advice *immediately* from a solicitor or your nearest Citizens Advice Bureau.

The Statutory Demand can be obtained or is available for inspection and collection from:

Name
Address

(Solicitor for) the creditor
Tel. No.   Reference

You have only 21 days from the date of the first appearance of this advertisement before the creditor may present a bankruptcy petition

Form 5
(prescribed form 6.11)

Affidavit of Personal Service
of Statutory Demand

(TITLE)

Date of statutory demand _____

(a) Insert name, address and description of person making the oath and whether the creditor or a person acting on his behalf

I, (a) _____
_____

make oath and say as follows:—

(b) Delete 'I' and insert name and address of person who effected service, if applicable

1. (b) [I] [_____]
did on (c) _____ (d) [before] [after]   hours, at (e) _____

(c) Insert date

(d) Insert time which must be either before or after 16.00 hours Monday to Friday or before or after 12.00 hours Saturday

(e) Insert address

(f) Delete words in [ ] if no acknowledgement of service has been received

(g) Give particulars of the way in which the debtor acknowledged service of the demand

_____
personally serve the above-named debtor with the demand dated
_____

(f) [2. That on (c) _____ the debtor acknowledged service of the demand by (g) _____]

3. A copy of the demand marked "A" (f) [and the acknowledgement of service marked "B"] is/are exhibited hereto.

Sworn at

Form 6
(prescribed form 6.12)

Affidavit of Substituted Service of Statutory Demand

(TITLE)

Date of Statutory Demand _____

(a) Insert name, address and description of person making the oath

I (a) _____
_____

make oath and say as follows:—

(b) Insert date
(c) Give particulars of the steps taken with a view to serving the demand and why they were ineffective and if the creditor has taken advantage of Rule 6.3(3) (newspaper advertisement) state the means of the creditor's knowledge for the purposes of that Rule and the date or dates on which, and the newspaper in which, the demand was advertised.

1. That on (b) _____ an attempt was made to serve the demand on the above named debtor by (c)

2. That on (b) _____ substituted service of the demand was effected in the following way:—

3. That to the best of my knowledge, information and belief the demand will have come to the attention of the above named debtor by

(b) _____

(d) Delete words in [ ] if no acknowledgement of service has been received

(d) [4. That on (b) _____ the debtor acknowledged service of the demand by (e) _____]

(e) Give particulars of the way in which the debtor acknowledged service of the demand

5. A copy of the demand marked "A" (d) [and the acknowledgement of service marked "B"] (f) [is] [are] exhibited hereto.

(f) Delete as applicable

Sworn at

Form 7
(prescribed form 6.4)

Application to Set Aside a Statutory Demand
(TITLE)

(a) Insert name and address of person to attend hearing

Let (a)

attend before the Registrar as follows:—

Date _____

Time _____ hours

Place _____

(b) Insert name of debtor

on the hearing of an application by (b) the applicant for an order that the statutory demand dated be set aside.

(c) Insert date

The grounds on which the applicant claims to be entitled to the order are set out in the affidavit of the applicant sworn on (c) a copy of which affidavit accompanies this application.

(d) State the names and addresses of the persons to be served

The names and addresses of the persons upon whom this application should be served are:— (d)

(e) State the applicant's address for service

The applicant's address for service is:— (e)

Dated _____

Signed _____
(Solicitor for the) Applicant

If you do not attend, the Court may make such order as it thinks fit

Form 8
(prescribed form 6.5)

Affidavit in Support of Application to Set Aside Statutory Demand

(TITLE)

(a) Insert name address and description of person making the oath

I (a) _____

_____

_____

_____

make oath and say as follows:—

(b) Insert date

1. That on (b) _____ the statutory demand exhibited hereto and marked "A" came into my hands.

(c) Insert one of the 8 following alternatives or if none of them are applicable state grounds on which you consider the statutory demand should be set aside

2. That I (c)

(1) "Do not admit the debt because..." [here state grounds] or
(2) "Admit the debt but not that it is payable immediately" [state reason], or
(3) "Admit the debt as to £   , and that this is payable but that the remainder is not immediately payable. I am prepared to pay the amount of £   immediately" [state reason], or
(4) "Admit the debt and am prepared to secure or compound for it to the creditor's satisfaction by ...." [state nature of satisfaction], or
(5) "Say that the debt is a secured debt" [give full details of security and its value], or
(6) "Have a counter-claim (or set-off or cross demand) for £   being a sum equal to (or exceeding) the claim in respect of" [here state grounds of counterclaim etc.], or

Form 8 contd.

(7) "Say that execution on the Judgment of the Court has been stayed" [give details], or

(8) "Say that the Demand does not comply with the Insolvency Rules in that .... " [state reason]

Sworn at

Form 9

Additional Paragraphs to Form 8 where Extension of Time Sought

(TITLE)

(Commence as in Form 8)

"**3.** That to the best of my knowledge and belief the creditor(s) named in the demand has/have not presented a petition against me.
"**4.** That the reasons for my failure to apply to set aside the demand within 18 days after service are as follows: . . .
"**5.** Unless restrained by injunction the creditor(s) may present a bankruptcy petition against me."

(Complete as in Form 8)

Form 10
(prescribed form 6.6)

Order Setting Aside Statutory Demand
(TITLE)

(a) Insert name and address of applicant

Upon the application of (a) _____
_____
_____

and upon hearing _____

and upon reading the evidence

It is ordered that the statutory demand dated _____ be set aside.

(b) Insert details of any further order in the matter

And it is ordered that (b) _____
_____
_____
_____
_____

Dated _____

**Form 11
(prescribed form 6.7)**

Creditor's Bankruptcy Petition on Failure to Comply with a Statutory Demand for a Liquidated Sum Payable Immediately.

(TITLE)

(a) Insert full name(s) and address(es) of petitioner(s).   I/We (a) _____

(b) Insert full name, place of residence and occupation (if any) of debtor   petition the court that a bankruptcy order may be made against (b) _____

(c) Insert in full any other name(s) by which the debtor is or has been known   [also known as (c) _____]

(d) Insert trading name (adding "with another or others", if this is so), business address and nature of business   [and carrying on business as (d) _____]

(e) Insert any other address or addresses at which the debtor has resided at or after the time the petition debt was incurred.   [and lately residing at (e) _____]

(f) Give the same details as specified in note (d) above for any other businesses which have been carried on at or after the time the petition debt was incurred.   [and lately carrying on business as (f) _____]

and say as follows:—

(g) Delete as applicable   1. The debtor has for the greater part of six months immediately preceding the presentation of this petition (g) [resided at] [carried on business at] _____

(h) Or as the case may be following the terms of Rule 6.9.   within the district of this court (h)

(j) Please give the amount of debt(s), what they relate to and when they were incurred. Please show separately the amount or rate of any interest or other charge not previously notified to the debtor **and the reasons why you are claiming it.**   2. The debtor is justly and truly indebted to me[us] in the aggregate sum of £(j) _____

Form 11 contd.

(k) Insert date on which judgment was obtained

(l) Insert date of execution

4. On (k) _____ judgment was obtained in (g) [the High Court of Justice _____ Division] [_____ County Court]. [or as the case may be] on an action the short title and reference to the record whereof is "A _____ " V. "B _____ " Number _____ in the sum of £ _____ following which execution was issued at the _____ court in respect of the debt and on (l) _____ the sheriff/county court (g) [made a return] [endorsed upon the writ a statement] to the effect that the execution was unsatisfied (g) [as to the whole] [as to part] and the above-mentioned debt represents the amount by which the execution was returned unsatisified.

5. I/We do not, nor does any person on my/our behalf, hold any security on the debtor's estate, or any part thereof, for the payment of the above-mentioned sum.

OR

I/We hold security for the payment of (g) [part of] the above-mentioned sum. I/We will give up such security for the benefit of all the creditors in the event of a bankruptcy order being made

OR

I/We hold security for the payment of part of the above-mentioned sum and I/we estimate the value of such security to be £ _____ This petition is not made in respect of the secured part of my/our debt.

Endorsement

This petition having been presented to the court on _____

it is ordered that the petition shall be heard as follows:—

Date _____

Time _____ hours

Place _____

(m) Insert name of debtor

and you, the above-named (m) _____ are to take notice that if you intend to oppose the petition you must not later than 7 days before the day fixed for the hearing:

(i) file in court a notice (in Form 6.19) specifying the grounds on which you object to the making of a bankruptcy order; and

(ii) send a copy of the notice to the petitioner or his solicitor.

(n) Only to be completed where the petitioning creditor is represented by a solicitor.

The solicitor to the petitioning creditor is:— (n)

Name _____

Address _____

_____

Telephone Number _____

Reference _____

Form 12
(prescribed form 6.8)

Creditor's Bankruptcy Petition on Failure to Comply with a Statutory Demand for a Liquidated Sum Payable at a Future Date

(TITLE)

(a) Insert full name(s) and address(es) of petitioner(s).

I/We (a) _____

(b) Insert full name, place of residence and occupation (if any) of debtor

petition the court that a bankruptcy order may be made against (b) _____

(c) Insert in full any other name(s) by which the debtor is or has been known

[also known as (c) _____]

(d) Insert trading name (adding "with another or others", if this is so), business address and nature of business

[and carrying on business as (d) _____]

(e) Insert any other address or addresses at which the debtor has resided at or after the time the petition debt was incurred.

[and lately residing at (e) _____]

(f) Give the same details as specified in note (d) above for any other businesses which have been carried on at or after the time the petition debt was incurred.

[and lately carrying on business as (f) _____]

and say as follows:—

(g) Delete as applicable

1. The debtor has for the greater part of six months immediately preceding the presentation of this petition (g) [resided at] [carried on business at] _____

(h) Or as the case may be following the terms of Rule 6.9.

within the district of this court (h)

(j) Please give the amount of debt(s), what they relate to and when they were incurred. Please show separately the amount or rate of any interest or other charge not previously notified to the debtor **and the reasons why you are claiming it.**

2. The debtor is justly and truly indebted to me[us] in the aggregate sum of £(j) _____

Form 12 contd.

(k) Insert date or dates when the debt becomes payable.

3. The above-mentioned debt is for a liquidated sum payable on (k) _____ and the debtor appears to have no reasonable prospect of being able to pay it.

(l) Insert date of service of statutory demand

4. On (l) _____ a statutory demand was served upon the debtor by

(m) State manner of service of the demand

(m) _____
in respect of the above-mentioned debt. To the best of my knowledge and belief the demand has neither been complied with nor set aside in accordance with the Rules and no application to set it aside is outstanding.

(n) If 3 weeks have not elapsed since service of statutory demand give reasons for earlier presentation of petition

(n)

5. I/We do not, nor does any person on my/our behalf, hold any security on the debtor's estate, or any part thereof, for the payment of the above-mentioned sum.

OR

(p) Delete as applicable

I/We hold security for the payment of (p) [part of] the above-mentioned sum. I/We will give up such security for the benefit of all the creditors in the event of a bankruptcy order being made.

OR

I/We hold security for the payment of part of the above-mentioned sum and I/we estimate the value of such security to be £   . This petition is not made in respect of the secured part of my/our debt.

Endorsement
This petition having been presented to the court on _____
it is ordered that the petition shall be heard as follows:
Date _____
Time _____ hours
Place _____

(q) Insert name of debtor

and you, the above-named (q) _____ are to take notice that if you intend to oppose the petition you must not later than 7 days before the day fixed for the hearing:

(i) file in court a notice (in Form 6.19) specifying the grounds on which you object to the making of a bankruptcy order; and

(ii) send a copy of the notice to the petitioner or his solicitor.

(r) Only to be completed where the petitioning creditor is represented by a solicitor.

The solicitor to the petitioning creditor is:— (r)

Name _____

Address _____

_____

Telephone Number _____

Reference _____

Form 13
(prescribed form 6.9)

Creditor's Bankruptcy Petition Where Execution or Other Process on a Judgment has been Returned in Whole or Part

(TITLE)

(a) Insert full name(s) and address(es) of petitioner(s).

I/We (a) _____

(b) Insert full name, place of residence and occupation (if any) of debtor

petition the court that a bankruptcy order may be made against (b) _____

(c) Insert in full any other name(s) by which the debtor is or has been known

[also known as (c) _____]

(d) Insert trading name (adding "with another or others", if this is so), business address and nature of business

[and carrying on business as (d) _____]

(e) Insert any other address or addresses at which the debtor has resided at or after the time the petition debt was incurred

[and lately residing at (e) _____]

(f) Give the same details as specified in note (d) above for any other businesses which have been carried on at or after the time the petition debt was incurred

[and lately carrying on business as (f) _____]

(g) Delete as applicable

(h) Or as the case may be following the terms of Rule 6.9.

and say as follows:—

1. The debtor has for the greater part of six months immediately preceding the presentation of this petition (g) [resided at] [carried on business at] _____ within the district of this court (h)

2. The debtor is justly and truly indebted to me[us] in the aggregate sum of

(j) Please give the amount of debt(s), what they relate to and when they were incurred. Please show separately the amount or rate of any interest or other charge not previously notified to the debtor **and the reasons why you are claiming it.**

£(j) _____

3. The above mentioned debt is for a liquidated sum payable immediately and the debtor appears to be unable to pay it.

Form 13 contd.

(k) Insert date of service of a statutory demand

4. On (k) _____ a statutory demand was served upon the debtor by

(l) State manner of service of demand

(l) _____
in respect of the above-mentioned debt. To the best of my knowledge and belief the demand has neither been complied with nor set aside in accordance with the Rules and no application to set it aside is outstanding

(m) If 3 weeks have not elapsed since service of statutory demand give reasons for earlier presentation of petition

(m)

5. I/We do not, nor does any person on my/our behalf, hold any security on the debtor's estate, or any part thereof, for the payment of the above-mentioned sum

OR

(n) Delete as applicable

I/We hold security for the payment of (n) [part of] the above-mentioned sum. I/We will give up such security for the benefit of all the creditors in the event of a bankruptcy order being made.

OR

I/We hold security for the payment of part of the above-mentioned sum and I/we estimate the value of such security to be £ _____ This petition is not made in respect of the secured part of my/our debt.

Endorsement

This petition having been presented to the court on _____ it is ordered that the petition shall be heard as follows:—

Date _____

Time _____ hours

Place _____

(p) Insert name of debtor

and you, the above-named (p) _____, are to take notice that if you intend to oppose the petition you must not later than 7 days before the day fixed for the hearing:

 (i) file in court a notice (in Form 6.19) specifying the grounds on which you object to the making of a bankruptcy order; and

 (ii) send a copy of the notice to the petitioner or his solicitor.

(q) Only to be completed where the petitioning creditor is represented by a solicitor

The solicitor to the petitioning creditor is:— (q)

Name _____

Address _____

_____

Telephone Number _____

Reference _____

Form 14
(prescribed form 6.10)

Bankruptcy Petition for Default in Connection with Voluntary Arrangement

(TITLE)

(a) Insert full name(s) and address(es) of petitioner(s).

I/We (a) _____

(b) Insert full name, place of residence and occupation (if any) of debtor

petition the court that a bankruptcy order may be made against (b) _____

(c) Insert in full any other name(s) by which the debtor is or has been known

[also known as (c) _____]

(d) Insert trading name (adding "with another or others", if this is so), business address and nature of business

[and carrying on business as (d) _____]

(e) Insert any other address or addresses at which the debtor has resided at or after the time the petition debt was incurred

[and lately residing at (e) _____]

(f) Give the same details as specified in note (d) above for any other businesses which have been carried on at or after the time the petition debt was incurred

[and lately carrying on business as (f) _____]

and say as follows:—

(g) Delete as applicable

1. That the debtor has for the greater part of six months immediately preceding the presentation of this petition (g) [resided at] [carried on business at] _____

(h) Or as the case may be following the terms of Rule 6.9.

within the district of this court (h)

(j) Insert date the debtor entered into voluntary arrangement

2. On (j) _____ a voluntary arrangement proposed by the debtor was approved by his creditors and I am (g) [a person who is for the time being bound by the said voluntary arrangement and (k) _____

(k) Insert name of supervisor.

is the supervisor] [(k) _____ the supervisor of the said voluntary arrangement]

Form 14 contd.

(l) Give details of the default in connection with the composition or scheme, being the grounds under section 276(1) IA86 upon which the bankruptcy order is sought

3. (l)

Endorsement
This petition having been presented to the court on _____
it is ordered that the petition shall be heard as follows:—
Date _____
Time _____ hours
Place _____

(m) Insert name of debtor

and you, the above-named (m) _____ are to take notice that if you intend to oppose the petition you must not later than 7 days before the day fixed for the hearing:

(i) file in court a notice (in Form 6.19) specifying the grounds on which you object to the making of a bankruptcy order; and

(ii) send a copy of the notice to the petitioner or his solicitor.

(n) Only to be completed where the petitioning creditor is represented by a solicitor.

The solicitor to the petitioning creditor is:— (n)

Name _____

Address _____

_____

Telephone Number _____

Reference _____

APPENDIX 3

Form 15
(prescribed form 6.13)

Affidavit of Truth of Statements in Bankruptcy Petition

(TITLE)

(a) Insert name, address and description of person making oath

I (a) _____

_____

_____

make oath and say as follows:—

[1. I am the petitioner. The statements in the petition now produced and shown to me marked "A" are true to the best of my knowledge, information and belief.

(b) If petition is based upon a statutory demand, and more than 4 months have elapsed between service of the demand and presentation of the petition, give reason(s) for delay and explanation of circumstances which have contributed to the late presentation of the petition.

2. (b)   ]

OR

(c) State the capacity eg. director, secretary, solicitor etc.

[1. I am (c) _____ of the petitioner; or

(d) Delete as applicable

2. I am duly authorised by the petitioner to make this affidavit on (d) [its] [his] behalf.

(e) State means of knowledge of matters sworn to in the affidavit

3. I have been concerned in the matters giving rise to the presentation of the petition and I have the requisite knowledge of the matters referred to in the petition because (e)

4. The statements in the petition now produced and shown to me marked "A" are true to the best of my knowledge, information and belief.

5. (b)   ]

Sworn at

**Form 16
(prescribed form 6.15)**

Order for Substituted Service of a Bankruptcy Petition

(TITLE)

Mr Registrar   in chambers

(a) Insert date   In the matter of a bankruptcy petition filed on (a)

(b) Insert full name, address and description of applicant   Upon the application of (b)

(c) State name, address and description of person making oath   And upon reading the affidavit of (c)

(d) State class of postage to be used   It is ordered that the sending of a sealed copy of the above-mentioned petition together with a sealed copy of this order by (d) prepaid post addressed to

at

and/or by publication in the London Gazette and/or in the   newspaper of the presentation of such petition and the time and place fixed for hearing the petition shall be deemed to be good and sufficient service of the said petition on the above-named debtor on the   day after completing such posting and/or publication as aforesaid.

Dated _____

Form 17
(prescribed form 6.16)

Substituted Service of Bankruptcy Petition—Notice in Gazette

(TITLE)

(a) Delete as applicable   In the (a) [High Court of Justice] [_____
                            County Court]

                            In Bankruptcy

(b) Insert full   To (b) _____
particulars of debtor
as in petition   _____

                            Take notice that a bankruptcy petition has been presented against you in this court
(c) Insert name(s) and   by (c) _____
address(es) of
petitioner(s)   _____

                            _____

                            _____

(d) Insert terms of   and the court has ordered that (d) _____
order of substituted
service   _____

                            _____

                            shall be deemed to be service of the petition upon you.

                            The said petition will be heard at this court on:—

                            Date _____

                            Time _____ hours

                            Place _____

                            Important

                            If you do not attend the hearing of the petition the court may make a bankruptcy
                            order against you in your absence.

                            The petition can be inspected by you on application at this court, whose offices
(e) Insert address   are at (e) _____

                            _____

                            _____

                            Dated _____

Form 18
(prescribed form 6.17)

Affidavit of Personal Service of Bankruptcy Petition

(TITLE)

(a) Insert date — In the matter of a bankruptcy petition filed on (a)

(b) Insert full name, address and description of person making oath — I (b)

(c) Insert name and address — and for the purpose of service instructed by (c)

(d) Delete as applicable — (d) [Solicitor(s) for] the

make oath and say as follows:—

1. That I did on (a)   serve the above-named debtor with a copy of the above-mentioned petition, duly sealed with the seal of the court by delivering the same personally to the said (e)

(e) Insert name of debtor as in title

(f) State exact place of service — at (f)

(g) Sealed copy must be marked as an exhibit — 2. A sealed copy of the said petition is now produced and shown to me marked "A" (g)

Sworn at

NOTE: This affidavit and exhibit should be filed in court immediately after service (Rule 6.15.(2))

Form 19
(prescribed form 6.18)

Affidavit of Substituted Service of Bankruptcy Petition

(TITLE)

(a) Insert date   In the matter of a bankruptcy petition filed on (a)

(b) Insert full name, address and description of person making oath   I (b)

(c) Insert name and address   and for the purpose of service instructed by (c)

(d) Delete as applicable   (d) [Solicitor(s) for] the

make oath and say as follows:—

(e) Set out terms of order for substituted service   1. That I did on (a)   serve the above-named debtor with a sealed copy of the above-mentioned petition, together with a sealed copy of the order for substituted service thereof, by (e)

(f) Sealed copy must be marked as an exhibit   2. A sealed copy of the said petition is now produced and shown to me marked "A" (f)

3. A sealed copy of the said order is now produced and shown to me marked "B" (f).

NOTE: This affidavit and exhibits should be filed in court immediately after service (Rule 6.15 (2))

Form 20
(prescribed form 6.19)

Notice by Debtor of Intention to Oppose Bankruptcy Petition
(TITLE)

(a) Insert name   Take note that I (a) _____
intend to oppose the application to make a bankruptcy order on the following grounds:—

_____

_____
_____

Dated _____

To the   court
and to the [solicitors for] the petitioner.

Form 21
(prescribed form 6.20)

Notice of Intention to Appear on Bankruptcy Petition

(TITLE)

In the matter of a bankruptcy petition filed

(a) Insert date   on (a) _____

to be heard on (a) _____

(b) Insert full name and address, or if a firm, the name of the firm and address

I (b) _____

_____

_____

(c) State amount and nature of debt eg. goods supplied

(d) Delete as applicable

a creditor of the above-named debtor in respect of (c) _____ intend to appear on the hearing of the above-mentioned petition and to (d) [support] [oppose] the petition.

Signed _____

Dated _____

Name in BLOCK LETTERS _____

(e) If creditor's solicitor or other agent please give name and address of firm

Position with or relationship to creditor (e) _____

_____

_____

Telephone No _____

Reference No _____

(f) Insert name(s) and address(es) of petitioner(s)

To (f) _____

_____

_____

Form 22
(prescribed form 6.21)

List of Creditors Intending to Appear on the Hearing of the Bankruptcy Petition

(TITLE)

(a) Insert date

In the matter of a bankruptcy petition filed on (a) ―――――

The following creditors have given notice that they intend to appear on the hearing of the above-mentioned petition on (a) ―――――

Name of creditor	Address of creditor	Amount owed to creditor	Creditor's Solicitors (if any)	Whether intending to support or oppose the petition

―――――
[Solicitors for the] Petitioning creditor (b) ―――――

(b) Insert name and address

Form 23
(prescribed form 6.23)

Order of Adjournment of Bankruptcy Petition

(TITLE)

(a) Insert date   In the matter of a bankruptcy petition filed on (a)

(b) Delete as applicable   Upon the (b) [adjourned] hearing of the petition today

And upon hearing

And upon reading the evidence

It is ordered that the further hearing of this petition be adjourned to:

Date _____

Time _____ hours

Place _____

Dated _____

Form 24
(prescribed form 6.24)

Notice to Debtor and Creditors of Order of Adjournment of Bankruptcy Petition
(TITLE)

(a) Insert date   In the matter of a bankruptcy petition filed on (a)

Take notice that by order of the court dated _____
the further hearing of the petition has been adjourned to:

Date _____

Time _____ hours

Place _____

Signed _____

Dated _____

Name in BLOCK LETTERS _____

(b) Insert name and
address of debtor and
creditors   To (b) _____

APPENDIX 3

**Form 25
(prescribed form 6.28)**

Statement of Affairs (Debtor's Petition)
Insolvency Act 1986

NOTE:
These details will be the same as those shown at the top of your petition

In the _____

In Bankruptcy   No _____ of 19____

Re _____

The 'Guidance Notes' Booklet tells you how to complete this form easily and correctly

Show your current financial position by completing all the pages of this form which will then be your Statement of Affairs.

AFFIDAVIT

This Affidavit must be sworn before a Solicitor or Commissioner of Oaths or an officer of the court duly authorised to administer oaths when you have completed the rest of this form

(a) Insert full name and occupation

I (a) _____

_____

(b) Insert full address

of (b) _____

_____

_____

Make oath and say that the several pages exhibited hereto and marked _____ are to the best of my knowledge and belief a full, true and complete statement of my affairs at today's date.

Sworn at _____

Date _____   Signature(s) _____

Before me _____

_____
A Solicitor or Commissioner of Oaths or Duly authorised officer

Before swearing the affidavit, the Solicitor or Commissioner is particularly requested to make sure that the full name, address and description of the deponent are stated, and to initial any crossings-out or other alterations in the printed form. A deficiency in the affidavit in any of the above respects will mean that it will be refused by the court, and will need to be re-sworn.

A

LIST OF SECURED CREDITORS

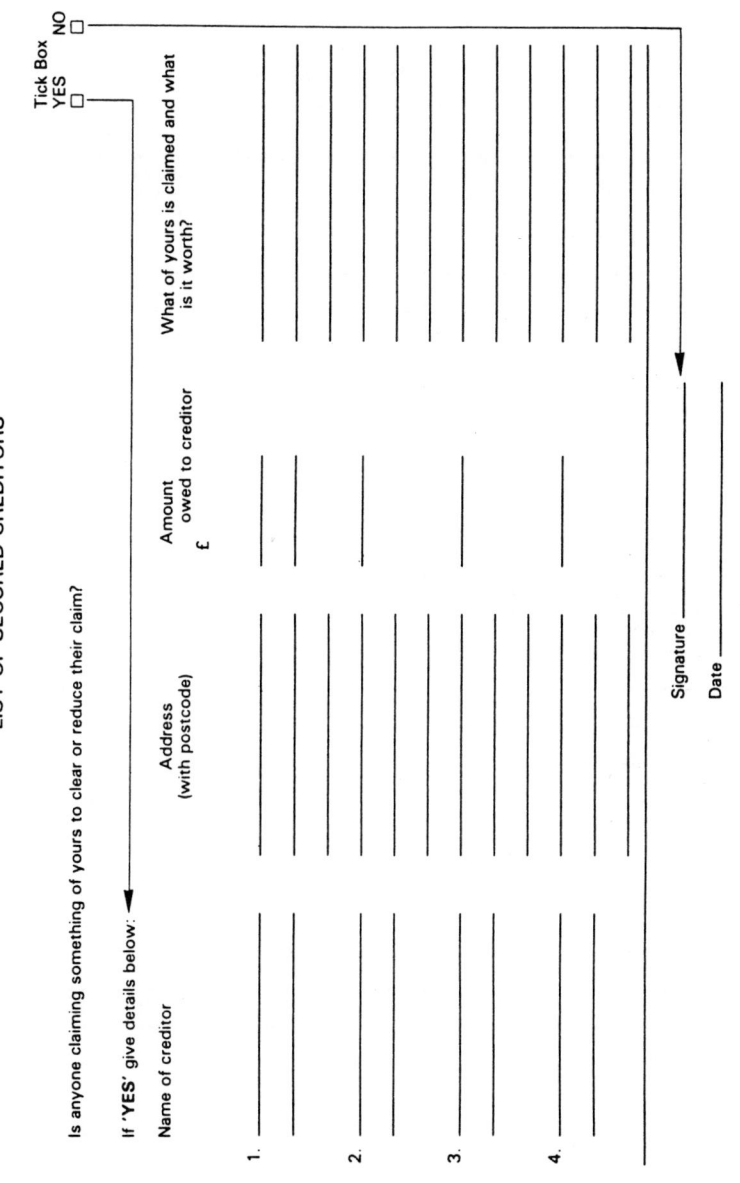

Is anyone claiming something of yours to clear or reduce their claim?

Tick Box
YES ☐
NO ☐

If 'YES' give details below:

Name of creditor	Address (with postcode)	Amount owed to creditor £	What of yours is claimed and what is it worth?
1.			
2.			
3.			
4.			

Signature _____

Date _____

B

LIST OF UNSECURED CREDITORS

1 No.	2 Name of creditor or claimant	3 Address (with postcode)	4 Amount the creditor says you owe him/her £	5 Amount you think you owe £

Signature _____   Date _____

C1

ASSETS

	Tick Box	
	Yes	No
Do you have any bank accounts or an interest in one? If **'YES'** state where they are, how much is in them and how much is your share.	☐	☐

_____
_____
_____
_____

Do you have any business bank accounts, including joint accounts? Yes ☐ No ☐
If **'YES'** state the name of the accounts, where they are
and how much is in them.

_____
_____
_____

Do you have any building society accounts or an interest in one? Yes ☐ No ☐
If **'YES'** state where they are and how much is in them
and how much is your share.

_____
_____
_____
_____
_____

Signature _____   Date _____

APPENDIX 3

C2

ASSETS

	Tick Box
	Yes No

Do you have any other savings?
If **'YES'** give details

_____
_____
_____
_____
_____

Do you use a motor vehicle?   Yes No
If **'YES'** who owns it and what is it worth?

_____
_____
_____
_____

Have you an interest in any other motor vehicles?   Yes No
If **'YES'** give details and their value.

_____
_____
_____
_____
_____

Signature _____ Date _____

C3

ASSETS

Now show anything else of yours which may be of value:

£

a) Household furniture and belongings _____
b) Life policies _____
c) Money owed to you _____
d) Stock in trade _____
e) Other property (see Guidance Notes): _____

TOTAL

Signature _____ Date _____

APPENDIX 3

D

1. State the name, age (if under 18), and relationship to you of your dependants

   1 _____   6 _____
   2 _____   7 _____
   3 _____   8 _____
   4 _____   9 _____
   5 _____   10 _____

2. Has distress been levied against you by or on behalf of any creditor?
   If **'YES'** give details below:—

   Tick Box
   Yes ☐ No ☐

Name of creditor	Amount of claim £	Date Distress levied	Description and estimated value of property seized
_____	_____	_____	_____
_____	_____	_____	_____
_____	_____	_____	_____
_____	_____	_____	_____
_____	_____	_____	_____
_____	_____	_____	_____
_____	_____	_____	_____
_____	_____	_____	_____

Signature _____   Date _____

E

3. At the date you present your bankruptcy petition, is any court judgment or other legal process outstanding against you that has been made by any court in England and Wales?
   If **'YES'** give details below:—

   Tick Box Yes ☐ No ☐

Name of creditor	Amount of claim £	Type and date of process issued	Description and estimated value of any property involved
_____	_____	_____	_____
_____	_____	_____	_____
_____	_____	_____	_____
_____	_____	_____	_____
_____	_____	_____	_____
_____	_____	_____	_____
_____	_____	_____	_____

4. At the date you present your bankruptcy petition, is any attachment of earnings order in force against you?
   If **'YES'** give details below:—

   Tick Box Yes ☐ No ☐

Name of creditor	Date of order	Court	Amount of instalment payable under order (per month/week) £	Total amount paid under order £	Date order expires (if applicable)
_____	_____	_____	_____	_____	_____
_____	_____	_____	_____	_____	_____
_____	_____	_____	_____	_____	_____

Signature _____   Date _____

F

5(a) Have you, before you presented your petition, tried
to come to any agreement with your creditors generally for payment of your debts?   Tick Box Yes ☐ No ☐

(b) If the answer to 5(a) is **'YES'**, what terms were offered to the creditors:—

    (1) Time for repayment _____

    (2) Total pence in £ _____

        receivable by creditors

    (3) When was the offer made? _____

(c) Did the attempt fail because the creditors refused to accept the terms offered?   Tick Box Yes ☐ No ☐

If **'NO'** why did it fail? _____

_____

_____

6. Do you think that you will be able to introduce a voluntary arrangement for your creditors under Part VIII of the Insolvency Act 1986, which is likely to be acceptable to them?   Tick Box Yes ☐ No ☐

If **'YES'**, give brief details _____

_____

_____

_____

Signature _____   Date _____

Form 26

Application to Stay Advertisement of Bankruptcy Order and to Rescind or Annul the Bankruptcy Order

(TITLE)

Between _____

Applicant _____
and
Respondent _____

Take notice that I intend to apply to the Judge/Registrar on:

Date

Time   hours

Place

(a) Set out the grounds

for an order that the advertisement of the bankruptcy order made herein on the   day of   199   and proceedings thereunder be stayed to enable an application to be made to rescind such bankruptcy order on the ground (a) or to enable an appeal to be entered.

OR

(b) Set out the grounds
(c) Set out the grounds

for an order rescinding the bankruptcy order made on the   day of   199   on the grounds (b) *or* to annul the bankruptcy order made on the   day of   199   on the grounds (c) and that the bankruptcy order herein be rescinded and the petition dismissed.

Signed:
(SOLICITOR FOR THE) APPLICANT

My/Our address for service is:—

Form 26 contd.

(d) Give the name(s) and address(es) of the person(s) (including the respondent) on whom it is intended to serve the application

To: (d)

OR

It is not intended to serve any person with this application

If you do not attend, the court will make such order as it thinks fit

**Form 27
(prescribed form 8.4)**

Proxy (Winding up by the Court or Bankruptcy)
(TITLE)

Notes to help completion of the form	
Please give full name and address for communication	Name of creditor/contributory _____ Address _____
Please insert name of person (who must be 18 or over) or the "Official Receiver". If you wish to provide for alternative proxy-holders in the circumstances that your first choice is unable to attend please state the name(s) of the alternatives as well.	Name of proxy-holder _____ 1 _____ 2 _____ 3 _____
Please delete words in brackets if the proxy-holder is only to vote as directed ie he has no discretion	I appoint the above person to be my/the creditor's/contributory's proxy-holder at the meeting of creditors/contributories to be held on _____, or at any adjournment of that meeting. The proxy-holder is to propose or vote as instructed below [and in respect of any resolution for which no specific instruction is given, may vote or abstain at his/her discretion].

Form 27 contd.

Please complete paragraph 1 if you wish to nominate or vote for a specific person as trustee/liquidator

Voting instructions for resolutions

1. For the appointment of _____ of _____

_____

Please delete words in brackets if the proxy-holder is only to vote as directed ie he has no discretion

as liquidator of the company/trustee of the bankrupt's estate.

[in the event of a person named in paragraph 1 withdrawing or being eliminated from any vote for the appointment of a liquidator/trustee the proxy-holder may vote or abstain in any further ballot at his/her discretion]

Any other resolutions which the proxy-holder is to propose or vote in favour of or against should be set out in numbered paragraphs in the space provided below paragraph 1. If more room is required please use the other side of this form.

_____
_____
_____
_____
_____
_____
_____
_____
_____
_____
_____
_____
_____

This form must be signed

Signature _____ **Date** _____

Name in CAPITAL LETTERS _____

Only to be completed if the creditor/contributory has not signed in person

Position with creditor/contributory or relationship to creditor/contributory or other authority for signature _____

_____

_____

Remember: there may be resolutions on the other side of this form.

Form 28
(prescribed form 6.37)

Proof of Debt–General Form
(TITLE)

Date of Bankruptcy Order   No

1	Name of Creditor	
2	Address of Creditor	
3	Total amount of claim, including any Value Added Tax and outstanding uncapitalised interest as at the date of the bankruptcy order	£
4	Details of any documents by reference to which the debt can be substantiated. [Note: the official receiver or trustee may call for any document or evidence to substantiate the claim at his discretion]	
5	If the total amount shown above includes Value Added Tax, please show:— (a) amount of Value Added Tax (b) amount of claim NET of Value Added Tax	£ £
6	If total amount above includes outstanding uncapitalised interest please state amount	£
7	If you have filled in both box 3 and box 5, please state whether you are claiming the amount shown in box 3 or the amount shown in box 5(b)	
8	Give details of whether the whole or any part of the debt falls within any (and if so which) of the categories of preferential debts under section 386 of, and schedule 6 to, the Insolvency Act 1986 (as read with schedule 3 to the Social Security Pensions Act 1975)	Category Amount(s) claimed as preferential £

Form 28 contd.

9	Particulars of how and when debt incurred	
10	Particulars of any security held, the value of the security, and the date it was given	
11	Signature of creditor or person authorised to act on his behalf	
	Name in BLOCK LETTERS	
	Position with or relation to creditor	

Admitted to vote for

£

Date

Official Receiver/Trustee

Admitted preferentially for

£

Date

Trustee

Admitted non-preferentially for

£

Date

Trustee

Form 29
(prescribed form 6.39)

Affidavit of Debt

(TITLE)

(a) Insert full name, address and description of person making oath

I (a)

make oath and say:

(b) Delete as applicable

(1) That (b) [I am a creditor of the above-named bankrupt] [I am (c)

(c) State capacity eg director, secretary, solicitor etc

of (d)

(d) Insert full name and address of creditor

a creditor of the above-named bankrupt.

(e) State means of knowledge of matters sworn to in affidavit

I have been concerned in this matter (e)

and am authorised by the creditor to make this affidavit on its/his behalf]

(f) Insert name of bankrupt

(2) That the said (f)

(g) Insert date

on (g)   the date of the bankruptcy order, was and still is justly and truly indebted (b) [to me] [to the said creditor] in the sum of £   as shown in the proof of debt exhibited hereto marked "A".

Sworn at

Form 30

Notice of Rejection of Proof of debt

(TITLE)

<small>(a) If proof wholly rejected, strike out following words
(b) Insert amount of claim</small> Take notice that, as trustee   of the above named debtor, I have this day rejected your claim against the debtor (a) [to the extent of £(b)   ] on the following grounds;

EITHER

That in spite of repeated requests you have neglected to produce evidence in support of your claim.

OR

That your claim represents the invoice price of work done for the debtor in an unsatisfactory and incomplete manner as a result of which the debtor had to have the work re-done and completed by another contractor.

OR

That your claim is barred by the provision of the Limitation Act 1980.

OR

<small>(c) State other grounds on which rejection of the claim is based</small> (c)

And further take notice that subject to the power of the court to extend the time, no application to reverse or vary my decision in rejecting your proof will be entertained after the expiration of 21 days from this date.

Form 30 contd.

Signed _____
(Trustee)

Dated _____

(d) Insert name and address of claimant

To (d) _____
_____
_____
_____

Form 31

Application to Reverse or Vary Trustee's Decision on Proof

(TITLE)

(*Commence as in Form 34*)

(a) Insert creditor's name
(b) Insert creditor's address

On the hearing of an application by (a)_____ of (b)_____ [claiming to be] a creditor of the abovenamed for an order that the decision of the Respondent, the trustee of the abovenamed

EITHER

in rejecting the Proof of the Applicant (a)_____ in the above matters for the sum of £   may be reversed and the said Proof may be ordered to be admitted in full.

OR

in rejecting the Proof of the Applicant (a)_____ in the above matters for the sum of £   to the extent of £   may be varied and that the said Proof may be ordered to be admitted [in full *or* for the further sum of £   ].

OR

(c) Insert name and address of creditor whose proof has been challenged

in admitting the Proof of (c)_____ in the above matters may be reversed and the said Proof Ordered to be rejected [in full *or* as to £   ] AND that the said trustee may be ordered to pay the costs of and incidental to this application.

(Conclude as in Form 34)

Form 32

Affidavit in Support of Summons to Reverse Trustee's Decision on Proof

(TITLE)

(a) Insert name, address and description of person making the oath

I (a) _____

_____

make oath and say as follows:—

(b) Insert date
(c) Insert name of trustee

1. That a bankruptcy order against the above was made on (b)_____ and by an Order dated (b)_____ (c)_____ was appointed trustee.

(d) Insert amount claimed

2. On (b)_____ I lodged with the trustee Proof for the sum of £(d) in respect of goods sold and delivered, particulars of which were annexed to the said Proof, a copy of which, together with the said particulars, is now produced and shown to me marked 'AB1'.

3. On (b)_____ I received a notice of rejection of the said Proof from the trustee, a copy of which is now produced and shown to me marked 'AB2' which states as the ground of rejection that (e)

(e) Specify the ground as in Form 28

(f) State the applicant's answer to the trustee's contention

4. (f) _____

_____

_____

sworn at

Form 33

Order Reversing or Varying Rejection of Proof or Giving Leave to Amend Proof

(TITLE)

<table>
<tr><td>

(a) Insert date
(b) Insert name and address of applicant
(c) Delete as applicable
(d) Insert name of the applicant

(e) Insert name of trustee

(f) Insert name of the deponent

</td><td>

Upon the application, by summons dated (a)_____ _____ of (b)_____ (c)[*or* Upon motion this day made unto this Court by Counsel on behalf of (d)_____]

And upon hearing Counsel for the Applicant and for (e)_____ the Trustee (the Respondent)

And upon reading the bankruptcy order dated (a)_____ (appointing the Trustee) the Proof of Debt of the Applicant filed (a)_____ the Notice dated (a)_____ by the Respondent as such Trustee rejecting the Proof of Debt the Affidavit of (f)_____ filed (a)_____ _____ and the exhibit in the said affidavit referred to

</td></tr>
</table>

It is ordered that the decision of the Respondent as such Trustee rejecting the said Proof of Debt of the Applicant (c)[for the said sum *or* to the extent] of £_____
be (c)[reversed *or* varied] and that such Proof be admitted in the bankruptcy for the [said] sum of £_____

OR

It is ordered that the Applicant be at liberty to amend his said Proof of Debt so as to prove in the bankruptcy as a creditor for the sum of £_____

And it is ordered that the Respondent as such trustee do admit the said Proof as so amended to rank for dividend in the bankruptcy for the said sum of £_____

THEN

And it is ordered that the costs of the Applicant (d)_____ of the said application be taxed (if not agreed) and paid out of the assets of the said bankrupt

Form 34
(prescribed form 6.61)

Notice of Disclaimer under section 315 of the Insolvency Act 1986

(TITLE)

PART 1

(a) Insert name of trustee

I, (a) _____
the trustee of the above-named bankrupt's estate, disclaim all my interest in:

(b) Insert full particulars of property*

(b) _____

Dated _____

Signed _____

Name in BLOCK LETTERS _____

Address _____

PART 2

NOTE:

(c) Insert name of court
(d) Insert date that notice filed in court

This is a copy of a notice filed at (c) _____ Court

on (d) _____

Seal of the Court

PART 3

(e) Insert name and address of person to be sent copy notice under Rule 6.179 or 6.180

To: (e) _____

_____

_____

This is a copy of a notice of disclaimer filed by the trustee in the above matter at (c) _____ Court.

NOTE: 1. Part 1 is to be completed by the trustee and filed in court with a copy
Part 2 is to be completed by the court and returned to the trustee
Part 3 is to be completed by or on behalf of the trustee when sending out copy notice under Rule 6.179 or 6.180
2. The attention of a recipient of this notice is drawn to sections 315–321 of the Insolvency Act 1986.
*3. Where the property concerned consists of land or buildings the nature of the interest should also be stated (eg whether leasehold, freehold etc).

Form 35

Authority to Trustee to Pay Dividends to another person

(TITLE)

(a) Insert name of trustee
(b) Insert name of bankrupt
(c) Insert name of intended recipient
(d) Insert address of intended recipient

To [the Official Receiver] *or* [(a) the trustee of (b)]

Sir,

    I/We hereby authorise and request you to pay to (c) of (d)_____ (a specimen of whose signature is given below), all dividends as they are declared in the above named matter, and which may become due and payable to me/us in respect of the proof of debt for the sum of £   against the above named debtor, made by/on our behalf.

    And I/we further request that the cheque or cheques drawn in respect of such dividends may be made payable to the order of the said (c) whose receipt shall be sufficient authority to you for the issue of such cheque or cheques in his name. It is understood that this authority is to remain in force until revoked by me/us in writing.

[*Signature*]

Witness to the signature of creditor

Dated this   day of   199

(*specimen of the signature of intended recipient appointed as above*)

Form 36
(prescribed form 7.1)

Originating Application
(TITLE)

Between
Applicant _____
and
Respondent _____

(a) Insert name and address of respondent

Let (a)

attend before the Judge/Registrar on:—

Date _____

Time _____ hours

Place _____

(b) Insert name of applicant

On the hearing of an application by (b) the applicant for an order in the following terms:—

(c) State the terms of the order to which the applicant claims to be entitled

(c)

The grounds on which the applicant claims to be entitled to the order are:—

(d) Set out grounds or refer to an affidavit in support

(d)

The names and addresses of the persons upon whom it is intended to serve this application are:—

(e) State the names and addresses of the persons intended to be served

(e)

OR

It is not intended to serve any person with this application.

(f) State the applicant's address for service

The applicant's address for service is: (f)

Dated _____

Signed: _____
(SOLICITOR FOR THE) APPLICANT

If you do not attend, the court may make such order as it thinks fit.

**Form 37
(prescribed form 7.2)**

Ordinary Application
(TITLE)

**Between
Applicant** _____
**and
Respondent** _____

Take notice that I intend to apply to the Judge/Registrar on:

Date _____

Time _____ hours

Place _____

(a) State nature and grounds of application

for (a)

Signed: _____
(SOLICITOR FOR THE) APPLICANT

My/Our address for service is:—

(b) Give the name(s) and address(es) of the person(s) (including the respondent) on whom it is intended to serve the application

To: (b)

OR

It is not intended to serve any person with this application

If you do not attend, the court will make such order as it thinks fit

Form 38
(prescribed form 4 in IPO)

Written/ Statutory Demand by Creditor
The Insolvent Partnerships Order 1994

(Title)

(a) Insert name of partnership	**In the matter of (a)** _____ **and in the matter of the Insolvent Partnerships Order 1994**

WARNING TO DEBTOR – READ THE FOLLOWING NOTES CAREFULLY

- This is an important document. Please read the demand and the notes entitled "How to comply with a demand" and "How to have a demand set aside (applicable to individual members only)" on page 5 below.
- If the partnership has received this, the partnership must act upon it **within 21 days** or a winding-up order could be made against the partnership.
- If a corporate member of the partnership has received this, that member must act upon it **within 21 days** or a winding-up order could be made against the company.
- If, having received this as an individual member of the partnership, you wish to have this demand set aside, you must make application to do so **within 18 days** from its service on you. If you do not apply to set aside **within 18 days** or otherwise deal with this demand as set out in the notes **within 21 days** after its service on you, you could be made bankrupt and your property and goods taken away from you.

  If you are in any doubt about your position you should seek advice **immediately** from a solicitor or your nearest Citizens Advice Bureau.

To: _____

Address: _____
_____
_____

This DEMAND is served on you by the creditor:

Name: _____

Address: _____
_____
_____

Form 38 contd.

Notes for Creditor

- If the creditor is entitled to the debt by way of assignment, details of the original creditor and any intermediary assignees should be given in part B on page 4.
- If the amount of the debt includes interest not previously notified to the partnership as included in its liability, details should be given, including the grounds upon which interest is charged. The amount of interest must be shown separately.
- Any other charge accruing due from time to time may be claimed. The amount or rate of the charge must be identified and the grounds on which it is claimed must be stated.
- In either case the amount claimed must be limited to that which has accrued due at the date of the demand.
- If the creditor holds any security, the amount of the debt should be the sum the creditor is prepared to regard as unsecured for the purposes of this demand.
  Brief details of the total debt should be included and the nature of the security and the value put upon it by the creditor, as at the date of the demand, must be specified.
- If signatory of the demand is a solicitor or other agent of the creditor, the name of his/her firm should be given.

DEMAND

The creditor claims that the partnership owes the sum of £_____, full particulars of which are set out on page 3;

The creditor demands that the partnership or a member or former member of the partnership named in part C of this notice do pay the above debt or secure or compound for it to the creditor's satisfaction.

[The creditor making this demand is a Minister of the Crown or a Government Department and it is intended to present a winding-up and/or bankruptcy petitions in the High Court in London]

[Delete if inappropriate]

Signature of individual _____

Name _____
(BLOCK LETTERS)

Date _____

*Position with or relationship to creditor:
_____

*I am authorised to make this demand on the creditor's behalf.

Address _____
_____
_____

Tel. no. _____ Ref. _____

N.B. The person making this demand must complete the whole of this page, page 3, page 4 and page 5.

*Delete if signed by the creditor himself.

Form 38 contd.

Particulars of Debt.
These particulars must include (a) when the debt was incurred, (b) the consideration for the debt (or if there is no consideration the way in which it arose), and (c) the amount due as at the date of this demand

Notes for Creditor
Please make sure that you have read the notes on page 2 before completing this page.

Note:
If space is insufficient continue on reverse of page and clearly indicate on this page that you are doing so.

Form 38 contd.

PART A

The individual or individuals to whom any communication regarding this demand may be addressed is/are:–

Name _____
(BLOCK LETTERS)
Address _____

Telephone number _____

Reference _____

PART B

For completion if the creditor is entitled to the debt by way of assignment

	Name	Date(s) of Assignment
Original creditor		
Assignees		

PART C

It is intended that a demand in respect of the debt shown on page 2 will also be served on the following:–

_____
_____
_____
_____

Form 38 contd.

HOW TO COMPLY WITH A DEMAND

If the partnership or a corporate member wishes to avoid a winding-up petition being presented against it, it must pay the debt shown on page 2, particulars of which are set out on page 3 of this notice, within the period of **21 days after** its service. Alternatively, the partnership can attempt to come to a settlement with the creditor. To do this the partnership should:

- inform the individual (or one of the individuals) named in part A above immediately that it is willing and able to offer security for the debt to the creditor's satisfaction; or

- inform the individual (or one of the individuals) named in part A immediately that it is willing and able to compound for the debt to the creditor's satisfaction.

If the partnership disputes the demand in whole or in part it should:

- contact the individual (or one of the individuals) named in part A immediately.

> **REMEMBER!** The partnership has only 21 days after the date of the service on it of this document before the creditor may present a winding-up petition against the partnership and winding-up or bankruptcy petitions against those members listed in part C of this notice.

HOW TO HAVE A DEMAND SET ASIDE (applicable to individual members only)

If you are an individual member of the partnership and you consider that you have grounds to have this demand set aside or if you do not quickly receive a satisfactory written reply from the individual named at part A whom you have contacted you should **apply within 18 days** from the date of service of this demand on you to the (a) [High Court of Justice, Strand, London WC2A 2LL] [(b) _____ County Court whose address is

_____]

to have the demand set aside.

Any application to set aside the demand (Form 6.4 in Schedule 4 to the Insolvency Rules 1986) should be made within 18 days from the date of service upon you and be supported by an affidavit (Form 6.5 in Schedule 4 to those Rules) stating the grounds on which the demand should be set aside. The forms may be obtained from the appropriate court when you attend to make the application.

> **REMEMBER!** From the date of service on you of this document
> - you have only 18 days to apply to the court to have the demand set aside, and
> - you have only 21 days before the creditor may present a bankruptcy petition against you.

(a) Delete as applicable
(b) Insert name and address of court

APPENDIX 3

Form 39
(prescribed form 7 in IPO)

Creditor's Bankruptcy Petition against Individual Member (Presented in Conjunction with Petition against Partnership)

The Insolvent Partnerships Order 1994

(Title)

(a) Insert name of individual member subject to petition

In the matter of (a) _____

_____

and in the matter of the Insolvent Partnerships Order 1994

(b) Insert title of court and number of proceedings (to be allocated by court)

To (b) _____

_____ No: _____ of _____

(c) Insert full name(s) and address(es) of petitioner(s)

I/We (c) _____

_____

_____

_____

(d) Insert full name, place of residence and occupation of individual member

petition the court that a bankruptcy order may be made against (d) _____

_____

_____

_____

(e) Insert in full any other name(s) by which the member is or has been known

[also known as (e) _____

_____]

(f) Insert trading name (adding "with another or others", if this is so), business address and nature of business

[and carrying on business as (f) _____

_____

_____

_____]

(g) Insert any former address(es) at which the member has resided after the time at which the petition debt of the partnership (j) was incurred

[and lately residing at (g) _____

_____

_____

_____]

(h) Give the same details as specified in note (f) above for any other businesses which have been carried on at or after the time at which the petition debt of the partnership (j) was incurred or at which the member may have incurred debts or liabilities still unpaid or unsatisfied

[and lately carrying on business as (h) _____

_____

_____

_____]

Form 39 contd.

(j)	Insert name of partnership subject to winding-up petition	
(k)	Delete as necessary. If the partnership has a principal place of business in both England and Wales and in Scotland the relevant period is 1 year. In any other case it is 3 years	
(l)	Insert appropriate date	
(m)	State date and manner of service of demand	

On the grounds that:
he is a member of (j) _____
which has carried on business in England and Wales at some time during the period of (k) [3 years] [1 year] ending with (l) _____ , the day on which a winding-up petition was presented to this court against the partnership.
The partnership is justly and truly indebted to me [us] in the aggregate sum of £ _____

The above-mentioned debt is for a liquidated sum payable immediately.

On (m) _____ a demand was served upon the member and the partnership by (m) _____

_____

_____

in respect of the above-mentioned debt.

To the best of my knowledge and belief the demand has neither been complied with nor set aside in accordance with the Rules and no application made to set it aside is outstanding.

The partnership is unable to pay its debts, and in the circumstances a bankruptcy order should be made against (a) _____

_____

Note 1:
Petitions are also being presented against the following members of the partnership:

NAME	ADDRESS	TYPE OF PETITION (WINDING-UP OR BANKRUPTCY)	DATE DEMAND SERVED

Note 2:
It is intended to serve this petition on (a) _____

Form 39 contd.

(n) Insert name of member

(o) Only to be completed where the petitioning creditor is represented by a solicitor

> **ENDORSEMENT**
> This petition having been presented to the court on _____ it is ordered that the petition shall be heard as follows:
>
> Date _____
>
> Time _____
>
> Place _____
>
> _____
>
> and you, the above-named (n) _____ are to take notice that if you intend to oppose the petition you must not later than 7 days before the date fixed for the hearing:
>
> (i) file in court a notice in Form 6.19 of the Insolvency Rules 1986 specifying the grounds on which you object to the making of a bankruptcy order; and
>
> (ii) send a copy of the notice to the petitioner or his solicitor.
>
> The solicitor to the petitioner is (o):
>
> Name _____
>
> Address _____
>
> _____
>
> _____
>
> Tel. no. _____
>
> Reference _____
>
> [whose agents are:
>
> Name _____
>
> Address _____
>
> _____
>
> _____
>
> Tel. no. _____
>
> Reference _____]

Form 40

Application for Interim Order (non-bankruptcy case)

IN THE   COUNTY COURT   No   of 199
BANKRUPTCY

Re:
Between:
Applicant _____
and
Respondent _____

Take notice that I intend to apply to the District Judge on:

Date   day of   199

Time   hours

Place

for an interim order in respect of

pursuant to Section 252 of the Insolvency Act 1986.

The grounds upon which I claim to be entitled to the order are set out in my Affidavit sworn on the   day of   199 .

Dated the   day of   199 .

Signed_____

Form 41

Affidavit in Support of Application for Interim Order (non-bankruptcy case)

IN THE LEEDS COUNTY COURT   No   of 199
BANKRUPTCY

Re:
Between:
Applicant _____
and
Respondent _____

AFFIDAVIT

I, _____
of _____
make oath and say as follows:

1. I am currently employed as:

I verily believe that I am insolvent but the excess of my liabilities over my assets can be reduced by way of an individual voluntary arrangement pursuant to the provisions of Part VIII of the Insolvency Act 1986.

2. I am unaware of any bankruptcy petitions presented against me. A statutory demand was however served by _____ _____ although no steps to bankruptcy have been taken. In addition _____ have a judgment against me in the sum of _____. In addition, _____ have issued a Writ against me in the sum of _____. A Writ has also been issued against me by _____ in the sum of _____.

3. I am able to petition for my own bankruptcy.

4. No previous application for an interim order has been made by or in respect of me in the period of 12 months prior to the date of this Affidavit.

5. The Respondent is a person who is qualified to act as an insolvency practitioner in relation to my affairs and he is willing to act as nominee in relation to the proposals which I intend to make.

6. A copy of the notice which I have given to the Respondent and which is endorsed with his agreement so to act is now produced to me and marked 'A'.

SWORN etc
Before me,

A Solicitor.

This Affidavit is filed on behalf of the Applicant.

Form 42

Application for Interim Order (bankruptcy case)

IN THE LEEDS COUNTY COURT   No   V of 199
IN BANKRUPTCY

Re:
Between:
Applicant_____
and
Respondent_____

Let
of_____
and the Official Receiver of_____attend before the District Judge
on:_____
Date_____
Time_____
Place_____
on the hearing of an application by_____
of_____
the Applicant for an Interim Order in respect of
pursuant to Section 252 of the Insolvency Act 1986.

The grounds upon which the Applicant claims to be entitled to the order are set out in the Affidavit of the Applicant sworn on the_____.

The names and addresses of the persons upon whom this application should be served are_____
of_____
and the Official Receiver of_____.

The Applicant's address for service is_____
_____

Dated this   day of   199

Signed_____
        Applicant

If you do not attend the Court may make such Order as it thinks fit.

Form 43

Affidavit in Support of Application for Interim Order (bankruptcy case)

IN THE   COUNTY COURT   No of 199
IN BANKRUPTCY

Re:
Between:
Applicant _____
and
Respondent _____

AFFIDAVIT

I, _____
of _____
MAKE OATH and say as follows:

1. I have traded:
I verily believe that I am insolvent but that the excess of my liabilities over my assets can be reduced by way of an individual voluntary arrangement pursuant to the provisions of Part VIII of the Insolvency Act 1986.

2. On the_____199 I was adjudicated bankrupt upon the petition of the_____.
I have also received further Writs and Summonses and copies of all such documents that I am aware of are now produced to me and marked 'A'.

3. No previous application for an interim order has been made by or in respect of me in a period of 12 months prior to the date of this Affidavit.

4. The First Respondent is a person who is qualified to act as an Insolvency Practitioner in relation to my affairs and he is willing to act as Nominee in relation to the proposals which I intend to make.

5. A copy of the Notice which I have given to the First Respondent and which is endorsed with his agreement so to act is now produced and shown to me marked 'B'.

6. In accordance with the provisions of Rule 5.4(5) of the Insolvency Rules, the Second Respondent will be served with this Affidavit and the application to which it relates.

Sworn etc

This Affidavit is filed on behalf of the Applicant.

Form 44

Proposals for Voluntary Arrangement

**Insolvency Act 1986
Section 253
Proposal for Individual Voluntary Arrangement**

Name of debtor:_____
Address:_____
_____

Name of Nominee_____
Date of Proposal_____

Telephone

1. **Introduction**
I wish to enter into a voluntary arrangement with my creditors and detailed below are my proposals for a voluntary arrangement. I consider that my creditors will be expected to agree with these proposals on the following grounds:
   a. Costs will be less than those which would obtain in bankruptcy since no DTI fees will be incurred.
   b. That the realisation and distribution of funds will take place more expeditiously than under bankruptcy proceedings.

2.1 **Proposals**
The statement of affairs herewith contain details of all my assets showing estimated gross and net realisable values (after deducting amounts due to secured creditors).

2.2 All of my assets have been included in the arrangements save for those items that would be excluded in bankruptcy. I understand that should my Supervisor locate assets of mine, not disclosed in these proposals, then the supervisor would be able to petition for my bankruptcy.

2.3 No assets other than my own are to be included in the arrangement.

2.4 The Supervisor will hold all realisations on trust for the benefit of my creditors.

2.5 The statement of affairs details all known liabilities to be included in the arrangement.

2.6 I am currently employed as a_____
with_____and my salary is £_____
per annum. I have been employed by the company since_____.

2.7 It is proposed to deal with the claims of preferential creditors as follows:

Whilst I am unaware of any preferential creditors should such creditors emerge then preferential creditors will be defined in Sections 386, 387 and Schedule 6 of the Insolvency Act 1986. It is intended that those creditors whose debts are preferential will be paid in full, but without interest, out of assets comprising this arrangement.

Form 44 contd.

It is proposed to deal with unsecured creditors as follows:
I will pay to my Supervisor £   per month for the period of 2 years and, after payment of the costs of the arrangement and any preferential creditors, the balance will be accepted by creditors in full settlement of their claims against me.

2.8 In the event that the Supervisor is unable to agree with any creditor the extent of their claim, then it is proposed that the Supervisor may apply to the Court for directions. The directions of the Court will be accepted as a final decision by the creditors.

2.9 I am unaware of any circumstances which in the event of my bankruptcy might give rise to claims under Section 339 (transactions at an undervalue), Section 340 (preferences), Section 343 (extortionate credit transactions).

2.10 The attached statement of affairs details guarantee creditors.

2.11 The claims of my associates are to be postponed to the claims of the ordinary unsecured creditors.

2.12 The duration of the proposed voluntary arrangement is 2 years.

2.13 In the event of my income exceeding £   then I will pay   % of the excess after tax to the Supervisor as a contribution to the arrangement.

2.14 It is proposed that the Nominee should receive £   plus VAT by way of remuneration together with disbursements and legal costs in connection with this matter. The Supervisor's remuneration shall be calculated by reference to the time spent by the Supervisor and his staff. The Supervisor will be reimbursed for all his expenses in relation to his administration. All fees and disbursements are to be deducted from funds held for the purposes of the arrangement. The Supervisor's fees and expenses shall rank ahead of the claims of all creditors and after the costs payable to the Nominee.

2.15 It is not intended my Supervisor's duty shall extend to the arrangement of any credit facilities which I may seek outside the scope of the arrangements.

2.16 The proposed functions of the Supervisor are to agree the creditors' claims and to realise my assets and distribute the funds to be included in the arrangements. The Supervisor is to keep such records of his receipts and payments and of his acts and dealings as are required by law.

2.17 It is proposed that the funds held for the purposes of the arrangement shall be banked by the Supervisor in an interest bearing account. Any funds held by the Supervisor pending distribution to creditors may be placed on deposit or invested in recognised securities for the benefit of creditors.

2.18 I propose that the Supervisor shall retain at any given time sufficient funds, until the arrangement is completed, to enable him to petition for my bankruptcy in the event that I am in default under the terms of the arrangement.

2.19 It is proposed that the Supervisor of the arrangement shall be Mr   . Mr   is qualified to act as an insolvency practitioner.

2.20 I acknowledge that I commit an offence if I make any false representations to the creditors in these proposals, or at any meeting of the creditors for the purposes of obtaining the creditors' approval to these proposals, punishable by imprisonment and a fine.

3. I_____, the above-named debtor hereby confirm this document fairly sets out my proposals to my creditors for a voluntary arrangement and that to the best of my knowledge and belief all statements herein are true. I further acknowledge that although I have received professional assistance in drafting these proposals, contents remain my sole responsibility and the implications of all proposals have been carefully explained to me.

Dated this_____day of_____199 .

Signed_____

Form 45

General Title (High Court)

IN THE HIGH COURT OF JUSTICE
IN BANKRUPTCY

                                                No.   of 19

(a) Insert name of debtor   *Re* (a)_____

(b) Insert name of debtor or creditor or the Official Receiver or the Trustee as the case may be   [*Ex parte* (b)_____]

Form 46

General Title (county court)

IN THE_____COUNTY COURT
IN BANKRUPTCY

                                        No.   of 19

(a) Insert name of debtor   *Re* (a)_____

              [*Ex parte* ((b)_____ as in Form 39)]

Form 47
(prescribed form 8.1)

Proxy (Company or Individual Voluntary Arrangements)

(TITLE)

Notes to help completion of the form

(a) Please give full name and address for communication

Name of creditor/member (a) _____

Address_____

(b) Please insert name of person (who must be 18 or over) or the "chairman of the meeting" (see note below). (c) If you wish to provide for alternative proxy-holders in the circumstances that your first choice is unable to attend please state the name(s) of the alternatives as well

Name of proxy-holder (b) _____

(c)1 _____

2 _____

3 _____

(d) Please delete words in brackets if the proxy-holder is only to vote as directed ie he has no discretion

I appoint the above person to be my/the creditor's (d) [member's] proxy-holder at the meeting of creditors/members to be held on_____, or at any adjournment of that meeting. The proxy-holder is to propose or vote as instructed below (d)[and in respect of any resolution for which no specific instruction is given, may vote or abstain at his/her discretion].

Form 47 contd.

Voting instructions for resolutions

(e) Please delete as appropriate

1. For the (e) acceptance/rejection of the proposed voluntary arrangement [with the following modifications:—]

(f) Any other resolutions which the proxy-holder is to propose or vote in favour of or against should be set out in numbered paragraphs in the space provided below Paragraph 1. If more room is required please use the other side of this form

(f) _____

_____

_____

_____

_____

_____

(g) This form must be signed

(g) **Signature** _____ **Date** _____

Name in CAPITAL LETTERS _____

(h) Only to be completed if the creditor/member has not signed in person

(h) **Position with creditor/[member] or relationship to creditor/[member] or other authority for signature**

_____

_____

Remember: there may be resolutions on the other side of this form.

Index

Accounts—
  failure to keep proper, 111
  requirement to submit, 48–9
Adjustment of prior transactions—
  assignment, avoidance of, 104
  avoidance of general assignment, 104
  credit transactions, extortionate, 104
  defrauding, 102
  distress, 105–6
  enforcement procedures, 105
  execution, 105
  extortionate credit transactions, 104
  general assignment, avoidance of, 104
  gifts, 98
  liens, 106
  orders, 103–4
  passive acts, 101
  proceeds of sale orders, 103
  property adjustment orders, 101–2
  relevant time, 103
  seizure of goods, 105
  time, relevant, 103
  undervalue, transactions at, 101–2
  voidable preferences, 102–3
Advertisement—
  anullment order, 53
  application to stay advertisement of order, 217
  discharge of bankrupt, 95
  dividend, intention to declare, 85
  petitons, of, 43
  statutory demand, 182
  substituted service, 200
Affairs of Bankrupt, *see* Statement of affairs
After-acquired property, 71–2, 78
Annulment of bankruptcy order, *see* Bankruptcy order
Appeals—
  appellants, 119
  documents, 118, 122
  extension of time, 120
  generally, 118–19

Appeals—*contd*
  hearing, 123
  hierarchy, 118
  lodging documents, 118
  necessity, 118
  notice of appeal, 121
  offical receiver, against, 118–19
  out of time, 121
  Practice Direction, 118
  procedure—
    documents, 122
    generally, 121
    hearing, 123
    notice of appeal, 121
    respondent's notice, 122
    security for costs, 122
    service of notice of appeal, 121
    setting down, 122
    stay of execution, 123
  rehearing, 119–20
  respondent's notice, 122
  Secretary of State's decisions, 118–19
  security for costs, 122
  service of notice of appeal, 121
  setting down, 122
  stay of execution, 123
  time limits, 118, 120–1
Arrangement, deeds of, *see* Deeds of arrangement
Arrest, power of, 114–15
Automatic review—
  introduction of provisions, 2

Bankrupt—
  business of, 72
  estate of, *see* Estate of bankrupt
  home, *see* Home of bankrupt
  inquiry into dealings and property, 115–16
  statement of affairs, *see* Statement of affairs
  vesting of estate, 70–1

INDEX

Bankruptcy—
  courts, 159–64
  effect, 1
  meaning, 1
  offences, *see* Offences, bankruptcy
  order, *see* Bankruptcy order
  truth of statements affidavit, 198
Bankruptcy Department of the Board of Trade, 1
Bankruptcy order—
  annulment—
    advertisement, 53, 217
    application for, 51–2
    contents of application, 51
    generally, 51
    grounds, 51, 52
    interim order, 52
    jurisdiction of court, 52–3
    locus standi, 51
    official receiver's action upon, 53
    power, 51
    report of affairs, 52
    satisfaction of court, 52
    seal, release under, 52
  application for, 50
  creditor's petition—
    grounds for making, 33–5
    offer to secure debt, 33–4
    refusal, 33–5
  debtor's petition—
    action following order, 41
    certificate of summary administration, 40
    making of order, 40
    procedure, 40
  destruction of only asset through, 35
  discretionary nature, 50–1
  extortion, used for, 34
  generally, 50–1
  grounds for making, 33–5
  partner's own petition, 135–6
  preparation, 35
  procedure, 35–6
  rescission—
    justification, 50
    power, 50
  sealed copies, 35
Bill of exchange, 7, 85
Business—
  bankrupt's, 72
  definition, 5

Certificate—
  debt, of, 32–3
Champerty, 127
Charges—
  home of bankrupt, on, 74–5
Charging orders, 75

Chief land registrar—
  notice of petition sent to, 26
Company—
  creditor, as, 21
Company Voluntary Arrangement, *see* Voluntary arrangement
Compounding debt, 33
Conditional fee agreements, 127
Consolidation, 137–8
Contempt of court, 112
Contingent debts, 89, 91–2
Costs—
  rules, 131
  security for, 28, 122
County court—
  areas, 159–64
  jurisdiction, 10, 20
Court—
  alternative, 165–7
  areas, 159–64
  bankruptcy, 159–64
  County, 10, 20
  powers, *see* Court's powers
Court's powers—
  absconding, 114
  arrest, 114–15
  general, 14
  inquiry into dealings and property, 115–16
  property seizure, 115
  redirection of mail, 117
  seizure of bankrupt's property, 115
  special manager, 116–17
Creditor—
  amendment of petition by, 21
  assignees, 22
  committee, *see* Creditor's committee
  company, 21
  definition, 21
  defrauding, 102
  executors, 22
  joint, 22
  married women, 22
  meaning, 21
  meeting of, *see* Trustee in bankruptcy
  mentally disordered persons, 21
  minors, 22
  partners, 21
  secured, 21, 87
  trustee—
    bankruptcy, in, *see* Trustee in bankruptcy
    bare, 22
    debt, of, 22
Creditor's committee—
  absence, 69
  appointment—
    creditor's meeting, at, 63
    sanctioning of trustee's powers, 67
  dealings with members, 68

Creditor's committee—*contd*
  establishment—
    membership, 66
    right to, 66
  expenses of members, 69
  functions, 66–7
  meaning, 66
  meetings, 67
  membership, 66, 68
  none appointed, 69
  postal resolutions, 68
  removal of member, 68
  remuneration of trustee determined, 66–7, 124–5
  report of trustee to, 67
  resignation of member, 68
  resolutions by post, 68
  right to establish, 66
  rights, 66–7
  role, 66–7
  Secretary of State, functions vested in, 69
  supervisory role, 66–7
  termination of membership, 68
  vacancies, 68
Creditor's petition—
  affidavit, 23–4
  amendment of petition, 21, 29
  appropriate court, 19–20
  chief land registrar, notice to, 26
  completion, 24–5
  conditions, 20
  consolidation, 28
  contents, 19, 20–1
  costs, security for, 28
  court, appropriate, 19–20
  creditor, *see* Creditor
  death of debtor, 27–8
  debtor identification, 22–3
  dismissal, 32, 34–5
  extortion, petition presented for purposes of, 34
  fee, 25
  filing, 25–6
  forms, 20–1, 190–6
  guidelines for completion, 24–5
  hearing, *see* Hearing of petition
  identification—
    debt, of, 23
    debtor, of, 22–3
  judgment debts, 35
  notice to chief land registrar, 26
  presentation—
    appropriate court, 19–20
    conditions, 8
    court, appropriate, 19–20
    fee, 25
    High Court, 19
    procedure, 25–6

Creditor's petition—*contd*
  presentation—*contd*
    requirements, 8, 25–6
    voluntary arrangement in force, 19
    wrong court, to, 20
  prior, 25
  sealing, 26
  searches for prior petitions, 25
  security for costs, 28
  service—
    affidavit of personal service, 201
    death of debtor before, 27–8
    generally, 26
    personal, 26
    proving, affidavit, 27
    substituted, 26–7, 179, 202
    timing, 26
  statutory demand, *see* Statutory demand
  transfer between courts, 20
  verification, 23–4
  withdrawal, 32
Criminal court action, 112–13
Crown—
  petition by, 69
  set-off, 92

Death of debtor—
  administration of estate, 27–8
  insolvent estate, *see* Deceaseds' insolvent estates
  service, before, 27–8
Debt—
  affidavit of, 223
  bankruptcy level, 6
  bill of exchange, 7, 85
  certificate of, 32
  classes, 82–3
  compound, offer to, 34
  conditions for petition, 6
  contingent, 89, 91–2
  deferred, 82, 83
  family proceedings, 83–4
  fines, 83
  future, 11, 84, 178–81
  identification in petition, 23
  illegal considerations, founded on, 7
  interest—
    after order, 86
    before order, 86
    judgment rate, 86
  judgment, 7, 174–7
  liability orders, 7
  liquidated sum, 6
  maintenance arrears, 7
  periodic, 84–5
  preferential, 82–3
  promissory notes, 85

INDEX

Debt—*contd*
  proof—
    admission, 85–6
    affidavit verifying, 83
    bills of exchange, 85
    contents, 84
    dividends, 85
    expunging, 86
    form, 83, 221–2
    future date, payable at, 84
    meaning, 83
    notice of application to reverse rejection, 85, 226
    periodic debts, 84–5
    promissory notes, 85
    provable debts, 83–4
    purpose, 83
    rejection, 85–6, 224
    rent, 84
    reversal of rejection, 85, 226–8
    secured creditor, 87
    summons reversing, 226–8
    time limits, 85
    timescale for dealing with, 85
    VAT, 86–7
    voting purposes, acceptance for, 85
  provable, 83–4
  ranking priority, 83
  reasonable prospect of paying, 8–9
  rent, 84
  secured, 6, 82
  shortfall in security, 6
  statute barred, 7
  unliquidated damages, 83
  unsecured, 82, 83
  VAT, 86–7
Debtor—
  ability to pay debts, 33–4
  carried on business in England, 5
  death—
    administration of estate, 27–8
    service, before, 27–8
  definition, 4
  domicile, 4–5
  foreigners, 4
  identification in petition, 22–3
  married women, 6
  meaning, 4
  mentally disordered persons, 6
  minors, 5–6
  ordinarily resident, 5
  partnership, *see* Partnership
  petition, *see* Debtor's petition
  place of business, 5
  secure debt, offer to, 33–4
Debtor's petition—
  abuse of process, 40
  appropriate court, 10

Debtor's petition—*contd*
  contents, 37–8
  court, appropriate, 37
  expedited petition, 37
  filing, 37
  form, 37–8
  grounds, 37
  hearing of petition, 39
  insolvency practitioner's report, 39
  issue procedure, 38
  making of order, 40
  presentation, 37
  procedure on issue, 38
  small bankruptcies, 39
  statement of affairs, 37, 38, 208–16
  voluntary arrangement in force, 38
Deceaseds' insolvent estates—
  administration begun by personal representative, 139–40
  funeral expenses, 139
  generally, 139
  good faith actions of personal representative, 141
  individual voluntary arrangements, 144
  inquiry into affairs, 142
  Insolvency Administration Order petitioned, 141
  insolvency practitioners, 139
  modification of law, 141
  offences, bankruptcy, 142
  pending petition, 140
  petition—
    not pending, 141
    pending, 140
  preferential debts, 142
  provisions governing, 139
  qualifcation as executor/administrator, 139
  statement of affairs, 140
Deeds of arrangement—
  accounts—
    audit, 157–87
    transmission, 157
  advantages, 155
  appointment of trustees, 157
  assent, effect of, 157
  audit of accounts, 157–8
  avoidance, 156
  classes of instruments, 156
  creditors, 156, 157
  Department of Trade and Industry, transmission of accounts to, 157
  essentials, 155–6
  generally, 155
  meaning, 155
  nature, 155–6
  non-compliance with statutory conditions, 156
  payment of undistributed money, 158

INDEX

Deeds of arrangement—*contd*
  protection of trustee, 158
  registration, 156
  security, 157
  statutory conditions, non-compliance with, 156
  trustees—
    appointment, 157
    audit of accounts, 157–8
    creditors, transmission of accounts to, 157
    Department of Trade and Industry, transmission of accounts to, 157
    payment of undistributed money, 158
    protection, 158
    security, 157
    transmission of accounts, 157
    undistributed money, 158
    void deed, 158
  undistributed money, 158
  uses, 155
  void, 158
Deferred debt, 82, 83
Defrauding creditors, 102
Department of Trade and Industry—
  deeds of arrangement, 157
  historical involvement, 1–2
  trustee, control over, 125–6
Discharge—
  advertisement, 95
  application—
    effective date, 95
    exclusions, 94–5
    hearing, 95
    notice, 95
    order, 95
    procedure, 94
    report of official receiver, 95
    requirement, 94
  automatic—
    conditions, 93
    date of bankruptcy, 93
    origins, 2
    rules, 93
  certificate, 95
  effect, 96
  historical background, 2
  income payments orders and, 73
  lifting suspension, 94
  personal injury compensation liability, 40
  release from obligations, 96
  suspension, 93–4
  transitional provisions, 93
Disclaimer—
  after-acquired property, 78
  application for leave to, 78
  communication, 79
  damage resulting from, 81

Disclaimer—*contd*
  dwelling house—
    effective date, 79–80
    occupation, 80
    vesting order, 80
  effect, 81
  effective date, 78
  ex parte grant of leave, 78
  exercise of power, 7
  extension of time limit, 78
  general power, 77
  guarantors, 81
  hearing of application, 78, 81
  interested parties, 78
  leaseholds, 79
  leave to, 78
  loss resulting from, 81
  notice of, 77, 78, 229
  onerous property, 77
  operation, 81
  personal property, 78
  power—
    exercise, 77
    general, 77
  prescribed form of notice, 77
  procedure, 77–8
  rentcharge, land subject to, 80
  subsequent trustee, 78
  third party rights, 81
  time limits, 78
  vesting order—
    affidavit supporting, 81
    categories of applicant, 80
    dwelling house, 80
    leasehold property, 80
    requirements for grant, 80
    time limits, 80
Dispositions—
  court order as, 42
  debt, payment of, 42
  restrictions on, 42–3
  statutory demand, notice of, 42
  third party, payments to, 42
  void, 42–3
Distress levied, 43, 105–6
Dividends—
  advertisement of intention to declare, 85, 87
  assignment of right, 88
  authority to pay, 230
  distribution, 88
  failure to lodge proof, 88
  final distribution, 88
  inability to declare, 88
  method of payment, 88
  partially secured creditor, 88
  proof of debt and, 85
  refusal to pay, 88

INDEX

Domicile—
  debtor's, 4–5
Dwellinghouse—
  disclaimer, 79–80
  occupation rights, 80
  see also Home of debtor

Enforcement of orders, 129
Estate of bankrupt—
  administration, *see* Trustee in bankruptcy
  after-acquired property, 71–2
  business of bankrupt, 72
  composition, 70–1
  control of, 74
  exclusions, 70, 71
  extent, 70–1
  home, charge on, 74
  income, 71
  income payment orders, 71, *see also* Income payments orders
  notice for after-acquired property, 71
  occupational pension scheme, 70
  personal pension plans, 71
  priority of expenses payment, 76
  property defined, 71
  vesting, 70–1
Evidence—
  affidavit, 129
  generally, 129
  offences, bankruptcy, 112
Examination—
  bankrupt, of, public, *see* Public examination
  court's powers, 115–16
  public, *see* Public examination
Executions—
  benefit of, 43–4
Executor—
  petition presented by, 22
Expenses—
  priority of payment, 76
Extortion—
  petiton presented for, 34
Extortionate credit transactions, 104

Family proceedings, 83–4
Fees—
  applicable, 3
Foreigners, 4
Funeral expenses, 139

Gambling, 111–12
General procedure, *see* Procedure
Gifts, 109

Hearing of petition—
  adjournments, 30–1, 206, 207
  amendment of petition, 29

Hearing of petition—*contd*
  appearances—
    failure of petitioning creditor, 30
    notice of intention, 29–30, 204
    other creditors, 30
    petitioning creditor, 29–30
  bankruptcy order, *see* Bankruptcy order *and* Creditor's petition
  carriage, change of, 31–2
  certificate of debt, 32–3
  change of carriage of petition, 31–2
  creditors intending to appear, 205
  date, 29
    adjournments, 30–1
    extensions, 30
  debtor's opposition, 29
  dismissal, 32
  extensions, 30
  notice of intention to appear, 29–30, 204
  opposition by debtor, 29, 203
  substitution of petitioner, 31
  withdrawal, 32
High Court—
  jurisdiction, 10
Historical background, 1–3
Home of bankrupt—
  bankrupt's rights, 98–9
  charge on, 74–5, 97, 99
  children living in, 98
  creditors' interests, 97–8
  extent of interest, 99–100
  joint names, 99
  occupation rights—
    bankrupt's, 98–9
    exceptional circumstances, 98
    spouse's, 97–8
  payments towards liabilities, 99
  "rent" required, 98–9
  sale, order for, 97
  sole name, in, 100
  spouse's occupation rights, 97–8

Income payments orders—
  application, 73
  circumstances, changes in, 74
  discharge, 73, 74
  employers and, 73
  fees, 73–4
  income defined, 73
  level of, 73
  meaning, 72–3
  notice of hearing, 73
  payer of income, 73–4
  power to make, 72–3
  procedure, 73
  variation, 74
Individual Voluntary Arrangement (IVA)—
  see Voluntary arrangement

INDEX

Inquiry into dealings of bankrupt, 115–16
Insolvency—
  deceased's estate, *see* Deceaseds' insolvent estates
  partnership, *see* Partnership
  practitioner—
    debtor's petition, report required for, 39
    interim receiver, appointment as, 44, 45
Interim order, 241–4
  see also Voluntary arrangement
Interim receiver—
  affidavit supporting, 45
  application for appointment, 45
  contents of order, 45
  debtor's obligations, 45
  form, 45
  insolvency practitioner appointed as, 44, 45
  limitations on powers, 44
  need for, 44
  obligation of debtor, 44–5
  official receiver appointed as, 44, 45
  remuneration, 45
  restrictions on powers, 44
  termination of appointment, 45–6
IVA, *see* Voluntary arrangements

Joint creditors—
  petition presentation, 22
Judgment debt, 7, 174–7
Jurisdiction—
  relevant law, 2–3

Leaseholds—
  disclaimer of, 79
  vesting order, 80
Liability orders, 7
Liens, 106
London Insolvency District, 19–20

Maintenance arrears, 7
Maintenance, principle of, 127
Married women—
  creditor, as, 22
  debtor, as, 6
Mentally disordered persons—
  bankruptcy, liability to, 6
  creditor, as, 21
  debtor as, 6
  public examination of, 55
Minors—
  bankruptcy, 5–6
  creditor, as, 22
  necessaries, 6
  partnership member, 6

Objects of law, 1
Occupational pension schemes, 70

Offences, bankruptcy, 107
  absconding, 110, 114
  accounts, failure to keep proper, 111
  arrest power, 114–15
  books—
    concealment, 108–9
    delivery, 109
  business, engaging in, 110–11
  concealment, 108, 114
  contempt of court, 112
  credit, fraudulent dealing with property, 110
  criminal court action, 112–13
  deceased debtor, 142
  defence of innocent intention, 107–8
  delivery up of books, 109
  engaging in business, 110–11
  evidence, 112
  examination, failure to attend, 114
  explanations, 108–9
  false statements, 109
  fraudulent disposal of property, 109
  gambling, 111–12
  generally, 107
  information, nondisclosure of, 108
  innocent intention defence, 107–8
  liability to prosecution, 107
  nondisclosure of information, 108
  obtaining credit, 110–11
  power of arrest, 114
  property, concealment of, 108
  prosecution liability, 107
  punishment, 107, 111
  removal of goods, 114
  renting property, 111
  warrant for arrest, 114
Official receiver—
  anullment of order, action on, 53
  appeals against decisions of, 118–19
  historical background, 2
  immunity from action, 46
  interim receiver, appointment as, 44, 45
  investigatory duties, 49
  origin, 2
  remuneration, 76
  suspension of action by, 36
Onerous property, 77
Ordinary application, 232
Originating application, 231

PAO, 132
Paper requirements, 130
Partnership—
  consolidation, 137–8
  creditor, as, 21
  debtor, as, 5, 6
  disqualification, 132

Partnership—*contd*
  insolvent—
    consolidation, 137–8
    disqualification of partners, 132
    individual partners—
      creditor's petition, 238–9
      partner's own petition, 135–6
      some partners, 136
      winding up and, 134–5
    meaning, 134
    partner's petition for bankruptcy order, 135–6
    Partnership Administration Order, 132
    Partnership Voluntary Arrangement, 132, 133
    POA, 132
    prescribed form, 133
    PVA, 132
    rights lost, 138
    rules, 132
    statutory demand, 233–7
    treatment, 132
    winding up petition—
      bankruptcy petition and, 133–5
      before, procedure, 132–3
      corporate partner, against, 134
      expedited petitions, 135
      individual partners, 134–5
      manner, 133
      non-corporate partner, against, 134
      partners request, 133
      place of service of demand, 134
      secured creditors, 135
  loss of rights, 138
  member, 5
  minors, 6
  rights lost, 138
  statutory demand, 9
Partnership Administration Order, 132
Partnership Voluntary Arrangement, 132, 133
Pension—
  occupational, 70
  personal, 71
Personal pension plans, 71
Petition—
  advertisement, 43
  conditions for, 6
  creditor's, *see* Creditor's petition
  debtor's, *see* Debtor's petition
  hearing, *see* Hearing of petition
  presentation, 4, 8
Preferential debts, 82–3, 142
Prior transactions—
  see Adjustment of prior transactions
Procedure—
  access to court file, 130
  applications, 128–9
  computation of time, 130

Procedure—*contd*
  costs, 131
  enforcement, 129
  evidence, 129
  fee on issue, 129
  file, access to, 130
  forms, 130
  hearing of applications, 128
  paper, 130
  postal service, 130
  review of orders, 131
  service by post, 130
  title of proceedings, 128, 248
  transfer of proceedings, 129
Proceedings—
  restrictions on, 43–4
Professional privilege, 116
Promissory notes, 85
Proof of debt, *see* Debt
Property—
  adjustment orders, 101–2
  after-acquired, 71–2, 78
  concealment of, 108
  fraudulent disposal of, 109
  incidental entitlements, 71
  onerous, *see also* Disclaimer
  personal pension plans, 71
Proxies—
  authorisation, 61
  contents of forms, 61
  eligibility, 61
  faxed, 62
  forms, 59, 61, 219–20, 249–50
  holder, 61
  individual voluntary arrangements and, 149
  lodging, 61–2
  necessity, 61
  purposes, 61
  solicitation for, 60, 62
  voting by holders, 62
  winding up, 219
Public examination—
  adjournment—
    discharge, effect on, 56–7
    general, 56–7
    power of, 56
  affidavit supporting application, 55
  application, 54
  bankrupt unfit for examination, 55
  creditor requesting, 54
  expenses, 57
  form of order, 55
  hearing—
    adjournment, 56–7
    disallowal of questions, 56
    participants, 55–6
    procedure, 55–6
    representation, 56

INDEX

Public examination—*contd*
  hearing—*contd*
    written record, 56
    leave to serve order, 55
    notice of requirement, 54
    order, 54–5
    participants, 55–6
    procedure at hearing, 55–6
    security for costs, 57
    unfitness of bankrupt, 55
PVA, 132, 133

Reasonable prospect of paying debt, 8–9
Receiver—
  interim, *see* Interim receiver
  trustee, pending appointment of, 46
Redirection of mail, 117
Rehearings, 119–20
Rentcharge, land subject to—
  disclaimer of, 80
Rescission of bankruptcy order, *see* Bankruptcy order
Residence—
  debtor's, 5
Restrictions—
  dispositions, 42–3
  proceedings, 43–4
Review of orders, 131

Secured creditor—
  definition, 21–2
  petition by, 21
  proving debt, 87
  set-off right, 91
Secured debt, 6
Security for costs, 28, 122
Set-off—
  allowable, 90
  classes of debt, 91
  contingent liabilities, 89, 91–2
  Crown, 92
  definition, 90
  future debts, 90
  generally, 89
  joint debts and seperate debts, 90
  mandatory nature, 90
  mutual credits—
    application of provisions, 90
    definition, 90
  mutual dealings, application of bankruptcy law, 89
  mutual debts, definition, 90
  not allowable, 90–1
  requirements for, 90
  right, 89
  same right requirement, 90
  secured debts, 91
  trustee, debts due to or from, 90–1

Set-off—*contd*
  unascertained liabilities, 89
Small bankruptcies—
  insolvency practioner's report, 39
  level, 39
  relevant law, 3
Special manager, 116–17
Statement of affairs—
  accounts, 48–9
  affidavit verification, 47
  assistance in preparation, 48
  completion of forms, 47
  contents, 47
  debtor's petition, 49, 208–16
  deceaseds' insolvent estates, 140
  extension of time, 47
  failure to submit, 48
  form, 47
  further disclosure, 49
  limited disclosure, 48
  release from submission, 47–8
  statute barred debts, 47
  submission, 47–8
Statute barred debts, 7
Statutory demand—
  acknowledgment of service, 12
  advertisement, 182
  affidavit of service, 12–13, 183, 184, 186
  appropriate court, 10
  assignment, 11
  calculation of compliance period, 13–14
  communications about, 11
  compliance, 11, 12, 13–14
  contents, 9–10
  court, appropriate, 10
  creditor, 9
  Crown, 10
  date, 10
  debt in, 9–10
  debtor, 9
  defects, 14
  foreign currency claimed, 10
  form, 9
  forms, 168 *et seq*
  future debt, 11, 178–81
  identification of debt, 10
  immediately payable debt, 170–3
  information, 11
  judgment debts, forms when, 174–7
  meaning, 8
  name and address, 9
  overstated debts, 10
  partnerships, 9
  proof of service, 12
  purpose explained, 11
  security, 10
  service—
    acknowledgment, 12

260

INDEX

Statutory demand—*contd*
  service—*contd*
    advertisement, 12
    affidavit, 12–13
    date, 13
    deemed date, 13
    generally, 11–12
    intention to rely, 12
    judgment debts, 12
    methods, 11
    outside jurisdiction, 12
    personal, affidavit of, 183
    proof, 12
    rules, 12
    substituted, 11, 13, 184
  setting aside—
    adjournment of application, 17
    affidavit in support, 15
    application—
      adjournment, 17
      affidavit supporting, 14, 186–8
      documents, 14
      extension of time limit, 15, 188
      form, 185, 186
      hearing of, 16–17
      procedure, 14–15
      where made, 14
    appropriate court, 10
    compounding debt, 16
    conditional, 17
    dismissal of application, 15, 18
    grounds, 15–16
    hearing of application, 16–17
    judgment debts, 17
    order for, 18, 189
    other grounds, on, 17
    overstated debt, 17
    reasons for, 15
    secured debt, 17
    substantial disputes, 17
    time extension, 15
  signature, 10
  three weeks for compliance, 13–14
  time for compliance, 11–14
Summary administration, certificate of, 40

Time, computation of, 130
Title of proceedings, 128
Transfer of proceedings, 129
Trustee—
  bare, 22
  debt, of, 22
Trustee in bankruptcy—
  accounts kept by, 126
  administration of estate—
    acquisition of control, 74
    control, acquisition of, 74
    estate of bankrupt, *see* Estate of bankrupt

Trustee in bankruptcy—*contd*
  administration of estate—*contd*
    income payments orders, *see* Income payments orders
  appointment—
    certification, 63
    creditor's meeting, *see* creditor's meeting *below*
    date of effect, 58
    eligibility, 58
    exercise of power, 58
    joint trustees, 58
    meeting, 58–9
    power to make, 58
    qualifications, 58
  certification of appointment, 63
  champerty, 127
  conditional fee agreements, 127
  control of—
    court, by, 125
    creditors, by, 124–5
    Department of Trade and Industry, by, 125–6
    ex parte James, rule in, 126
  court control, 125
  creditor's committee, *see* Creditor's committee
  creditors control of, 124–5
  creditor's meeting—
    attendance of bankrupt, 63
    business at first, 62–3
    chairman, 60
    creditor's committee apointment, 63
    decision to hold, 58–9
    first, 59, 62–3
    individual voluntary arrangements, *see* Voluntary arrangements
    nominees and, 149
    notice, 59
    official receiver's appointment as trustee, 63
    permitted resolutions, 62–3
    proof of debt requirement, 60
    proofs of debt, 59
    proxies, *see* Proxies
    purpose, 62
    qualifications for appointment as trustee, 63
    quorum, 60
    rejection of proof, 60
    requirement to hold, 59
    rules governing, 60
    secured creditor, 60
    timing, 59
    trustee's appointment and, 59
    unliquidated crditors, 60
    venue, 59
    voting procedure, 60

Trustee in bankruptcy—*contd*
  Department of Trade and Industry control, 125–6
  disclaimer, *see* Disclaimer
  duty, 70
  ex parte James, rule in, 126
  expenses, priority of payment, 76
  functions, 70
  home, charge on, 74
  joint, 58
  maintenance, 127
  meeting to appoint, 58–9
  permission for exercise of powers, 75–6
  powers, 75
  qualification, 58, 63
  receivership pending appointment, 46
  records of administration, 126
  removal from office—
    generally, 64
    grounds, 64–5
    interested person's application, 64–5
    order for meeting, 64
    procedure, 64–5
    release, grant of, 64, 65
    Secretary of State, by, 65
    sufficient cause for, 64–5
  remuneration, 124–5
    determination of, 66–7
  resignation, 63–4
  vesting of bankrupt's estate, 70–1

Undervalue, transactions at, 101–2
Unsecured debt, 82

Value added tax, 86–7
VAT, 86–7
Vesting—
  bankrupt's estate, 70–1
  order—
    disclaimer and, *see* Disclaimer
    immediate on bankruptcy order, 46
Voidable preferences, 102–3
Voluntary arrangement—
  application—
    affidavit accompanying, 146
    fee, 146
    interim order, 145–6
    proposal, 144–5
    steps in, 143–4
  approval, 153
  background, 143
  bankruptcy petition, 196, 197
  challenging meeting's decision, 152
  creditors' meeting, 149
    adjournment of meeting, 150
    approval of proposals, 150–1
    chair, 149
    challenging, 152
    conduct, 149

Voluntary arrangement—*contd*
  creditors' meeting—*cont*
    costs, 149
    documents, 149
    insufficient notice, 148–9
    modifications to proposals, 150
    notices calling, 148–9
    partially secured creditors, 149
    preferential creditors, 150–1
    proxy form, 149
    rent arrears, 149
    report, 151
    resolutions, 150
    voting, 149–50
  creditor's petition and, 19
  debtor's default, 154
  debtor's petition and, 40
  default by debtor, 154
  implementation, 153–4
  individual, meaning of, 143
  interim order—
    action following, 147–8
    affidavit accompanying application, 146
    application, 145–6
    duration, 147
    effect of, 145
    form of application, 145–6
    hearing of application, 146–7
    nominee's consent exhibited, 145
    precedent of application, 146
    purpose, 145
    requirement, 145
    service of application, 146
  nature, 143
  nominee, 143
  non-bankruptcy cases, procedure in, 151
  notice of hearings, 148
  offence, 154
  proposal—
    basic conditions, 145
    conditions, 145
    contents, 144–5
    deceaseds' insolvent estates, 144
    form, 245–7
    information needed in, 144–5
    joint debtors, 144
    whom made by, 144
  proxy form, 149
  purpose, 41, 143
  report of nominee, 147–8
  second hearing, 148
  statement of affairs, 147
  supervisor, 143
    duties, 153
    implementation by, 153
    responsibilities, 153
    trustee, appointment as, 40
  third hearing, 151